Lecture Notes
in Business Information Processing   344

Series Editors

Wil van der Aalst
  RWTH Aachen University, Aachen, Germany
John Mylopoulos
  University of Trento, Trento, Italy
Michael Rosemann
  Queensland University of Technology, Brisbane, QLD, Australia
Michael J. Shaw
  University of Illinois, Urbana-Champaign, IL, USA
Clemens Szyperski
  Microsoft Research, Redmond, WA, USA

More information about this series at http://www.springer.com/series/7911

Julia Kotlarsky · Ilan Oshri ·
Leslie Willcocks (Eds.)

Digital Services and Platforms

Considerations for Sourcing

12th Global Sourcing Workshop 2018
La Thuile, Italy, February 21–24, 2018
Revised Selected Papers

 Springer

Editors
Julia Kotlarsky ⓘ
University of Auckland
Auckland, New Zealand

Ilan Oshri ⓘ
University of Auckland
Auckland, New Zealand

Leslie Willcocks ⓘ
London School of Economics
and Political Science
London, UK

ISSN 1865-1348 ISSN 1865-1356 (electronic)
Lecture Notes in Business Information Processing
ISBN 978-3-030-15849-1 ISBN 978-3-030-15850-7 (eBook)
https://doi.org/10.1007/978-3-030-15850-7

Library of Congress Control Number: 2019934737

This Springer imprint is published by the registered company Springer Nature Switzerland AG
The registered company address is: Gewerbestrasse 11, 6330 Cham, Switzerland

Preface

This edited book is intended for use by students, academics, and practitioners who take interest in outsourcing and offshoring of information technology and business services. The book offers a review of the key topics in sourcing of services, populated with practical frameworks that serve as a toolkit to students and managers. The range of topics covered in this book is wide and diverse, offering micro and macro perspectives on successful sourcing of services. More specifically the book examines sourcing decisions and management practices around digital platforms, giving specific attention to digital aspects of innovation in sourcing. The book also explores new sourcing trends such as automation, which is gaining attention by academics and practitioners alike. Aspects such as partnership and motivation receive further attention in this book. Topics discussed in the book combine theoretical and practical insights regarding challenges that industry leaders, policy makers, and professionals face or should be concerned with. Case studies from various organizations, industries, and countries are used extensively throughout the book, giving it a unique position within the current literature offering.

The book is based on a vast empirical base brought together through years of extensive research by leading researchers in information systems and strategic management.

December 2018

Julia Kotlarsky
Ilan Oshri
Leslie Willcocks

Organization

The Global Sourcing Workshop is an annual gathering of academics and practitioners.

Program Committee

Julia Kotlarsky	The University of Auckland, Auckland, New Zealand
Ilan Oshri	The University of Auckland, Auckland, New Zealand
Leslie Willcocks	London School of Economics, London, UK

Contents

Partnering for Digital Innovation:
A Competence-Based Study

Daria Arkhipova$^{(\boxtimes)}$ and Giovanni Vaia

Ca' Foscari University of Venice,
San Giobbe 873, Cannaregio, 30121 Venice, Italy
{daria.arkhipova,g.vaia}@unive.it

Abstract. Drawing on the attention-based view of the firm and research on microfoundations of organizational capabilities, we develop and empirically analyze a theoretical model that examines the role of cognition of IT leadership in achieving organizational-level digital maturity and the mechanisms through which it affects the innovative outcomes of the exploration-focused outsourcing projects. We find that Chief Information Officers' (CIOs) internal beliefs regarding the importance of capabilities for the IT function seem to not directly affect the innovation outcomes of third-party collaborations. Instead, this relationship is mediated by the degree of digital maturity the company has managed to achieve.

Keywords: Digital transformation · Digital maturity · Sourcing decisions

1 Introduction

Over the past decade, both scholars and practitioners emphasized the growing importance of digital transformation as a means for achieving and sustaining competitive advantage [1, 2]. As a result, organizational IT departments – and senior-level IT executives as their primary representatives - have been demanded to lead and execute the process of transformation, and many have acknowledged the challenges associated with this new role [3]. First, as leaders of the transformation, IT executives find themselves under ever increasing pressure to "determine the values and cultures of the IT function and instill the belief that an IT's staff first duty is to the contribution of achieving business solutions" [4]. To that end, the intrinsic beliefs of IT executives as to which capabilities need to be prioritized set an overall direction for the organizational IT function and eventually define which level of "digital maturity" the company will be able to achieve.

Second, organizational IT is expected to go beyond its traditional role as a "functional subordinate to business" and to participate in digital innovation process on par with the business instead [5, 6]. Doing so requires an entirely new set of competences from IT that might be not readily available internally. To address the resultant capability gap, IT managers may choose to access lacking capabilities externally by building value-enhancing partnerships with the third-parties in order to jointly develop innovations of strategic importance [7–10].

© Springer Nature Switzerland AG 2019
J. Kotlarsky et al. (Eds.): Global Sourcing 2018, LNBIP 344, pp. 1–18, 2019.
https://doi.org/10.1007/978-3-030-15850-7_1

Drawing on the attention-based view of the firm [11, 12] and research on micro-foundations of organizational capabilities [13–15], we develop and empirically analyze a theoretical model that examines the role of cognition of IT leadership in achieving organizational-level digital maturity and the mechanisms through which it affects the innovative outcomes of the exploration-focused outsourcing projects.

Our results demonstrate that the relationship between the managerial beliefs regarding the importance of IT capabilities and the degree of digital maturity is capability-specific. We find that IT managers assigning higher importance to strategic planning and management aspects in their profession in the digital era exhibit higher levels of digital maturity. Conversely, placing excessive importance on operational support activities was found to be characteristic of the companies that are lagging behind with respect to digital maturity. With regards to innovation outcomes, we find that digitally mature companies are more likely to develop exploratory innovations through third-party collaborations.

The paper is organized as follows. We start by reviewing the extant literature on mental representations in management research and proceed by examining the specifics of IT profession during digital transformation. We then discuss the characteristics of a digital enterprise and capability sourcing decisions its IT managers are expected to make. Next, we formulate a set of hypotheses and devise a structural model. We conclude by discussing our results and their theoretical and practical implications.

2 Background

2.1 Managerial Representations and Exploratory Outsourcing Projects

According to the behavioral theory of the firm, managers are considered to be boundedly rational agents that act upon the simplified representations of the environment [16, 17]. Managerial internal representations (or mental models) are defined as knowledge structures stored in an individual's mind with regards to how the business environment works [14] and reflect managerial perception and understanding of the relative importance of the different elements of this environment and causal relationships between them. As such, mental models form the basis for developing beliefs that influence managerial decisions and drive the development of new capabilities [13, 14].

To that end, senior-level executives reallocate organizational attention and resources towards capabilities whose importance is consistent with their internal representations and, consequently, away from those that they believe to be less critical [11, 12, 18]. However, because mental representations are constructed based on an individual's past experiences, it becomes particularly challenging for managers to adapt their mental models if the initial circumstances change [19]. As a result, when confronted with novel situations representing a significant departure from the *status quo*, managers tend to continue relying on their existing mental models and often remain committed to an inertial course of action that leads to failure in the "new" environment [15, 20–22].

In this regard, digitalization presents a radical shift for senior managers in domain of IT in that it increases the significance of IT in developing strategic digital innovation [5, 23, 24]. Doing so successfully requires IT managers to revisit their existing mental models as to what falls into their professional "jurisdiction" [25] in order to be able to accurately interpret signals from the business environment and make appropriate strategically relevant choices [14]. That is, managerial understanding of which components of their profession have become more (or less) salient as a result of digitalization will determine how much attention IT will allocate to developing each capability [11, 12].

In what follows, we identify five major capabilities constituent of IT profession and formulate a series of hypotheses with regards to how allocation of managerial attention towards each of these aspects affects the likelihood of achieving innovation in outsourcing.

Strategic Planning. In the past, IT has been typically involved in strategic-decision making within its functional boundaries, e.g. in developing strategy plans regarding IT resources required for supporting business operations [26]. As digital technologies have become critical for creating and sustaining competitive advantage, IT leaders are now expected to participate in strategic decision-making on an organizational level and use their technical knowledge to devise innovative, technology-enabled business solutions for customers [3]. Academic literature in IS and management field provides an ample evidence that CIOs demonstrating strategic orientation have achieved more profitable returns [27], derived greater value from IT investments [28] and developed a superior understanding of the mechanisms of business value creation and capture [5]. To that end, IT managers that acknowledge the role of strategic orientation for their profession will be better aligned with the business goals and therefore better equipped for steering the exploratory efforts of the innovation team in the more promising directions. Hence, we posit:

H1a: IT managers that allocate more attention to strategic planning capabilities are more likely to achieve innovation through third-party collaborations.

Technical Development. IT profession historically required technical background and mastery of "hard" skills such as hardware installation and maintenance, software programming and system integration [29]. That is, the ability to design, develop, test and implement software as well as knowledge of well-established practices, methodologies and techniques have been considered critical for IT profession [25]. To that end, [27] have empirically demonstrated the importance of technical capability on a senior level and provided empirical evidence that firm performance was higher for the firms whose CIO had a technical background as opposed to those where CIO had general management background. Yet, with the advent of cloud technologies, software development and infrastructure maintenance has become increasingly commoditized and procured externally thus reducing the internal need for technical skills [30]. In this regard, maintaining excessive focus on developing technical capabilities that can be more efficiently procured from outside can divert the attention from exploratory activity and derail the innovation focus within the project. Hence, we posit:

H2a: IT managers that allocate more attention to technical development capabilities are less likely to achieve innovation through third-party collaborations.

Operational Support. Until recently, the predominant idea about the role of IT within an organization was that it is confined to "process improvement, streamlining operations and effective, reliable and secure functioning of the organization" [25]. Despite of the recent claims that IT managers need to focus more on strategic priorities, some studies indicate that the majority of CIOs continue spending substantial amount of time on operational work [3]. To that end, IT managers that prioritize operational efficiency will tend to exhibit exploitative (rather than explorative) approach to innovation and are more likely to remain devoted to familiar, low-risk domains thereby reducing the likelihood of achieving innovation when partnering with third-parties. Hence, we posit:

H3a: IT managers that allocate more attention to operational support capabilities are less likely to achieve innovation through third-party collaborations.

IT Enablement. Prior research has demonstrated that a company's propensity for IT-enabled business innovation increases if CIOs are "boundary-spanners" that are actively involved in cross-functional interactions within as well as beyond the boundaries of an organization [31]. The underlying mechanisms are as follows. First, by actively engaging in information exchange with the employees outside IT department, CIOs get a better understanding of organizational-level issues that can be solved with the help of IT thus enhancing their mental representations of what capabilities they need to address them. Second, increased interaction with the customers stimulates exploratory behavior within a firm and enables managers to maximize the effectiveness of their actions in response to a technological change [32]. Finally, frequent and repetitive interactions with suppliers enhance managerial familiarity with the type of knowledge that resides in vendor firms and increases the propensity to achieve innovation outcomes through collaboration with them [33]. To sum up, prior evidence seems to suggest that IT managers assigning higher importance to IT enablement capabilities will allocate their attention to activities that favor the development of innovation in outsourcing. Hence, we posit:

H4a: IT managers that allocate more attention to IT enablement capabilities are more likely to achieve innovation through third-party collaborations.

IT Management. Managerial capabilities for IT leaders are defined as "*capabilities stemming from deep understanding of the organization's business environment and from mastery of general management skills*" [34] and have been shown to be instrumental for exploiting existing IT resources to support ongoing business activity [35] as well as for exploring new sources of IT-enabled business value [36]. To that end, [36] have found that CIO supply-side managerial capabilities (e.g. cost-effectiveness and stability) are antecedent to developing demand-side capabilities aimed at exploration and innovation. Furthermore, recent findings have pointed out that digital innovations require developing new approach towards managing third-party collaborations [37].

That is, acknowledging the increased importance of and, consequently, allocating more attention to managerial capabilities in IT is likely to be beneficial for achieving innovation in the outsourcing projects. Hence, we posit:

H5a: IT managers that allocate more attention to managerial capabilities are more likely to achieve innovation through third-party collaborations.

2.2 Mediating Role of Digital Maturity

Recent theoretical work has provided a more nuanced understanding of the factors that determine the use of external sourcing in building new knowledge [39, 40] and of the modes that facilitate integration of new knowledge and increase the effectiveness of combining internal and external sourcing modes [41, 42]. One of the key determinants that drives the external sourcing decision relates to the difference in the existing internal capability levels [43]. Furthermore, the extent to which a firm will be able to leverage the complementarities between external and internal knowledge sourcing has been attributed to the firm's absorptive capacity [44], the type of the firm's prior experience [45], and the firm's ability to recombine knowledge and reduce knowledge coordination costs [46].

Prior research has highlighted the importance of adjusting the existing logic of organizing for digital innovation [47, 48] suggesting that *"developing digital innovation capability requires fundamentally rethinking how the business is organized, how it makes decisions, with whom it partners, and how those partnerships are managed ... managing innovation concerns by opening up opportunities for collaboration with external partners without disturbing existing internal innovation practices"* [37]. That is, the success of achieving innovation through external collaboration is predicated upon the ability of a client to create conditions that will take into account the specifics of the digital innovation process which we review below.

First, an organization needs to have a superior understanding of technological landscape and have experience with using technology to create additional customer value [49]. Second, to increase the likelihood of success of digital innovation process, an organization needs to adjust its governance structure in a way that grants IT leaders substantial decision-making authority with regards to strategically relevant digital innovations [50, 51]. Third, process of digital innovation requires more computing power and better network connectivity for the new solutions to be tested and implemented. To that end, an organization aspiring for digital innovation needs to have a technologically advanced IT infrastructure in-place [52]. Forth, as many digital innovations often do not have a clear goal that can be specified in the contract upfront, an organization needs to have sufficient familiarity with software development methodologies (e.g. agile) that facilitate interactions and information exchange between client and supplier innovation teams [53]. Finally, the success of digital innovation is increased if an organization nurtures people skill development and fosters experimentation culture that favours creativity and innovation at all levels [24]. In this paper we refer to the organizations that have sufficiently developed the characteristics enumerated above as *digitally mature* organizations.

To that end, we argue that the likelihood of achieving digital innovation through exploratory outsourcing projects will also depend on digital maturity of the client organization. That is, attention of IT leadership needs to be allocated towards certain capabilities in a way that reflects the changing role of IT within an organization. Doing so contributes to building digital maturity which, in turn, creates conditions that support an organization in achieving digital innovation through outsourcing. Hence, we hypothesize that the relationship between IT managers attention towards developing internal capabilities and the digital innovation outcome obtained through external collaborations will be mediated by the degree of digital maturity of the company:

H1b: Digital maturity will mediate the relationship between IT manager's attention to strategic planning capability and innovation outcome.
H2b: Digital maturity will mediate the relationship between IT manager's attention to technical development capability and innovation outcome.
H3b: Digital maturity will mediate the relationship between IT manager's attention to operational support capability and innovation outcome.
H4b: Digital maturity will mediate the relationship between IT manager's attention to IT enablement capability and innovation outcome.
H5b: Digital maturity will mediate the relationship between IT manager's attention to IT management capability and innovation outcome.

The complete theoretical model with hypothesized paths is depicted in Fig. 1.

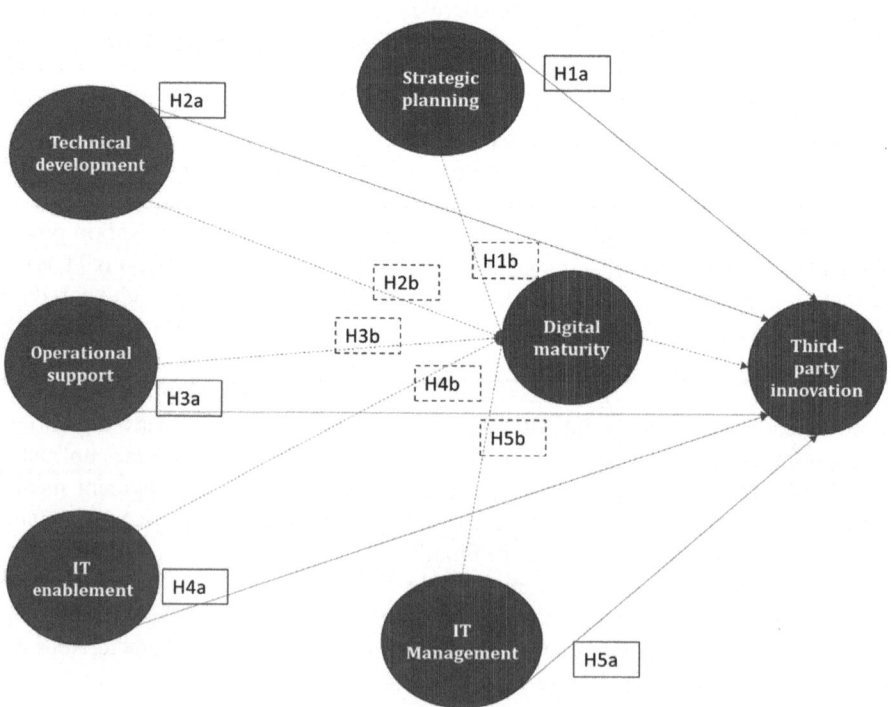

Fig. 1. Conceptual path model.

3 Data and Method

We have relied on survey method to collect our data. Our data comes from two different sources. First, we have solicited help from an independent market research firm for reaching out to the broader pool of respondents with the specifics characteristics we were interested in. Second, we have sent out the survey to the contacts of the Digital Enterprise Lab (DEL) of Ca' Foscari University of Venice. In both instances, our respondents were based in Italy and at a time of completing the survey occupied a senior managerial role in information technology department of their respective enterprise. We have obtained 105 observations in total.

To qualify for taking part in the survey, each respondent was asked to answer a series of screening questions. First, we were interested only in respondents that were employed in companies that have carried out or have been considering carrying out a digital transformation initiative. Second, to minimize the risk of non-response or randomizing, our respondents were supposed to be involved in the digital transformation initiative their companies were carrying out. Third, our respondents were supposed to be familiar with the involvement of the third parties in the process of digital transformation. Failure to respond affirmatively to the first and second screening questions or choosing an "I do not know" response option for the third screening question resulted in the exclusion of a respondent from the survey.

An overview of the key sample characteristics is presented in Table 1.

Table 1. Sample characteristics

Sample characteristics		Frequency	Percentage, %
Country	Italy	105	100
Industry sector	Retail, distribution and transport	8	7.62
	Manufacturing	16	15.24
	Financial and professional services	9	8.57
	Public sector, defense and education	7	6.67
	ICT	52	49.52
	Resources, utilities and construction	4	3.81
	Others	9	8.57
Revenue	Less than €2 millions	1	0.95
	€2 millions–€10 millions	21	20.00
	€10 millions–€50 millions	33	31.43
	More than €50 millions	47	44.76
	No answer	3	2.86
Firm size	Small (<250 employees)	11	10.48
	Medium-large (250–999 employees)	48	45.71
	Large (1,000–3,000 employees)	30	28.57
	Extremely large (>3,000 employees)	16	15.24

3.1 Exogenous Variables

Our model includes five exogenous capability-related variables: (1) strategic planning, (2) technical development, (3) operational support, (4) IT enablement and (5) IT management. As a point of departure, we have used the list of 40 competences identified for professionals in information technology and communication (ICT) domain by the European e-Competence Framework. In the questionnaire, our respondents were asked to assign an importance score for each competence for their job on a scale from 1 ("this skill is not at all important") to 4 ("this skill is critical"). We have retained the original classification of the competences into five main ICT business areas, as proposed by the Framework, but have modified the variable labels such as to conform with terminology used in the prior academic research. As a result, the number of measurement items per construct initially varied from four to 12. To refine our measures, we used the results of convergent and discriminant validity tests as a guidance for dropping and retaining the items for each construct (see the next section for more details).

3.2 Endogenous Variables

As the concept of digital maturity has initially originated from in the practitioners' literature, most of the existing measurements are limited to executives' self-assessment of the digital maturity levels of their organizations with respect to the industry peers [54–56]. Although we recognize the benefits of using self-reported single measures, they are prone to respondents' cognitive biases and subjective interpretations. To that end, we have identified nine items that reflect the multi-dimensional nature of the large-scale transition from a traditional to digital enterprise and developed measurement scales specifically for this study.

In so doing, we have followed three steps. As a first step, we have reviewed academic and practitioners' literature to gain a more nuanced understanding of the critical aspects of digital transformation and of what distinguishes a digitally mature enterprise from a digital "novice". Next, based on the literature review, we have developed a set of six measurement items and have validated them in a series of interviews with four senior-level managers with an extensive expertise in digital transformation and IT. Finally, our research team has critically evaluated the professionals' feedback, modified a set of existing items thereupon and added three new items – digital process innovation, real-time data personalization and data security - that have surfaced during the interviews. As a result, the construct of digital maturity was measured using a nine-item five-point Likert scale where 1 corresponded to "completely disagree" and 5 – to "completely agree" response options, respectively.

With regards to third-party involvement in digital transformation, we have adapted the measure of strategic innovation used in IS research [9, 38]. Whereas the original scale was used to measure innovation without making a specific reference to whether these innovations were digital or not, the modified scale was intended to elicit responses as to whether third parties were involved in the process of identifying an opportunity, co-developing and eventually jointly introducing new digital products on the market as well as experimenting with digital business models and digitalizing internal operations. The construct was measured by using six-item five-point Likert scale.

4 Analysis and Results

To test our hypotheses, we have relied on partial-least squares structural equation modelling (PLS SEM) technique[1]. Because PLS-SEM uses nonparametric bootstrapping procedure to test the significance of the relationships between the variables, it does not require the data to be normally distributed and allows to run the analysis for datasets with less than 200 observations [57, 58]. Hence, the choice of PLS-SEM method for analysis was deemed to be more appropriate for our dataset compared to more widely adopted, covariance-based SEM procedures.

4.1 Measurement Model

Before we proceed to testing the hypothesized internal relationships between the variables, we need to establish convergent and discriminant validity of the latent constructs included in our model first. We used reflective indicators to measure all our constructs – the assumption being that the changes in the individual indicators are caused by the variance in the focal latent construct and co-vary in the same direction [59]. Using the reflective scale determines the type of tests that need to be performed to validate the construct.

Table 2 reports convergent validity and internal consistency values for the five exogenous, competence-related constructs. It is noteworthy that Table 2 deliberately omits the information about the dropped indicators that failed to meet the accepted criteria and includes only those indicators that passed the validity tests. To establish convergent validity, we started by analyzing the magnitude and significance of the factor loadings for each construct first. As can be inferred from the table, we have retained only those indicators whose factor loadings were equal or exceeded the recommended threshold of 0.7 and were statistically significant at $p < 0.01$. Next, we analyzed average variance extracted (AVE) for each construct. Following [59], the calculated values of AVE should exceed the value of 0.5 to allow us to conclude that the amount of variance captured by the focal construct from its indicators is larger than the amount of variance caused by the measurement error. The reported AVE values for all constructs meet this criterion. Finally, we used Cronbach α and composite reliability (CR) scores to establish internal consistency between the constituent indicators for each construct. For each construct, both values pass the acceptance criteria as they exceed or are equal to 0.7.

Similarly, Table 3 contains convergent validity assessment for the two endogenous variables – digital maturity and third-party innovation. To decide whether a certain indicator needs to be retained or dropped, we have followed the exact same procedure and were guided by the identical cut-off value recommendations as in case of exogenous variables. As a result, we have retained all the items for the digital maturity

---

[1] Ringle, Christian M., Wende, Sven, and Will, Alexander (2005). SmartPLS 2.0.M3. Hamburg: SmartPLS, http://www.smartpls.de.

construct and all but one item for third-party innovation construct (Digital Process Innovation item, not reported here). As it can be inferred from the Table 3, convergent validity and internal consistency have been established for both endogenous variables.

Table 2. Convergent validity assessment criteria for the exogenous variables

Reflective constructs: exogenous	Factor loadings ($***p < 0.01$)	Cronbach α	CR	AVE
Strategic planning		**0.697**	**815**	**0.524**
Business plan development	0.694***			
Product/Service planning	0.735***			
Technology trend monitoring	0.709***			
Innovating	0.757***			
Technical development		**0.877**	**0.907**	**0.662**
Application development	0.815***			
Component integration	0.811***			
Testing	0.814***			
Solution deployment	0.779***			
Systems engineering	0.846***			
Operational support		**0.796**	**0.863**	**0.612**
User support	0.719***			
Change support	0.789***			
Service delivery	0.794***			
Problem management	0.824***			
IT enablement		**0.727**	**0.828**	**0.547**
Information security strategy development	0.787***			
Information and knowledge management	0.743***			
Needs identification	0.767***			
Sales proposal development	0.656***			
IT management		**0.766**	**0.850**	**0.588**
Relationship management	0.692***			
Business change management	0.709***			
Information security management	0.827***			
IS governance	0.829***			

To establish discriminant validity of our constructs we have analyzed cross-factor loadings, Fornell-Larcker criterion [60] and heterotrait-monotrait (HTMT) correlation ratio [61]. The core idea behind cross-factor loading analysis is that the loading of each indicator should be higher on the respective focal construct it intends to measure than on the other constructs in the model. The results (not reported here) demonstrate that the differences between factor and cross-factor loadings exceed 0.2 for all indicators thus suggesting that discriminant validity has been established. The results of Fornell-Larcker criterion reported in the upper section of Table 4 provide additional evidence in support of discriminant validity because the values of $\sqrt{AVE}$ for each construct (diagonal values in bold font) are larger than the values of pairwise correlations between the focal construct and other constructs in the model (off-diagonal values). Finally, HTMT criterion requires the ratio between the average of the correlations between indicators measuring different constructs and the average of the correlations between indicators measuring the same construct to be lower than 0.9 [61]. The results reported in the bottom section of Table 4 demonstrate that, with the exception of one, HTMT ratio values do not exceed the threshold value. We can therefore conclude that the discriminant validity has been established for all constructs in our model based on the three different criteria.

Table 3. Convergent validity assessment criteria for the endogenous constructs

Reflective constructs: endogenous	Factor loadings (***p < 0.01)	Cronbach α	CR	AVE
Digital maturity		0.930	0.941	0.641
Product innovation	0.778***			
Process innovation	0.785***			
IT-business partnership	0.808***			
New application integration	0.725***			
Personalized real-time data	0.731***			
Agile work processes	0.819***			
People development	0.835***			
Experimentation culture	0.826***			
Data security	0.887***			
Third-party innovation		0.788	0.854	0.540
New digital products development	0.777***			
Digital product experimentation	0.721***			
Digital business model design	0.774***			
New digital product commercialization	0.689***			
New market opportunity identification	0.701***			

4.2 Structural Model

After having established the construct and measurement validity of the latent constructs, we continue using PLS path modelling to examine the hypothesized relationship between them. We start by analyzing the model that simultaneously evaluates direct paths from the five exogenous variables to digital maturity as well as a direct path from digital maturity to third-party innovation (Table 5). The five exogenous capability attention variables jointly explain 32% of variance in digital maturity. The results indicate that none of the hypothesized direct paths is statistically significant and hence,

Table 4. Discriminant validity assessment criteria for the reflective constructs. Off-diagonal values are the correlations between the constructs in our model

	Fornell-Larcker Criterion						
	1	2	3	4	5	6	7
1. Strategic planning	**0.724**						
2. Technical development	0.313	**0.813**					
3. Operational support	0.414	0.762	**0.782**				
4. IT enablement	0.454	0.561	0.571	**0.740**			
5. IT management	0.588	0.481	0.585	0.576	**0.767**		
6. Digital maturity	0.483	0.290	0.195	0.358	0.427	**0.801**	
7. Third-party innovation	0.377	0.462	0.473	0.406	0.396	0.477	**0.735**
	Heterotrait-Monotrait Ratio (HTMT)						
	1	2	3	4	5	6	7
1. Strategic planning							
2. Technical development	0.380						
3. Operational support	0.549	0.909					
4. IT enablement	0.636	0.694	0.761				
5. IT management	0.807	0.557	0.729	0.795			
6. Digital maturity	0.581	0.298	0.205	0.416	0.492		
7. Third-party innovation	0.510	0.538	0.580	0.549	0.523	0.536	

contrary to our expectations, we get no support for our initial set of hypotheses suggesting the presence of direct relationship between attention allocation and digital innovation outcome.

With regards to the set of mediation hypothesis, we have obtained several interesting results. Our analysis revealed the presence of statistically significant indirect effects between strategic planning (b = 0.173, p < 0.01) and operational support (b = − 0.178, p < 0.01) and third-party innovation, respectively thus supporting Hypotheses H1b and H3b. To examine whether digital maturity mediates the relationship between the perceived competence importance and third-party involvement in digital transformation, we have temporarily removed the digital maturity construct and have run the model including only direct paths between five exogenous constructs and the third-party involvement[2]. The results have demonstrated that none of the antecedent attention

---

[2] We have used the bootstrapping procedure proposed in [62] to verify whether the mediation effect of digital maturity is statistically significant. Differently from the traditional four-step procedure [63] that necessarily requires the direct path between independent and dependent variables to be significant, bootstrapping procedure relaxes this assumption. Instead, the bootstrapping procedure requires generating a large number of samples with replacement and estimating indirect effect for each sample. The obtained values were then ranked from highest to lowest and confidence intervals were calculated – as the confidence interval excluded zero, we were able to conclude that the observed indirect effect is significant [62].

Table 5. PLS-SEM path coefficients: standard errors in parentheses; ***p < 0.01, **p < 0.05. R^2 calculates the amount of variance explained in endogenous latent variable(s) and serves as an approximate measure of the goodness of model fit

Hypothesized direct paths	Path coefficients
Strategic planning -> Third-party innovation (H1a)	0.175 (0.113)
Technical development -> Third-party innovation (H2a)	0.228 (0.185)
Operational support -> Third-party innovation (H3a)	0.129 (0.449)
IT enablement -> Third-party innovation (H4a)	0.127 (0.320)
IT management -> Third-party innovation (H5a)	0.063 (0.661)
Hypothesized indirect (mediation) paths	
Strategic planning -> Digital maturity -> Third-party innovation (H1b)	**0.173*** (0.063)**
Technical development -> Digital maturity -> Third-party innovation (H2b)	0.137 (0.084)
Operational support -> Digital maturity -> Third-party innovation (H3b)	**−0.178*** (0.071)**
IT enablement -> Digital maturity -> Third-party innovation (H4b)	0.054 (0.045)
IT management -> Digital Maturity -> Third-party innovation (H5b)	0.109 (0.059)
Direct paths	
Strategic planning -> Digital maturity	0.362*** (0.117)
Technical development -> Digital maturity	0.288 (0.157)
Operational support -> Digital maturity	−0.373*** (0.136)
IT enablement -> Digital maturity	0.113 (0.088)
IT management -> Digital Maturity	0.229** (0.109)
Digital maturity -> Third-party innovation	0.477*** (0.079)
R^2 (Digital maturity)	0.324
R^2 (Third-party innovation)	0.227

variables had a significant direct effect on the third-party involvement thus suggesting that achieving a certain degree of digital maturity is an important step between recognizing the value of IT capabilities for building a digital enterprise and involving external companies in the process of digital transformation.

We have also performed an *ex post* analysis of the relationships between exogenous variables and digital maturity. To that end, allocation of attention towards strategic planning has a positive and strongly significant effect on digital maturity (b = 0.362, $p < 0.01$). Furthermore, operational support was found to be negatively associated with digital maturity (b = −0.373, $p < 0.01$). Our model also indicates the presence of positive relationship between IT management variable and digital maturity (b = 0.229, $p < 0.05$). Finally, we found no statistically significant relationship between either technical development or IT enablement and digital maturity, respectively.

5 Discussion and Conclusion

Our findings have a series of theoretical and practical implications for companies embracing the digital transformation and using outsourcing as a strategic tool to leverage innovation.

Our first set of results identifies the type of activities that need to be prioritized in IT departments in the context of digital transformation. First, we have empirically confirmed that IT managers' beliefs regarding the importance of strategy-making and management activities for their job are imperative for achieving digital maturity. This evidence implies that in addition to strategic "planning" functions, IT leaders need to acknowledge the importance of the execution side of digital transformation. A clear understanding of the practical aspects of the large-scale digital transformation projects and familiarity with tools and mechanisms facilitating their execution are important for achieving digital maturity and extracting value from digital transformation initiatives. To sum up, whereas developing business acumen and strategic vision are necessary at the planning stage of digital transformation, building effective governance mechanisms and performance control systems become crucial at the implementation phase.

Conversely, we found that companies in which CIOs perceive providing operational support to business as their primary responsibility exhibit lower levels of digital maturity. That is, by adhering to a legacy of "backroom support" mindset, CIOs continue operating in silos and instilling cultural values which thwart the success of transformational initiatives. Surprisingly, we found no empirical evidence for the importance of activities from either technological development or IT enablement categories for digital maturity. As for the former, the possible explanation is that technical development of applications and related coding work has been procured from specialized providers even in the periods preceding digital era, and so whether or not these capabilities are retained important by CIOs remains irrelevant for digital transformation. Regarding the latter, the possible explanation is that IT enablement activities require the involvement of other organizational functions (e.g. procurement, HR) and therefore CIOs' individual beliefs about their respective importance do not directly affect digital maturity.

Our second set of results emphasizes the role of digital maturity in involving third parties in digital transformation projects. We find that digitally mature companies are more likely to co-create new products and services jointly with other companies within the industry ecosystem. The explanations of the observed results are several.

First, digitally mature companies have a clear vision of how to use technology for business value creation. As a result, they have an understanding of why external sourcing is required and which capability gaps they seek to address [42]. Second, they nurture the type of behavior among their employees that emphasizes the value of learning, sharing and collaboration thus facilitating the absorption of new knowledge [64]. Third, digital enterprises have more nimble governance structures and work processes in place that help to eliminate inefficiencies in communication and coordination of activities across two or more external stakeholders. As a result, they are more likely to reduce waste and obtain tangible outcomes. Last but not least, digitally mature companies have technology and infrastructure systems that enables them to test innovative solutions in a quick and responsible manner without making large investments up-front. Doing so also allows the company to obtain user feedback early on and reduce the risk of failure of a digital innovation.

Finally, with regards to the relationship between CIOs' priorities and the decision to source capabilities externally we have uncovered a more complex mechanism. That is, when it comes to digital transformation, the CIOs' internal beliefs regarding the importance of capabilities for the IT function seem to not directly affect the innovation outcomes of third-party collaborations. Instead, this relationship is contingent on the type of capability prioritized within IT and is mediated by the degree of digital maturity the company has managed to achieve.

References

1. Pavlou, P.A., El Sawy, O.A.: The "third hand": IT-enabled competitive advantage in turbulence through improvisational capabilities. Inf. Syst. Res. **21**(3), 443–471 (2010)
2. Fitzgerald, M., Kruschwitz, N., Bonnet, D., Welch, M.: Embracing digital technology: a new strategic imperative. MIT Sloan Manag. Rev. **55**(2), 1 (2014)
3. Weill, P., Woerner, S.L.: The future of the CIO in a digital economy. MIS Q. Executive **12** (2), 65–75 (2013)
4. Feeny, D.F., Willcocks, L.P.: Core IS capabilities for exploiting information technology. Sloan Manag. Rev. **39**(3), 9 (1998)
5. Bharadwaj, A., El Sawy, O.A., Pavlou, P.A., Venkatraman, N.V.: Digital business strategy: toward a next generation of insights. MIS Q. **37**(2), 471–482 (2013)
6. Wu, S.P.J., Straub, D.W., Liang, T.P.: How information technology governance mechanisms and strategic alignment influence organizational performance: insights from a matched survey of business and it managers. MIS Q. **39**(2), 497–518 (2015)
7. Weeks, M.R., Feeny, D.: Outsourcing: from cost management to innovation and business value. Calif. Manag. Rev. **50**(4), 127–146 (2008)
8. Lacity, M.C., Willcocks, L.P.: Beyond cost savings: outsourcing business processes for innovation. Sloan Manag. Rev. **54**(3), 63–69 (2013)
9. Oshri, I., Kotlarsky, J., Gerbasi, A.: Strategic innovation through outsourcing: the role of relational and contractual governance. J. Strateg. Inf. Syst. **24**(3), 203–216 (2015)
10. Aubert, B.A., Kishore, R., Iriyama, A.: Exploring and managing the "innovation through outsourcing" paradox. J. Strateg. Inf. Syst. **24**(4), 255–269 (2015)
11. Ocasio, W.: Towards an attention-based view of the firm. Strateg. Manag. J. **18**(S1), 187–206 (1997)
12. Ocasio, W.: Attention to attention. Organ. Sci. **22**(5), 1286–1296 (2011)
13. Gary, M.S., Wood, R.E., Pillinger, T.: Enhancing mental models, analogical transfer, and performance in strategic decision making. Strateg. Manag. J. **33**(11), 1229–1246 (2012)
14. Gary, M.S., Wood, R.E.: Mental models, decision rules, and performance heterogeneity. Strateg. Manag. J. **32**(6), 569–594 (2011)
15. Tripsas, M., Gavetti, G.: Capabilities, cognition, and inertia: evidence from digital imaging. Strateg. Manag. J. **21**(10–11), 1147–1161 (2000)
16. Simon, H.A.: A behavioral model of rational choice. Q. J. Econ. **69**(1), 99–118 (1955)

17. Cyert, R.M., March, J.G.: A Behavioral Theory of the Firm, vol. 2, pp. 169–187. Prentice-Hall, Englewood Cliffs (1963)
18. Shepherd, D.A., Mcmullen, J.S., Ocasio, W.: Is that an opportunity? An attention model of top managers' opportunity beliefs for strategic action. Strateg. Manag. J. **38**(3), 626–644 (2017)
19. Kiesler, S., Sproull, L.: Managerial response to changing environments: perspectives on problem sensing from social cognition. Adm. Sci. Q. **27**, 548–570 (1982)
20. Vuori, T.O., Huy, Q.N.: Distributed attention and shared emotions in the innovation process: how Nokia lost the smartphone battle. Adm. Sci. Q. **61**(1), 9–51 (2016)
21. Lucas Jr., H.C., Goh, J.M.: Disruptive technology: how Kodak missed the digital photography revolution. J. Strateg. Inf. Syst. **18**(1), 46–55 (2009)
22. Eggers, J.P., Kaplan, S.: Cognition and renewal: comparing CEO and organizational effects on incumbent adaptation to technical change. Organ. Sci. **20**(2), 461–477 (2009)
23. Nambisan, S., Lyytinen, K., Majchrzak, A., Song, M.: Digital innovation management: reinventing innovation management research in a digital world. MIS Q. **41**(1), 223–238 (2017)
24. Kane, G.C., Palmer, D., Phillips, A.N., Kiron, D., Buckley, N.: Strategy, not technology, drives digital transformation. MIT Sloan Manag. Rev. **14**, 1–25 (2015)
25. Tumbas, S., Berente, N., vom Brocke, J.: Digital innovation and institutional entrepreneurship: chief digital officer perspectives of their emerging role. J. Inf. Technol. 1–15 (2018)
26. Boynton, A.C., Zmud, R.W.: Information technology planning in the 1990's: directions for practice and research. MIS Q. **12**, 59–71 (1987)
27. Sobol, M.G., Klein, G.: Relation of CIO background, IT infrastructure, and economic performance. Inf. Manag. **46**(5), 271–278 (2009)
28. Aral, S., Weill, P.: IT assets, organizational capabilities, and firm performance: how resource allocations and organizational differences explain performance variation. Organ. Sci. **18**(5), 763–780 (2007)
29. Tippins, M.J., Sohi, R.S.: IT competency and firm performance: is organizational learning a missing link? Strateg. Manag. J. **24**(8), 745–761 (2003)
30. Malladi, S., Krishnan, M.S.: Cloud computing adoption and its implications for CIO strategic focus–an empirical analysis. In: Thirty Third International Conference on Information Systems (ICIS), Orlando (2012)
31. Saldanha, T., Krishnan, M.: Leveraging IT for business innovation: does the role of the CIO matter? (2011)
32. Khanagha, S., Volberda, H., Oshri, I.: Customer co-creation and exploration of emerging technologies: the mediating role of managerial attention and initiatives. Long Range Plan. **50**(2), 221–242 (2017)
33. Oshri, I., Arkhipova, D., Vaia, G.: Exploring the effect of familiarity and advisory services on innovation outcomes in outsourcing settings. J. Inf. Technol. 1–13 (2018)
34. Bassellier, G., Benbasat, I.: Business competence of information technology professionals: conceptual development and influence on IT-business partnerships. MIS Q. **28**, 673–694 (2004)
35. Heart, T., Maoz, H., Pliskin, N.: From governance to adaptability: the mediating effect of IT executives' managerial capabilities. Inf. Syst. Manag. **27**(1), 42–60 (2010)
36. Chen, D.Q., Preston, D.S., Xia, W.: Antecedents and effects of CIO supply-side and demand-side leadership: a staged maturity model. J. Manag. Inf. Syst. **27**(1), 231–272 (2010)

37. Svahn, F., Mathiassen, L., Lindgren, R.: Embracing digital innovation in incumbent firms: how Volvo cars managed competing concerns. MIS Q. **41**(1), 239–253 (2017)
38. Jansen, J.J., Van Den Bosch, F.A., Volberda, H.W.: Exploratory innovation, exploitative innovation, and performance: effects of organizational antecedents and environmental moderators. Manage. Sci. **52**(11), 1661–1674 (2006)
39. Rothaermel, F.T., Deeds, D.L.: Exploration and exploitation alliances in biotechnology: a system of new product development. Strateg. Manag. J. **25**(3), 201–221 (2004)
40. Chesbrough, H.: The logic of open innovation: managing intellectual property. Calif. Manag. Rev. **45**(3), 33–58 (2003)
41. Parmigiani, A., Mitchell, W.: Complementarity, capabilities, and the boundaries of the firm: the impact of within-firm and interfirm expertise on concurrent sourcing of complementary components. Strateg. Manag. J. **30**(10), 1065–1091 (2009)
42. Capron, L., Mitchell, W.: Selection capability: how capability gaps and internal social frictions affect internal and external strategic renewal. Organ. Sci. **20**(2), 294–312 (2009)
43. Kogut, B., Zander, U.: Knowledge of the firm, combinative capabilities, and the replication of technology. Organ. Sci. **3**(3), 383–397 (1992)
44. Cohen, W.M., Levinthal, D.A.: Absorptive capacity: a new perspective on learning and innovation. In: Strategic Learning in a Knowledge Economy, pp. 39–67 (2000)
45. Hoang, H.A., Rothaermel, F.T.: Leveraging internal and external experience: exploration, exploitation, and R&D project performance. Strateg. Manag. J. **31**(7), 734–758 (2010)
46. Grigoriou, K., Rothaermel, F.T.: Organizing for knowledge generation: internal knowledge networks and the contingent effect of external knowledge sourcing. Strateg. Manag. J. **38**(2), 395–414 (2017)
47. Yoo, Y., Henfridsson, O., Lyytinen, K.: The new organizing logic of digital innovation: an agenda for information systems research. Inf. Syst. Res. **21**(4), 724–735 (2010)
48. Yoo, Y., Boland Jr., R.J., Lyytinen, K., Majchrzak, A.: Organizing for innovation in the digitized world. Organ. Sci. **23**(5), 1398–1408 (2012)
49. Corso, M., Giovannetti, G., Guglielmi, L., Vaia, G.: Conceiving and implementing the digital organization. In: Bongiorno, G., Rizzo, D., Vaia, G. (eds.) CIOs and the Digital Transformation, pp. 181–203. Springer, Cham (2018). https://doi.org/10.1007/978-3-319-31026-8_10
50. Arkhipova, D., Vaia, G., DeLone, W., Braghin, C.: IT Governance in the Digital Era (2016)
51. Preston, D.S., Chen, D., Leidner, D.E.: Examining the antecedents and consequences of CIO strategic decision-making authority: an empirical study. Decis. Sci. **39**(4), 605–642 (2008)
52. Kaltenecker, N., Hess, T., Huesig, S.: Managing potentially disruptive innovations in software companies: transforming from on-premises to the on-demand. J. Strateg. Inf. Syst. **24**(4), 234–250 (2015)
53. Lee, G., Xia, W.: Toward agile: an integrated analysis of quantitative and qualitative field data on software development agility. MIS Q. **34**(1), 87–114 (2010)
54. Catlin, T., Scanlan, J., Willmott, P.: Raising your digital quotient. McKinsey Q. (2015)
55. Westerman, G., Tannou, M., Bonnet, D., Ferraris, P., McAfee, A.: The digital advantage: how digital leaders outperform their peers in every industry, pp. 2–23. MIT Sloan Management and Capgemini Consulting, Massachusetts (2012)
56. Kane, G.C.: Digital maturity, not digital transformation. MIT Sloan Manag. Rev. **14**, 1 (2017)
57. Chin, W.W.: The partial least squares approach to structural equation modeling. Mod. Methods Bus. Res. **295**(2), 295–336 (1998)

58. Hair, J.F., Ringle, C.M., Sarstedt, M.: PLS-SEM: indeed a silver bullet. J. Mark. Theor. Pract. **19**(2), 139–152 (2011)
59. MacKenzie, S.B., Podsakoff, P.M., Podsakoff, N.P.: Construct measurement and validation procedures in MIS and behavioral research: integrating new and existing techniques. MIS Q. **35**(2), 293–334 (2011)
60. Fornell, C., Larcker, D.F.: Evaluating structural equation models with unobservable variables and measurement error. J. Mark. Res. **18**, 39–50 (1981)
61. Henseler, J., Ringle, C.M., Sarstedt, M.: A new criterion for assessing discriminant validity in variance-based structural equation modeling. J. Acad. Mark. Sci. **43**(1), 115–135 (2015)
62. MacKinnon, D.P., Lockwood, C.M., Williams, J.: Confidence limits for the indirect effect: distribution of the product and resampling methods. Multivar. Behav. Res. **39**(1), 99–128 (2004)
63. Baron, R.M., Kenny, D.A.: The moderator–mediator variable distinction in social psychological research: conceptual, strategic, and statistical considerations. J. Pers. Soc. Psychol. **51**(6), 1173 (1986)
64. Rothaermel, F.T., Alexandre, M.T.: Ambidexterity in technology sourcing: the moderating role of absorptive capacity. Organ. Sci. **20**(4), 759–780 (2009)

The Barriers to Innovation: An Examination of the Effect of "Keeping the Lights on"

Ilan Oshri[✉]

Graduate School of Management, University of Auckland Business School,
University of Auckland, 12 Grafton Road, Auckland 1050, New Zealand
Ilan.oshri@auckland.ac.nz

Abstract. Innovation delivers a sustainable competitive edge if done right. The multi-million dollar boardroom question that CIOs are often left to address is, "how are we going to pay for this?" The problem is, ongoing operations consume 80%–90% of a typical IT budget. As you will see on the following pages, nearly 90% of IT decision makers believe their organizations ought to be spending more on innovation. We found most IT leaders (68%) say too much of the budget is being consumed by basic IT operations and maintenance. This excessive emphasis on just "keeping the lights on" is frustrating because it limits the IT organization's ability to pursue transformational initiatives that go beyond the basics. Technology leaders want to make sure the basics are covered but at a reasonable cost – with budget left over for trying new things and seeking technology-enabled business opportunities. They want core business systems managed in efficient ways that make the organization agile, creating possibilities rather than hindering progress. Our analysis validates an overarching point that investment in innovation requires a rebalancing of spending priorities today by shifting funds and resources away from simply maintaining and running the IT infrastructure. This is widely understood, but IT leaders struggle on how to make it happen. The innovative CIO must not only find the savings and free up resources from routine maintenance but also ensure the money is redirected to innovation initiatives. Innovation is not easy, but it is worth the effort because only exceptional effort, intelligence, and leadership will produce exceptional results.

Keywords: Innovations · Outsourcing · IT expenditure decisions

1 The State of Innovation

Innovation is key for the firm's growth and its competitiveness. Innovative firms are more likely to outperform their competition, attract superior talent and enjoy the trust of their customers and vendors. Innovative firms are known to be technology savvy, accustomed to rapidly integrating the latest technologies into successful services and products. High performing innovation companies are used to transformations and changes in their operating mode and consequently embrace new business models as a way of integrating innovative solutions into their corporate strategy. History has provided us with ample examples of firms that maintained their relevance by reinventing the sources of their competitiveness. Consider the top innovating firms in 2017

© Springer Nature Switzerland AG 2019
J. Kotlarsky et al. (Eds.): Global Sourcing 2018, LNBIP 344, pp. 19–34, 2019.
https://doi.org/10.1007/978-3-030-15850-7_2

according to FastCompany[1], among them Amazon, Google, Uber and Netflix. What they have in common is their commitment to seek new technological solutions that transform their products and services. For example, Uber was initially known for its superior app-based transportation platform that challenged the established taxi business, but now is experimenting with autonomous trucks to transform the economics of logistics. Amazon, originally known for selling books through its website has developed itself into a cloud-based service using artificial intelligence to provide a customer centric experience, including efficient delivery and timely and relevant information to make purchasing decisions. Uber and Amazon have continuously invested in new IT platforms, such as cognitive computing and artificial intelligence, to challenge their own business models as well as reshape existing business solutions. These innovations are radical in nature, completely revamping the service offering of these firms and helping them create new revenue streams.

Radical innovation is capital intensive, often requiring significant investment in resources to transform the knowledge and operational base of the firm. For this reason, radical innovation is often viewed by executives as a risky strategy that puts constraints on the firm's resources. While successful radical innovation is desired by firms, in reality, many firms either shy away from engaging in radical innovation or fail to successfully achieve it. Therefore, we observe that firms pursue incremental innovation either alongside their radical innovation investments or as an alternative strategy. Incremental innovation is characterized as small improvements aimed at improving the firm's services, products and processes. This type of innovation requires steady and often reasonable amounts of spending on improvements in IT assets. However, incremental innovation is unlikely to deliver a competitive edge, but rather maintain the firm's relatively advantageous position vis-à-vis its services and processes. Of particular concern is the relatively mid-to-long term outlook to see significant returns on the investment. A good example of a radical innovation is the current investments in artificial intelligence by many firms that is transforming their knowledge-base, operational and business model. These AI initiatives are not yet yielding significant returns but are expected to have significant impact on business performance in the next decade[2]. Similarly, investments made in robotic process automation since 2015 are only now showing returns for early adopters of the technology.

Executives are required to consider both incremental and radical innovations. Incremental innovations will provide support to existing platforms that drive contemporary business objectives while investments in radical innovations will offer a leapfrog advancement that transforms the firm's business model. As both types of innovation require significant investments of capital and knowledge, firms need to weigh all their strategies and trade-offs to fund their innovation strategy.

Another challenge for many firms is to keep up with the rapid introduction of technological innovations. While most new technologies deliver opportunities to reduce costs and reconstruct the firm's value proposition, it takes time to properly

---

[1] https://www.fastcompany.com/most-innovative-companies/2017.

[2] https://www.ibm.com/blogs/watson/2017/11/top-10-ways-ai-will-impact-business-in-the-next-decade/.

implement new technologies. Equally critical is the next step: redesigning the value chain to accommodate the changes needed in the firm's operational and strategic model to benefit from the value new technologies may bring. Consider the latest wave of technologies such as robotic process automation, cognitive computing and artificial intelligent. Undoubtedly, these technologies will transform the firm's operational model and, to some degree, the firm's business model. However, research[3] shows that since 2016, most firms have gained little innovative experimentation with robotic process automation, so far yielding very little impact on the firm's operations in terms of real cost savings. Similarly, apart from anecdotal examples, it is unclear the degree to which firms have benefited from implementing impactful innovative solutions that incorporate cognitive computing and artificial intelligence. Clearly, it will take few years for firms embracing such innovative technologies to yield results from their recent investments.

Innovation presents additional challenges. As innovation is by and large technology-driven, knowledge of the technology and its ability to support business solutions does not always reside within the firm and, if it does, in many cases it resides outside the decision makers' circle. We have observed greater reliance on advisory services and vendors as firms make important decisions about the nature of innovation. One likely outcome is that the firm is responding to a vendor's offering rather than constructing a clear roadmap of upcoming innovations that would ensure an alignment between the adopted technology, an existing architectural platform and the firm's strategic plan. Unfortunately, such a reactive approach often results in a scattered and decentralized innovation strategy, in which business units pursue their innovation agenda but without an orchestrated effort to bring new technologies together as part of the service platform.

While such challenges persist, firms undoubtedly require to plan for the introduction of new technologies in an informed and impactful manner to ensure growth and change vis-à-vis market conditions. As such, firms need to consider how they organize for innovation.

2 Investing in Innovation

Most firms claim to have the drive and ambition to be an innovator. However, many of them face challenges in achieving success through innovation s. But why is innovation so challenging?

First and foremost, companies struggle with shrinking to flat budgets to fund innovation. A recent study by Gartner[4] shows that firms have invested about 90% of their IT budget in 'keeping the lights on' and incremental innovation, while only 10% of the budget is allocated to transformative innovation. Our study confirms these concerns, with 77% of the executives stating that the biggest obstacle to achieving innovation is over-spending on 'keeping the lights on' (Fig. 1).

---

[3] https://www.horsesforsources.com/gartner-rpa-overhype_052317.

[4] https://www.gartner.com/doc/3830119/it-key-metrics-data-.

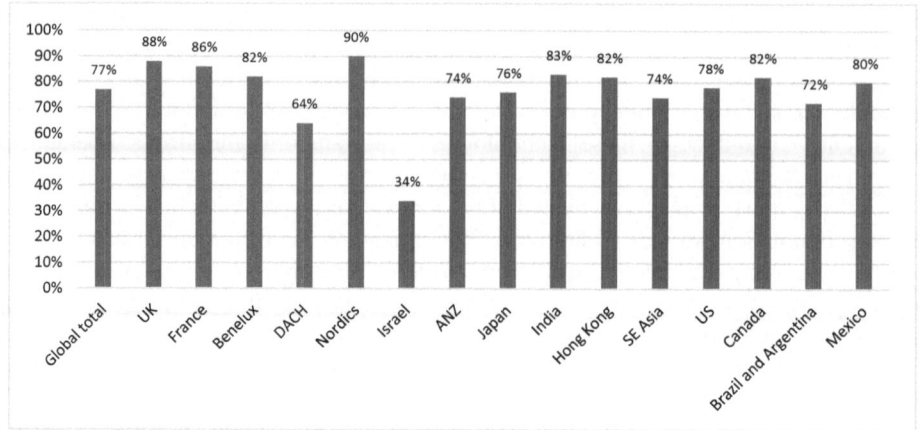

Fig. 1. Spending too much keeping the lights on is a blocker to innovation in organizations around the world

With the 1majority of IT budget invested in maintaining and running current IT systems, firms are losing on both drivers of success, i.e. operational excellence and transformative innovation. Reflecting that concern, 89% of the executives in this study clearly indicated that their organization should be spending more on innovation, and 68% said their organization is spending too much on "keeping the lights on" (see Figs. 2 and 3).

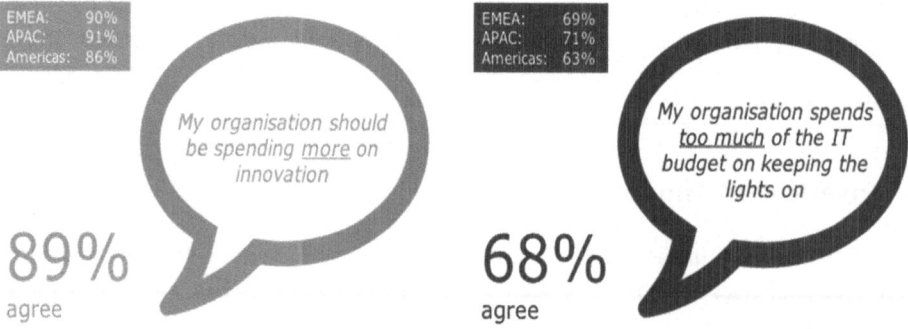

Fig. 2. Analysis of respondents who agree with the above statement, all respondents (900)

Fig. 3. Analysis of respondents who agree with the above statement, all respondents (900)

Considering that IT budgets are tight and spending on IT is expected to increase by only 2.7% by 2019[5] it is hard to see how firms will be able to cope with a lack of investment in both innovation and achieve operational excellence. Specifically, 71% of the executives are worried about investing adequately in IT innovation (Figs. 4 and 5).

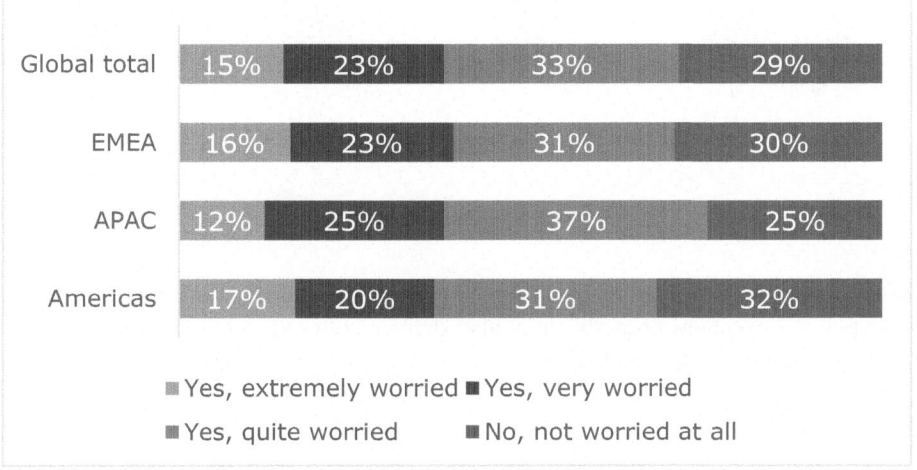

Fig. 4. 'Are you worried about how your organization will find the budget for innovation?' split by region

Allocating budget for IT innovation is a strategic matter. It goes beyond the financial exercise of computing budget allocation to various departments and requires the firm to align its strategic service and product roadmap with information about the value of emerging technological and business solutions. There must be a careful and realistic analysis of the benefits that IT innovation would deliver to the firm vis-à-vis its strategic roadmap. Executives in this study are confident that investing in innovation is a strategic priority (see Fig. 6) and plan to increase IT spending on innovation by 11% (globally).

Interestingly, executives believe that current allocation of IT budget to innovation initiatives falls short by about 5% to allow the firm to achieve its innovation goals. In budget terms, an additional allocation of 5% of the IT budget can be a substantial amount for medium and large firms.

Executives are confident in the returns on an investment in IT innovation, with 46% saying they have already seen improved productivity as a result, while 49% expect to see a reduction in operating costs. Further, executives reported that they have already benefited from a 14% increase in annual revenues and a 12% reduction in operating

---

[5] https://www.gartner.com/newsroom/id/3845563.

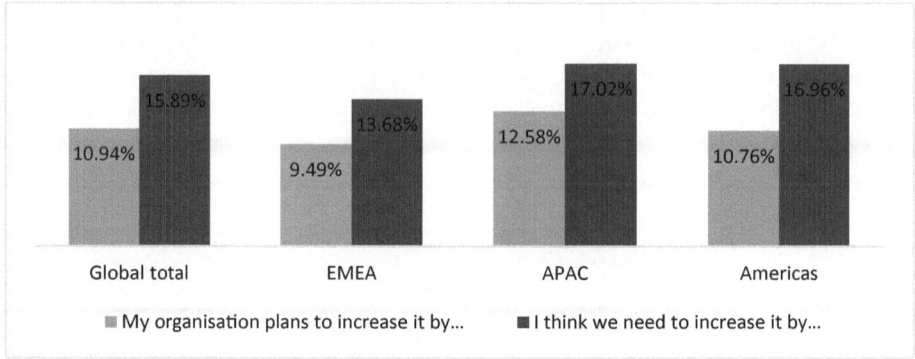

Fig. 5. Increase IT innovation budget by…..

costs as a result of spending on IT innovation, hinting that innovation, if planned, budgeted and executed properly, may also deliver both competitive edge and operational excellence (Figs. 7 and 8).

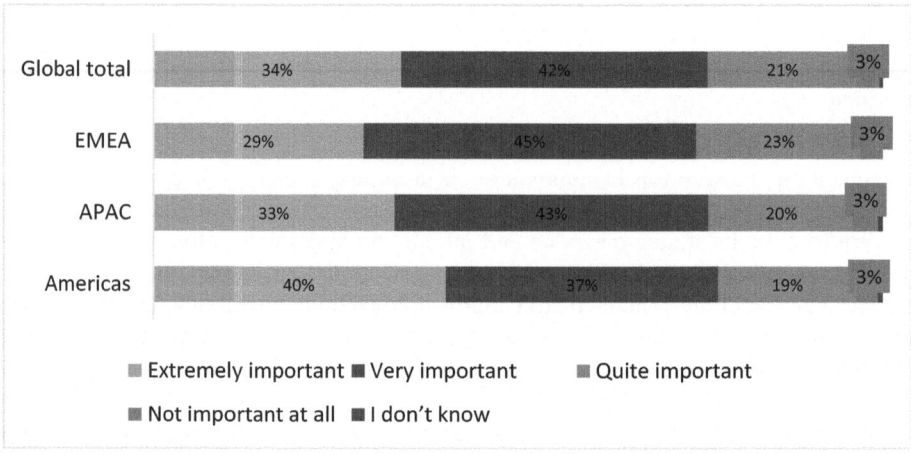

Fig. 6. 'How important a strategic priority is it for your organization to increase its spending on innovation?' split by region

While executives are convinced of the benefits of innovation; the results so far highlight serious concerns about the ability of firms to achieve their innovation objectives. When asked about the main roadblocks for innovation in their organizations, executives pointed to over spending on keeping the lights on (77%), complex legacy infrastructure that makes innovation difficult (76%), board support for significant investment in innovation (76%), and lack of skills critical to delivering innovation (74%).

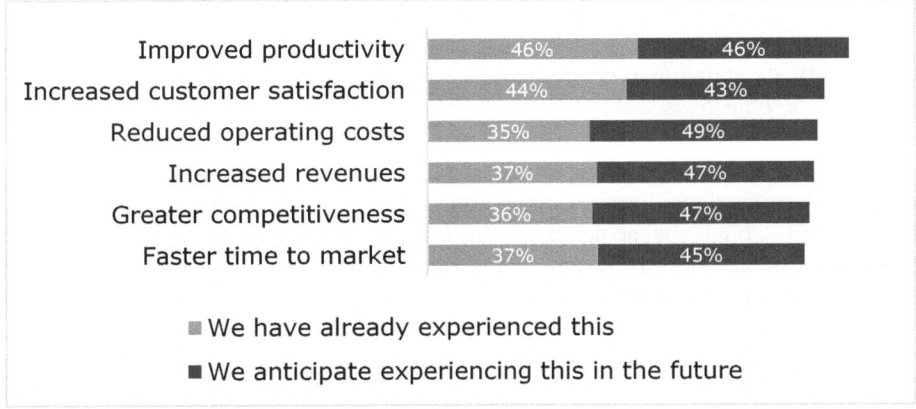

Fig. 7. The benefits that respondents' organizations have already experienced and the benefits anticipated in the future as a result of spending on innovation

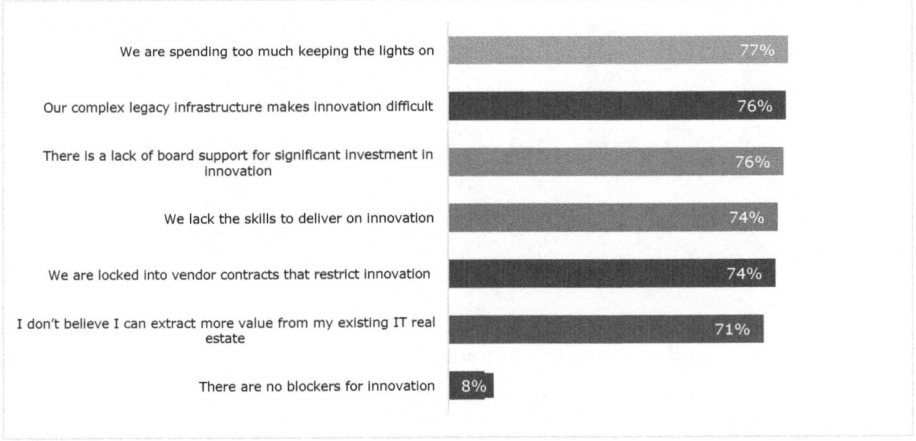

Fig. 8. What are the biggest blockers for innovation in your organization

These four areas highlight the difficult trade-offs many firms face and their inability to find the sweet spot to allocate budgets for transformative innovation while still improving their operational excellence. We will probe into each of these roadblocks for innovation in more detail in this report.

3 Leading the Innovation Effort

CEOs today are acting as both an innovation visionary and a facilitator, ensuring that the business objectives behind technological implementations are clear and well aligned with the firm's strategic roadmap and that resources are available for the team to deliver impactful innovation. However pursuing breakthrough IT innovation initiatives like artificial intelligence or cognitive computing may require revisiting the idea that the CEO should be at the helm. Such innovations require both technological knowledge and business relevance of the proposed solution to allow the innovation champion to make an informed decision.

Our study show that respondents were in the opinion that IT leaders, either the CTO (19%) or CIO (18%) should be leading IT innovation within the organization. They also reported that currently the CIO (20%), CEO (18%) and CTO (15%) are leading IT innovation initiatives (Fig. 9).

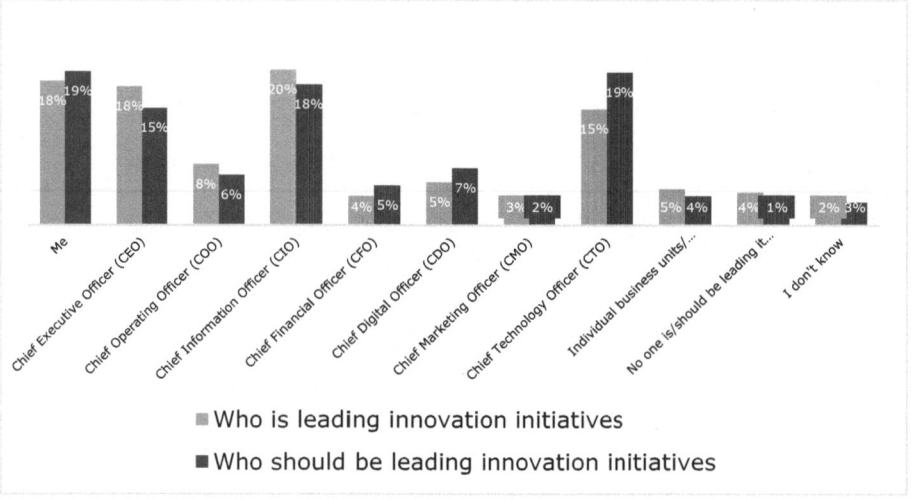

Fig. 9. 'Who is leading your organization's innovation initiatives?' asked to all respondents (900)

While our results show that there is innovation leadership at the board level, 50% of our respondents reported that they failed to convince the board that investing in innovation is critical for the business.

Respondents also felt that their role should be more strategic to delivering innovation initiatives (75%).

There was also an agreement among respondents that the board shies away from transformative projects that integrate the entire IT infrastructure (64%), is not confident that the firm has the skills to meet innovation objectives (57%), and is focusing on cost cutting rather than innovation (63%) (see Fig. 10).

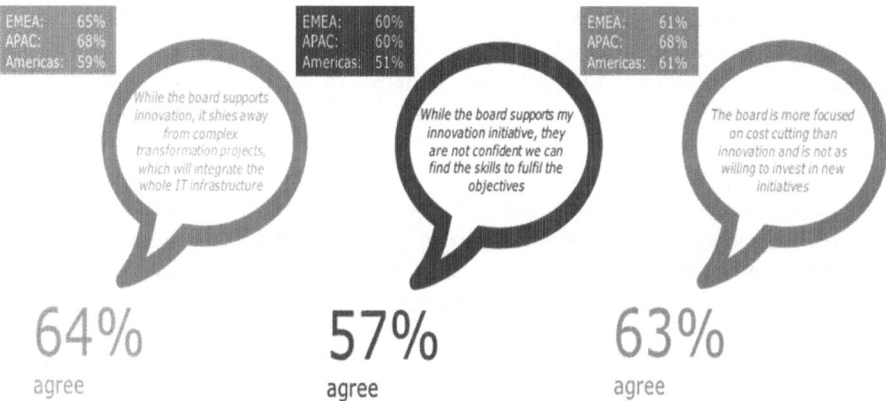

Fig. 10. Board-level attitudes to innovation

These results are alarming as the enterprise is facing tremendous challenges in keeping up with the recent wave of new technologies that require both innovation leadership and the ability to integrate knowledge and expertise. Innovation is becoming more complex than ever. While in the past a firm would have been expected to develop an innovative product or service by itself, now firms have to collaborate with other firms in order to bring in critical knowledge and capabilities unavailable in-house. In this regard, firms are required to develop a collaborative culture in which collaboration and competition are part of its operational mode. Put simply, firms need to train employees to reach out to external sources in search of innovation, while instilling the discipline to compete with their collaborator on market share and ideas. That is what makes organizing the firm for innovation in the 21st century so complex.

4   The State of Vendor Relationships

Historically, clients assumed that working with partners and third-party providers will benefit their operations and competitive positioning. After all, third-party providers possess wide experience of doing things better. But it is only relatively recently that client firms have paid greater attention to examining how closely working with their software vendors would deliver value-add to their operations. Several factors have contributed to this recent trend. First and foremost, long lasting engagements with software vendors have created trustful relationships between clients and vendors that allowed the parties to shift from focusing on transactional projects to value-add services. Secondly, some software vendors have seen delivering value-add services as a way of differentiating themselves from the crowd while deepening their relationships with the client and on some occasions increasing the client's dependency on their services and technologies. Last but not least, as pressure to deliver value to end-users mounts and client firms struggle to keep up with the pace of introducing new technologies, relying on software vendors who possess advanced business solutions, seems a reasonable and beneficial strategy.

Our study shows that while the idea of achieving innovation from your vendors is potentially beneficial, in reality our respondents expressed disappointment with their existing vendors in regard to the support offered in helping them to achieve their innovation objectives.

Clients are likely to entrust their service development with vendors when the relationships are based on a partnership between equals, in which the parties are creating opportunities to equally benefit from joint activities. Opportunistic behavior on behalf of either side is likely to diminish trust, resulting in lack of aptitude to engage in co-development activities. Fifty-four percent of our respondents reported that they have felt pressured to adopt the vendor's cloud strategy Similarly, 63% of the respondents reported that they felt locked in to their relationships with their vendors, hinting at their inability to make changes in the contract or service, despite changes in needs over time (Fig. 11).

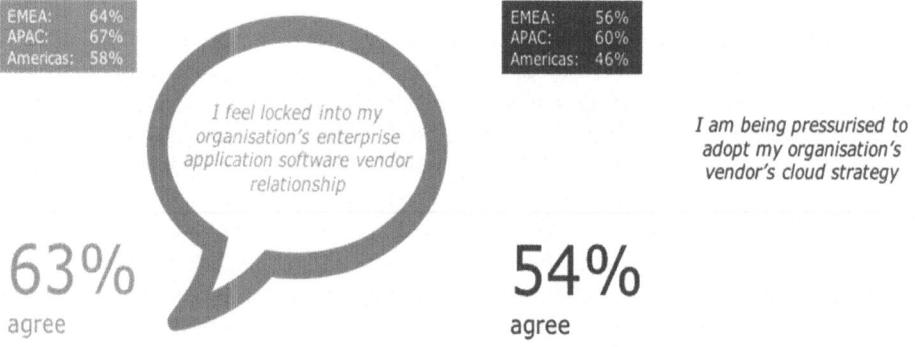

Fig. 11. Troubling vendor relationships

While many firms tend to auto-renew their engagement with their vendors, a healthy practice is to assess the needs and market offering well in advance of the end of the service contract. In doing so, client firms are required to re-assess their future needs and examine solutions available in the market, compared with the current levels of service and associated costs by the existing provider. Respondents (56%) indicated that they are under so much time pressure that they often allow software support contracts to auto-renew without properly evaluating the alternatives. This evidence is particularly worrying as we also see that the vast majority of the vendors took little interest in helping client firms benefit from value-add services. To conclude, it appears from this study that client firms are 'stuck' in a transactional relationship with their software vendors, expressing growing dissatisfaction with the vendors' intent and commitment to help them innovate and transform their IT service platforms.

5   The Future of IT Innovation

The future brings additional challenges. There are numerous disruptors that firms should mitigate in the form of either introducing technological innovation or new processes. Our respondents indicated the top three risks to their ability to innovate are cybersecurity (62%), legacy IT systems (57%) and moving to the cloud (42%). These issues require significant investment of both capital and knowledge that may drain the organizational resources and occupy management for long periods of time while the firm gradually develops and executes a plan to mitigate the risk.

Take the move to the cloud as an example Forty-two percent of respondents indicated that they will invest their IT innovation budget in moving to the cloud in the next 12 months. They estimated that, on average, it will take three years to move core systems to the cloud, at an expected average cost of $62.5 million USD. Thirty-one percent of the respondents have already started their cloud migration (Fig. 12).

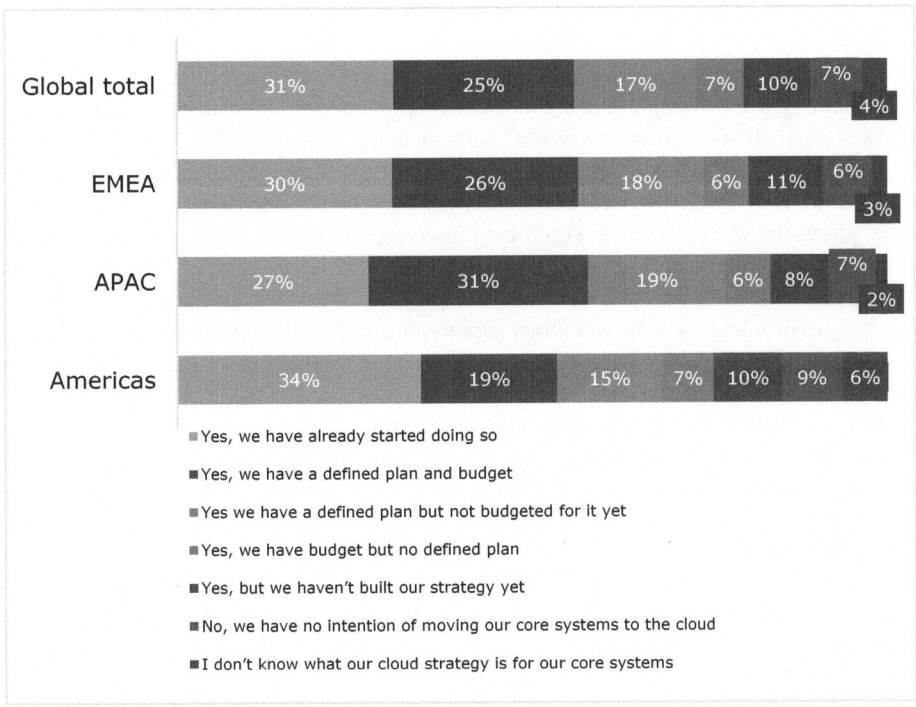

Fig. 12. Does your organization intend to move its core systems to the cloud?

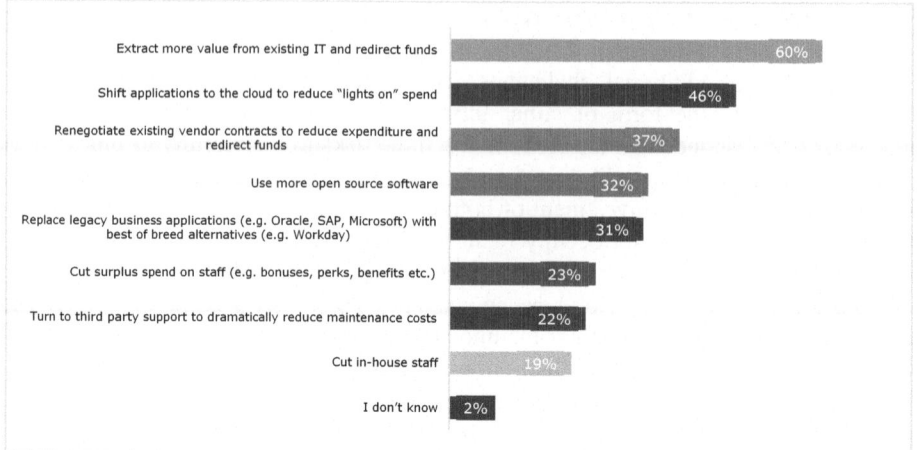

Fig. 13. How will your organization fund the desired increase in spending for IT innovation

However, these estimates by executives reveal the extreme challenge firms face in implementing their strategic plans. Consider that IT budgets are usually 3% (large firm) to 6% (small firm) of total revenues[6]. On average, a firm with $1 billion USD in revenue is likely to allocate about $40 million USD as their IT budget, thus needing to seek a significant budget increase of nearly 50% to finance the move to the cloud over three years. How can such a significant increase in the IT budget be realistically achieved over a short period of time?

Respondents weighed this question and predicted their top two strategies to solve the 'budget problem' will be to extract more value from existing IT in order to finance IT innovation (60%) and pursue cloud services to reduce costs associated with 'keeping the lights on' (46%) (Fig. 13).

But attempting to extract additional value from IT systems is in fact a call for incremental innovation in legacy systems that would require an investment prior to realizing a return. Moving applications to the cloud means, for many firms, greater concerns about data security, fear of being locked-in by the provider, concerns about access, and uncertainty about the cost of the service. These concerns persist in the mind of many decision makers despite advances in technological and business solutions relating to cloud services.

Renegotiating contracts is an option, supported by 37% of respondents. Yet it doesn't always deliver value to the client firm. A client might be able to renegotiate down the cost of the contract, but the vendor will very likely look for opportunities to safeguard its margins, either by slimming down its governance efforts, reassigning talent to more lucrative projects, or refraining from engaging in innovative projects. In the end, cost savings would be achieved, but less value will be delivered within the engagement. In other words, the result may be a lose-lose outcome for both parties.

---

[6] https://techvera.com/company-it-spend/.

Yet executives confirmed that despite the budget challenges they remain committed to introducing various initiates in order to embed innovation as a practice within the organization. These include investment in IT infrastructure (59%), professional development to enhance knowledge and skills (57%), and change management programs (39%). Such commitment is key to pursuing innovation. However, solving the 'budget problem' in which too much is currently invested in 'keeping the lights on' and too little is allocated into innovation' is still a challenge. We will next outline our proposal to tackle this challenge.

6 Solving the 'Budget Problem': The Service and Innovation Model

Firms nowadays sustain market position mainly because of their access to external sources of knowledge. Thinking of innovation as a collaborative effort that includes the involvement of end-users, stakeholders and vendors is imperative. Firms that have adopted this approach have sped up their innovation process, shortened the intervals between introductions of new services and shortened time to market. A key element in such a strategy is the ability of a firm to collaborate with its vendors. While client-provider relationships may often be portrayed as prone to disagreements and disputes, they also bear a great potential for success beyond the transactional contract. Our long examination of the relationships between contracting out services and innovation has revealed some specific conditions that can lead to success in terms of both service and innovation. Put simply, firms can enhance innovation by contracting out enterprise services. We identified two strategies to achieve this:

First, by contracting out the optimization of existing IT and software assets and redirecting savings to sponsor innovations. Second (and more promising), by incorporating innovation into the service contract.

While both strategies will result in the reduction of costs associated with 'keeping the lights on,' the latter likely will facilitate ongoing innovations delivered by the service provider. Both strategies require savvy vendor management capabilities on behalf of the client firm in which the client and vendor closely cooperate to achieve their objectives.

Strategy 1 – Reduce 'Keeping the Lights on' Costs. Firms can pursue multiple ways to reduce the costs involved in keeping enterprise systems and services up and running including exploring cloud computing, optimal license models, and third party support options to reduce expensive maintenance and support fees. Reducing IT costs by using in-house capabilities will require the firm to regularly optimize its software assets and licenses and continuously monitor the usage of applications to avoid servicing low-utilized assets and retire under-used applications. Developing such an internal capability is likely to be less efficient than current offerings on the market, as service providers have developed greater scale and technological abilities to perform such regular audits, thus outperforming most in-house services in this area.

Choosing the client-vendor collaborative path has both advantages and risks. On the one hand, working with a third-party has proven to deliver significant cost savings to client firms, often forming long-term relationships and commitments between vendors and clients that resulted in new sources of competitive advantage. On the other hand, this path can be risky, as clients and vendors might not always interpret the contract in a similar way, and expectations might lead to disappointments over time. Indeed, our research has shown that lack of commitment on behalf of the parties often leads to failure in collaboration. Thus, when choosing the collaborative path, the client firm needs to ensure that their software assets are ready to be serviced by an external vendor and carefully select the most suitable partner to assume responsibility for the service. A strong approach to governance on behalf of both parties and the on-going engagement in both maintaining and improving the service is likely to mitigate common risks.

While each of these options is likely to deliver costs-savings, it is the CIO's responsibility to ensure that savings gained are redirected back to value-add initiatives. With tight budgets, there is a possibility that the board will not be convinced that savings should be redirected to innovation activities. Money could instead be directed to the bottom line or to marketing and other departments outside of IT.

Strategy 2 – Blend Service with Innovation. The second strategy is to seek opportunities to blend innovation with outside services. Put simply, as part of the collaboration with a vendor, the client firm should seek to create conditions for the parties to collaborate on both incremental and radical innovations. In this way, innovation is generated within the engagement, by working closely with the vendor and leveraging the knowledge the vendor has acquired about the technological and business platforms of the clients.

One key challenge: the vendor's willingness to innovate for the client as part of the service engagement. Our research[7] into this issue reveals that many vendors shy away from engaging in innovation for their clients mainly because of the relatively high degree of uncertainty in innovation. Vendors are concerned that failing to meet the client's innovation expectations might negatively affect the service relationships. In return, clients are dissatisfied with vendors' efforts to innovate within the engagement, as we have seen in the results of this study.

Clients and vendors can and should create the appropriate conditions to achieve innovations within their service engagements. For one, the parties should design a contract that captures innovation opportunities throughout the lifecycle of the engagement. These can be sponsored via cost savings made within the engagement or as a co-sourcing model. Indeed, one major obstacle to achieving innovation is the lock-in position of client firms in contracts that do not accommodate innovation. But clients and vendors need to do more than just designing a contract that encourages collaboration. They must familiarize themselves with each other's technological and business

---

[7] Oshri, I., Kotlarsky, J. and Gerbasi, A. (2015) "Strategic Innovation Through Outsourcing: The Role of Relational and Contractual Governance," Journal of Strategic Information Systems, 24(3), pp. 203–216.

platforms and share the service roadmap to explore what technologies and methodologies may assist in the near and long-term future to achieve the firm's goals. Clients should articulate their objectives, be these cost savings, shorter time-to-market, or even improved strategic positioning in the market, and closely work with their vendor to explore avenues to achieve these goals. A software vendor needs to be attentive to the client's objectives and seek to develop standardized – but also customized – solutions that deliver value from the partnership. The collaborative innovation model is unique in assuming a long-term partnership between the parties in which greater familiarity and strong relationships allow the parties to meet their goals.

7 The Service – Innovation Model in Practice

The journey to ensure a productive use of IT assets while not compromising incremental and radical IT innovations requires executives to follow three key steps:

IT Innovation Roadmap. An IT Innovation roadmap is imperative to ensure clarity of future spending on IT innovation as well as to achieve alignment with contemporary and future business needs. CIOs should be in charge of developing a 5-year innovation roadmap to be annually reviewed in light of the introduction of new technologies and rapid changes in business models. The innovation roadmap will include the development of a multi-year plan of ongoing incremental innovations in existing platforms as well as a flagship radical innovation project that aims to transform the firm's market position in the mid to long term. The innovation roadmap will produce current spending on new IT projects and innovations as well as estimates of future spending needed to support the multi-year innovation plan.

An organization's technology roadmap benefits from clear visibility into the product roadmaps of technology vendors – an area where 81% of IT leaders surveyed said they wanted to see an improvement.

IT Maintenance/Innovation Spending Ratio Check. Input from the firm's innovation roadmap will be used to perform current and future maintenance/innovation (M/I) spending checks. A healthy M/I ratio should be an equal 50/50 spent on keeping the lights on, versus spending on innovation. In measuring maintenance spending, firms need to include the costs involved in maintaining IT hardware assets, application and enterprise software service packages, and cloud services, now and in the future. Of particular importance is the firm's commitment to spending on IT projects and the procurement of technological platforms in the future. Firms that currently or expect in the future to spend a greater amount on maintenance than on innovation should consider the following questions:

– Are we providing these IT services in-house or from a service provider?
– If in house, have we recently benchmarked the quality and cost of our in-house service against market offerings?
– If by service provider, have we recently benchmarked our service provider against current market offerings?
– Does the service require a premium offering or a standard one?

These guiding questions should allow the firm to realize its current spending position and consider making changes in the way the service is provided by considering on par quality but possibly more affordable offerings available in the market. Indeed, reducing the costs of 'keeping the lights on' will ensure a healthy M/I ratio and investment in innovation critical for the growth of the firm.

Collaborative Service – Innovation. Switching providers is not easy, but sometimes it is a necessity. Our research found out that nearly 50% of the firms that use service providers have changed providers. The main reason for changing providers was lack of value delivered by the provider. Benchmarking providers is therefore imperative. However, switching providers is only the starting point. Client firms ought to exploit the opportunity of a new contract to develop a collaborative service – innovation model with their service provider. Indeed, we advocate the approach that service and innovation should be woven together, creating a single fabric of collaborative relationships that benefits both service and innovation horizons. Some of the key enablers to achieve a successful collaborative Service-Innovation model are investment in familiarizing the vendor with the client's innovation road map and the client with the vendor's service roadmap. Knowledge sharing sessions can highlight contemporary business challenges the client is facing and the vendor's knowledge of current technological solutions that may address such challenges. Client and vendor should create 'spaces' to push forward innovation projects by considering the financial arrangements to support such initiatives. Last but not least, both parties need to be committed to achieve innovation by dedicating resources and capital to on-going exploration of value delivered through the engagement.

8   Conclusion

Nowadays, firms have to explore numerous avenues to ensure their IT assets are serviced in an efficient and productive manner while at the same time pursuing both incremental and transformative IT innovation.

Our survey showed the vast majority of IT decision makers believe their firms should be spending more on innovation. They say innovation is recognized by the organization as a strategic goal – but not always one that translates into budgeted funds and management priorities.

One of the biggest drains on innovation is "keeping the lights on" spending, which more than two thirds of those surveyed said consumes too high a proportion of their budget. That includes spending on ongoing enterprise vendor contracts, which many feel locked in to even though few IT leaders are fully satisfied with what the vendors are doing to contribute to innovation.

We make a clear case to seek partnership with specialized vendors who can free-up resources and capital to pursue innovations as well as getting involved directly in delivering incremental and radical innovations for their clients. It is through such collaborative innovations that the client firm will maintain its strategic edge in a fast-moving technological environment.

Exploring Determinants Influencing a Service-Oriented Enterprise Strategy: An Executive Management View

Albert Plugge[(✉)] and Marijn Janssen

Faculty of Technology, Policy and Management,
Delft University of Technology, Delft, The Netherlands
a.g.plugge@tudelft.nl

Abstract. Due to the convergence of rapid business developments and digitization challenges firms need to become more agile. A service-oriented enterprise (SOE) strategy is an approach that decomposes an enterprise into business services that are modular, accessible, and interoperable, in which parts can be provided in-house, or outsourced to the market. The SOE concept has mainly been approached from a technological view and little is known about what type of strategic SOE determinants are relevant. A firm's strategy to implement an SOE requires top management support. Therefore, insights at executive level are a prerequisite to identify strategic business directions. We conducted a literature review and a qualitative case study amongst eleven firms at executive level in various industries. Business services, business processes, and enabling technology were found in the literature as key determinants influencing a firm's SOE strategy. Subsequently, the interviews at executive level identified that organizational readiness, knowledge and skills, and governance also affect the SOE strategy of firms. We suggest that a holistic view is required to study the complexity of an SOE. By using an executive view we contribute to IS and business literature as strategic SOE determinants become more explicit.

Keywords: Service-oriented enterprise · Strategic decision-making ·
Business services · Business processes · Enabling technology

1 Introduction

Technology researchers paid attention to adopting a service-orientation enterprise (SOE) to improve business services in the period 2005 up to 2009. An SOE enabled the building of new products, end-user services, or business processes by composing them out of readily available and reusable building blocks which can be accessed using services [1–4]. These building blocks have an interface to initiate the execution of services. Large granular services, often involving humans and software, are often called *business services*. [5] argue that 'service-orientation is emerging at multiple organizational levels in business, and it leverages technology in response to the growing need for greater business integration, flexibility and agility', p. 356. Research interest to study the concept of service-orientation decreased after 2009 as the concepts of adaptability and agility were studied as a serious alternative to respond to changes

© Springer Nature Switzerland AG 2019
J. Kotlarsky et al. (Eds.): Global Sourcing 2018, LNBIP 344, pp. 35–55, 2019.
https://doi.org/10.1007/978-3-030-15850-7_3

easily [6, 7]. However, there is a renewed market interest in SOE as the convergence of rapid business developments and digitization challenges reflect firms' need to seek various approaches and become more agile [8, 9]. For example, [10] transformed their organization into an SOE to cater for market changes, and improve business value in which business services are managed from an integrated perspective. By means of establishing various types of shared business services (e.g. HR, Finance & Procurement, Business Operations) and supported by technology they are able to manage business processes globally, standardize scale and simplify work. As changes in, for instance, Finance and Procurement services occur, corresponding services (e.g. Information Technology) may be affected too, as a result of which an integrated change approach is required. As a result of an integrated management approach, [10] is able to accelerate business value and reduce cost that is reinvested in business areas.

By adopting an SOE, firms create business services that are modular, accessible and interoperable [11]. This enables them to reuse existing services and assemble them into new business services. As a result, firms are more able to become agile, respond to changing business circumstances, and, as such, decrease business development times, improve service quality, and reduce development cost. An SOE can be characterized as a set of cooperating business services that are loosely coupled and supported by dynamic business processes and applications that span organizations and multiple information systems [1]. Yet, little is known about *what* types of strategic SOE determinants are relevant, and subsequently, influence the implementation of an SOE strategy. Moreover, we may assume that a firm's strategy to implement an SOE requires top management support. Therefore, insights at executive level are a prerequisite. Given this void in research, we argue that a holistic approach is required to identify and analyze key determinants in the context of the implementation of a firm's SOE strategy. As literature is in its infancy we combine a literature review with empirical research by conducting interviews at the executive level. The leading research questions were:

- What SOE determinants are identified based on a literature review?
- What SOE determinants are identified at firms' executive level?

To address these questions an exploratory approach was conducted, consisting of a literature review and interviews conducted at executive level. In particular, we selected eleven firms in various industries. Firms deciding to adopt an SOE are studied by investigating their SOE strategy and corresponding determinants. By using an executive view we contribute to IS literature as strategic determinants become more explicit. This paper is organized as follows. In Sect. 2 the research is positioned vis-à-vis existing literature in the field of SOEs and next, the concepts business services, business processes, and enabling technology are presented. Section 3 explains the research approach. Next, the findings of our qualitative analysis are described in detail. Finally, our conclusions and limitations are listed in Sect. 5.

2 Literature Background

2.1 Service-Oriented Enterprise

The concept of an SOE gained momentum as the next generation of loosely coupled enterprise in which examples are recognized amongst various industries including computer industry, telecommunications, aircraft, and automotive industry [12–14] have defined an SOE as 'an enterprise that implements and exposes its business processes through a service-oriented architecture (SOA), and that provides frameworks for managing its business processes across a SOA landscape, p. 347". Literature shows that firms' aim to become an SOE is based on their business strategy. Strategic business drivers are, for instance, new service development [15], orchestrating new sources of value creation [16], and an increase enterprise agility [17]. In an effort to adapt to dynamic circumstances, today, firms deconstruct their enterprises and business processes into multiple business components that makes it more easy for businesses to focus on their core capabilities. Such business components can be characterized by a collection of activities or tasks in which resources produce services.

The decomposition of enterprises makes complexity manageable and, as such, services can be integrated and disintegrated. In this way business services can be provided by the own organization or by the market. As there are many business services, this results in sourcing strategies in which multiple modes of sourcing decisions are managed simultaneously [18]. Consequently, some sources, often related to the core competences, are provided in-house, whereas more commoditized services are outsourced. Examples include car manufacturers [19], external distribution channels [20], and IT process integration capabilities [21].

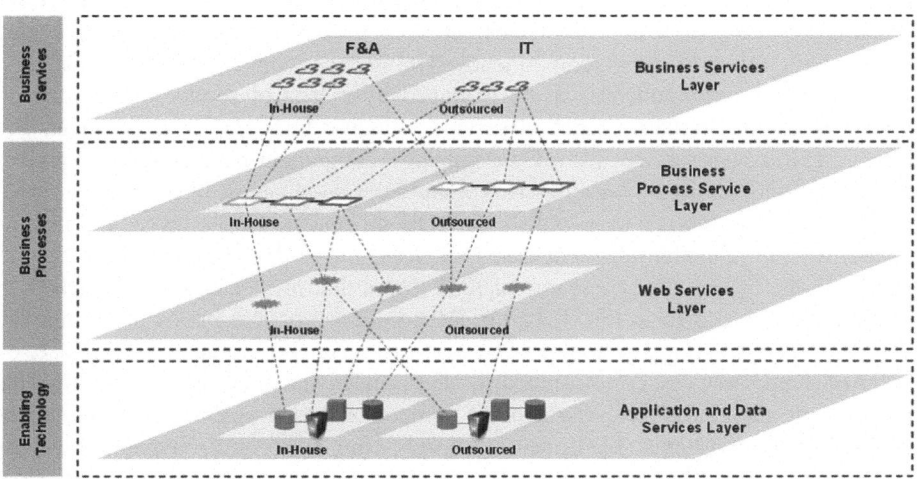

Fig. 1. Explaining a service-oriented enterprise by using layers

[22] points out that in order to become an SOE, firms must dismantle traditional stovepipes and design and implement modular services that can be reused dynamically. The authors argue that from an architectural perspective an SOE consists of various layers that comprise business services, business processes and IT infrastructure. Moving downward, business services, which reflect the first layer provide a firm essential support to produce and sell their products and goods. In turn, business services are supported by business processes, which form the second layer. Next, web services are used to establish relationships between business processes and enabling technology. The latter is seen as the third layer that consists of applications, data and IT infrastructure [23, 24]. The relationship between business services, business processes, and enabling technology is shown in Fig. 1.

The figure shows that services can be divided into business services and web services. Business services provide a business functionality and can be executed by software and/or humans, whereas web services are software-based services. At each layer there are services on different levels of granularity that can be combined to create new business services. By unbundling business services (e.g. F&A, IT) into loosely coupled business service processes, web services form the connection towards the application and data services layer. At each aggregated level (e.g. business services, business processes, enabling technology) a firm may decide to keep these tasks in-house or outsource these to the market.

2.2   Business Services

Previous studies show that a firm's SOE strategy is influenced by their business services [1, 22]. To focus on their core business competences business services are perceived as a federation of capabilities that collaborate with other business services in an ecosystem [1]. To improve effectiveness firms decompose their enterprise and corresponding business services into smaller autonomous business components that may interact with other business components. To manage complexity, the interaction between business components can be managed by means of services. Literature on services distinguishes varies types of services, ranging from business, technical, and software [5] to web services [25]. Consequently, component-based business services increase a firm's agility to cater for market and internal changes. In line with a firm's strategic business drivers to establish an SOE an analysis may reveal if business capabilities and related component-based services can be developed in-house or out-sourced to the market. Prior research of [26] shows that firms can decide which SOE related layers, as shown in Fig. 1, can be kept in-house or outsourced to the market. Literature reveals various examples of business services, both organized in-house, by means of shared services, or outsourced services, such as Finance and Accounting, HR, Procurement and IT [27, 28]. To support component-based business services, enterprise information systems (EIS) must be loosely coupled to create dynamic business processes [29] and, therefore, form a prerequisite for a strategic sourcing decision. Tightly coupled business services and EIS, on the other hand, may hinder the degree of SOE effectiveness.

2.3 Business Processes

Within traditional enterprises process flows are often sequential which may hinder reacting to internal and external changes adequately. Applying a service-orientation approach business processes are managed across a firm's organization that requires breaking down siloed business processes into modular independent services [5] that support dynamic processes. Considering dynamic processes, each subsequent process step may be based on the full or partial results of previous steps. This is in contrast with traditional processes that are designed from a predefined static sequence. From the perspective of a single service orchestration is concerned with the composition of services. To cater for changing circumstances business processes as applied within an SOE need to be orchestrated dynamically by means of choreographies, in which business processes are integrated to create end-to-end business processes. [13] argues that an SOE contains business-component-based, standardized process flows to encourage reusability [2]. To do so, a dynamic process design needs to build upon modular services that are supported by Enterprise Information Systems (EIS) that comprise applications, data, and infrastructure.

2.4 Enabling Technology

Literature shows that business processes are supported by enabling technology [2, 23, 24]. More specifically, EIS are used, based on the assumption that seamless integration of information is provided such as 'financial and accounting information, human resource information, supply chain information, and customer information' [30, p. 121]. [31] argue that 'EIS refer to organizational implementations of commercial software packages that enable the integration of transaction-oriented data and business processes throughout an organization (p. 152)'. An EIS is essential to respond to business and IT developments in IT-driven firms such as financial services and telecommunications [32]. As a result of changing firm and vendor relationships, supporting EIS need to be modified and enhanced [17]. This is related to the concept of modularization that can be applied to information systems as well as on an organizational level [33]. When business services are modularized the degree of complexity to manage these services is decreased. Moreover, EIS that support various loosely coupled modules and thus business services can be sourced both internally or to vendors. Consequently, the option to source a firm's EIS increases their level of adaptability, which, in turn, contributes to the manageability of an SOE. The concept of modularization supports organizations to interconnect their enterprise systems modules with other organizations modules. Interoperability across platforms is ensured as long as the interfaces between modules remain the same. This encourages seamless integration of information provided by various business services like finance and accounting, human resource, and procurement [30]. Thus modularized EIS can be configured to accommodate different business processes.

3   Research Method

The first phase in this research was based on a review of existing literature in the field of SOEs. On the one hand, the literature background focused on determinants that affect the implementation of a firm's SOE strategy. On the other hand, we may find indications for perceived determinants that can be studied specifically. The literature background provided necessary input for the second phase by conducting interviews and constructing a questionnaire that has been used to gather qualitative data in order to identify SOE determinants. Our qualitative method thus yielded an exploratory research [34]. This research design enabled the researchers to explore SOE determinants in a natural setting [35]. To acquire more insight in SOE determinants, it is necessary to consider different industries. In particular we have analyzed eleven firms in eight different industries.

We used two main criteria to select appropriate firms, namely: (A) the size of a firm, and (B) geography. Although there are differences between these eleven firms, they were selected due to similarities with regard to an SOE strategy. All of the selected firms are considered to be large companies and market leaders in their specific industry, operating in an intense and dynamic environment resulting in a need to be agile to cater for changing market circumstances and internal changes. This is related to the first criterion. The firms have at least two years of SOE experience and some of them are involved in a second generation SOE environment. Their geographical scope is based on operating on at least three geographies. The basic assumption is that business services must be agile by nature to provide these services in various countries. This is related to the second criterion.

3.1   Data Collection

Data was gathered between January 2015 and May 2016, and drew on various sources. These ranged from a literature review to a series of semi-structured interviews, both formal face-to-face and informal telephone interviews. First, we conducted eleven (11) in-depth interviews in total at executive level, as we want to investigate if an SOE strategy requires top management support. As the interviews were confidential, we anonymized the companies. All interviewed participants were executives or senior managers and had been engaged in establishing an SOE strategy. A semi-structured interview protocol was designed to gather data regarding the key constructs. Interviews varied from 60 min to 120 min in duration while some interviews were replicated for clarification purposes. Field notes were used during informal meetings to collect relevant background information. Second, a straightforward questionnaire was used to collect SOE-related information in which the key concepts were divided from the literature, namely: business services, business processes, and enabling technology. In addition, more generic client information was collected to create a better understanding of the sourcing context: strategic drivers, geographical coverage, and sourcing modes. The questionnaire was accompanied by a short cover letter that explained the purpose of this study. A short description of the questionnaire is provided in Appendix A.

Moreover, considering the need for clarity, and preventing the terminology from being interpreted differently, a glossary of definitions was included. By using multiple data sources we were able to increase the reliability of the data [36]. In this way we apply a cross-section between the firms to gain a richer insight in SOE determinants and to contribute to creating construct validity.

3.2 Data Analysis

The results of the case studies were written down in a case study report and sent to the participants to be validated. Interview data was stored in a case study data base. We analyzed the data in several systematic steps to ensure that the process is replicable. First, we studied context related information as well as construct data by grouping the statements (i.e. codes) into the construct categories. In doing so, we aim to create a basic understanding if determinants affect an SOE strategy. Second, a thorough analysis of the interview transcripts and field notes was done. Some data was verified by follow-up phone calls and emails. We consulted multiple sources of evidence, and strived for confirmation by triangulation of data. We used techniques as coding and clustering [34], sensitizing concepts and data displays [35]. We followed Miles and Huberman's advice to split the coding amongst two researchers, each coding the interview notes [35, p 64]. Then, we discussed the findings and clarified disagreements. As a result of the coding process we were able to identify links between concepts, so that we could fathom the data [37]. Patterns were gradually identified, which resulted in direct and indirect links between the constructs. Based on the analysis we were able to draw conclusions on how the constructs affected a firm's SOE strategy, and identified additional constructs.

4 Case Study Findings

4.1 Background Information

The questionnaire data revealed that the size of the firms ranges from 20,000 up to more than 100,000 employees, while the geography of the firms under study shows three dominant regions: North America, Europe and Asia Pacific. The SOE start of the firms varies from 2006 to 2014, and, by excluding the two firms that started in 2014, the vast majority of firms have a significant SOE experience. With regard to the headquarters location of the studied firms the questionnaire revealed that five out of eleven firms are located in the USA. SOE management reports to various reporting lines while the data does not indicate a specific relationship between the reporting line and sector, headquarters, size of the firm, start of the SOE, and geography. Moreover, the findings indicate that each firm allocates dedicated resources (e.g. SOE number of employees) to manage business services and related processes. Relevant background information is shown in Table 1.

Table 1. Background case study findings

Firm	Sector	Head quarters	Size of the firm	Responsible SOE manager	Reporting line	Start SOE	SOE geography	SOE number of employees
1	Pharma	USA	50,001 to 100,000	Director	CFO	2009	North America, Europe, Asia Pacific	100 to 500
2	Pharma	Switzerland	100,001 to 250,000	Director	CEO	2014	North America, Europe, Asia Pacific	5,001 to 10,000
3	Pharma	USA	20,001 to 50,000	Director	COO	2014	North America, Europe, South America, Asia Pacific	501 to 1,000
4	Food & Beverages	Mexico	100,001 to 250,000	Vice President	COO	2010	North America, South America	501 to 1,000
5	Diversified Conglomerate	Denmark	50,001 to 100,000	Director	COO	2007	Europe, Asia Pacific	100 to 500
6	Consumer Products	USA	20,001 to 50,000	Director	CEO	2006	North America, Europe, Asia Pacific	501 to 1,000
7	Food & Beverages	USA	20,001 to 50,000	Director	COO	2008	North America, Europe, South America, Asia Pacific, Middle East & Africa	1,001 to 2,000
8	Technology	USA	100,001 to 250,000	Director	Business Unit director	2006	North America, Europe, South America, Asia Pacific	1,001 to 2,000
9	Energy & Utilities	Norway	20,001 to 50,000	Senior Vice President	CFO	2006	North America, Europe, South America	1,001 to 2,000
10	Energy & Utilities	UK	50,001 to 100,000	Director	COO	2012	North America, Europe, South America, Asia Pacific, Middle East & Africa	1,001 to 2,000
11	Financial Services	Switzerland	50,001 to 100,000	Vice President	CFO	2011	North America, Europe, South America, Asia Pacific, Middle East & Africa	2,001 to 5,000

4.2   SOE Strategy and Business Services

The questionnaire indicates firms' strategic drivers to develop and implement an SOE strategy. Based on our questionnaire eight strategic drivers were assessed by the interviewees on a five-point scale (1 = low, 5 = high) (see Fig. 2). Importantly, the top three drivers indicate process excellence, the ability to scale up or down, and alignment of a firm's operating model. In an attempt to improve process efficiency interviews show that firms adapt their business processes continuously. Business services are often interdependent due to supporting interwoven business processes that need to be orchestrated dynamically. As a result, firms are able to cater for changes (e.g. improve their time-to-market and decrease lead times).

> 'We experienced that managing business processes is the key to sustain our business services. As multiple colleagues have to engage in performance process-related tasks it's key to decrease process complexity at all time. We strive to increase process performance day by day.' (Source: Director client 6)

Interviewees argue that in order to respond to environmental change effectively, business services are broken down in modular components. By integrating or disintegrating business components firms have the ability to scale up or down, depending on business needs. In doing so, flexible oriented business services contribute to enterprise agility.

> 'Based on our strategy 25% of F&A services are centralized in shared services centers to achieve standardization and flexibility. Our goal is to scale up to 75% within the three years... we expect that this ambition will lead to a 7% to 10% higher productivity.' (Source: Director client 3)

> 'As we have to adapt to market changes we have split our supporting processes in sub-processes to speed up time-to-market. Take for example our F&A function, we designed and implemented sub-processes in a modular way of working to support partial F&A activities, such as accounts payable, to align and integrate with other sub-processes easily.' (Source: Vice President client 4)

Moreover, as business services comprise modular components we find that firms have to make a critical decision at a strategic level how to source these business services. The questionnaire shows that all firms under study apply various modes (e.g. in-house and outsourced) of sourcing decisions that are managed simultaneously (see Table 2). This is consistent with prior research of [38] who argue that a firm's choice to select a sourcing mode is affected by the characteristics of a firm, such as their sourcing strategy, degree of risk aversion, internal capabilities, and market attractiveness.

Some firms opted to outsource large parts of specific business services, such as client 8 and 10 for Finance & Accounting and firm 5 for Information Technology. However, with the exception of client 6 and 10, all clients decided to provide data analytics services in-house.

> 'From a sourcing point of view we apply various models, including in-house, shared services and outsourced services, we have to! You know, it's impossible to acquire and maintain the knowledge and skills to support all our business services by ourselves. Besides that, we also have to be competitive in the market, so outsourcing tasks result in severe cost reductions.' (Source: CFO client 9)

Studying the interview data we find that in applying an SOE strategy executive management perceive organizational readiness to be an essential aspect. As business services are often interwoven and may span multiple functions (e.g. F&A, HR, IT) the complexity to organize and manage services will increase. In particular, sponsorship at executive level is required to create a buy-in from multiple stakeholders who are involved in managing various business services aspects, such as, business performance, change management, and financial goals and budgets. Interviews revealed that due to changing internal and external circumstances the clients under study developed a coherent approach over time to translate their SOE strategy into managerial conse-quences. Various executives experienced that a lack of stakeholder management may result in resistance that is difficult to overcome.

'The difficulty with business services is that responsibilities and budgets are dispersed amongst departments and geographies. That means that we have to pay a lot of attention to mutually align tasks and create a buy-in from all the stakeholders. This is an ongoing task and if we are not successful in this task, as a global organization we're not ready to provide business services.' (Source: Director client 10)

Fig. 2. Strategic drivers (N = 11)

With regard to organizational readiness we found that business services functions require involvement of the clients' employees in processes. To support procurement services, which are supported by EIS, employees have to exchange information between both services to ensure the availability and performance. As such, we found that from a content perspective the knowledge and skills of business employees are essential to manage and support these services. For example, employees need to have in-depth knowledge of business processes and the skills to operationalize these pro-cesses adequately.

'To support business services on a European scale we have to align business processes contin-uously to adapt to market conditions. As an example, we have appointed business process spe-cialists on a central level to exclude a much process waste as possible. We are only able to integrate business services as we streamline our processes to the max!' (Source: Director client 5)

Table 2. Modes of sourcing decision per business service

Client	Number of SOE functions	Finance & Accounting % outsourced	Information technology % outsourced	Human resources % outsourced	Procurement & supply chain % outsourced	Data analytics % outsourced
1	3	30%	40%		10%	
2	4	30%	60%	20%	10%	
3	2	50%		10%		
4	3	30%		10%	40%	
5	3	10%	80%	80%		
6	5	10%	10%	10%	10%	30%
7	2			10%	10%	
8	2	80%			10%	
9	3	20%	60%	30%		
10	4	80%		40%	40%	100%
11	3	50%		10%	50%	

On an operational level information was exchanged within and between EIS to support business services. We found that EIS employees dispose of technical knowledge to integrate and configure EIS modules as these systems are used to support various business services (e.g. SAP for F&A and HR services). Moreover, both technical and process-related knowledge was exchanged between internal departments and external vendors in case business services are (partially) outsourced to the market.

> *'Our IT department has to share technical information regarding our functional SAP services with external vendors. As part of our IT infrastructure is outsourced we have to implement our SAP modules for F&A services on the vendor's platform. This requires a lot of technical knowledge from our side (i.e. impact analysis, performance, reporting) to keep services running'. (Source: Director client 2)*

4.3 Business Processes

Based on the interviews we can distinguish four types of business processes that are applied by the selected clients to support business services (see Fig. 3). First, business processes can be implemented from a decentralized perspective. In this view an SOE function is performing business services on their own behalf. Second, some clients consolidate business processes tasks from a centralized perspective. As such, processes are managed by a centralized SOE function in which business units can be seen as internal customers.

> *'On a monthly basis all process owners meet at central level to discuss improvements and KPI's and assess if allocated budgets towards the business units are sufficient.' (Source: Director client 8)*

Third, business processes can be consolidated and managed by a regional SOE entity and operated as a business. In this case, a region can be perceived as geographical entities, for instance Europe. Next, we found examples of processes that were consolidated by a global SOE entity and, similar to a regional SOE entity, managed as a business towards regions. Finally, we identified clients who established business processes from a multifunctional perspective. In this case, business processes are managed across multiple SOE functions with an end-to-end ownership.

> 'We have to manage a complex set of various interrelated business processes, in particular in the supply chain and F&A domain. As internal responsibilities to manage these processes are fragmented we desperately need overview. That's why we have chosen to appoint global process owners who are responsible to manage and improve the performance of our end-to-end processes.' (Source: Vice President client 4)

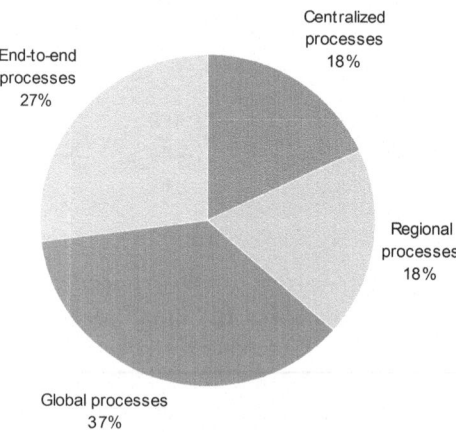

Fig. 3. Type of business processes (N = 11)

Importantly, interviewees argued that independent of the type of implemented business process governance is required to support the processes adequately. This means that clients have to pay more attention to developing governance mechanisms to manage interdependencies, for instance between front end and back end functions. Our findings reveal that clients have to deal with governance aspects, such as mutual tasks, responsibilities, and coordination mechanisms along the line of implemented business processes.

> 'We have organized the our F&A, HR, Procurement/Supply Chain services by means of bundles. To govern these bundles we have established centers of expertise (CoEs). IT, however, is governed separately based on a federative approach to coordinate the operational delivery of these services on a local level.' (Source: Director client 1)

This requires the existence of a coherent strategic blueprint that describes the position, role, and mandate of each party within the business process. By developing governance mechanisms that include internal and external stakeholders a governance strategy will improve the coordination of business process tasks and a such may overcome potential disputes between the parties involved. Consequently, a governance strategy may span inter-organizational mechanisms as external vendors maybe involved in the provisioning of business services.

4.4   Enabling Technology

The questionnaire data show that all clients use EIS to support their business services. With regard to the type of EIS SAP is applied predominantly, to enable business processes that provide business services in various regions (see Table 3). We find that the EIS, and particularly SAP, is highly modularized (instances), using standard interfaces to support multiple components of business processes.

> 'We use one SAP platform applying three instances that support in total four business functions, so IT integration is essential. Therefore, our goal is to use standard interfaces as much as possible to support a seamless integration approach.' (Source: Director client 7)

The EIS of the clients under study support at least two and ultimately five business services. Interviewees argued that the use of modularized EIS is essential as business services have to be adapted regularly to cater for changes and the EIS provide the technology to support these adjustments. EIS complexity is influenced by technology issues, such as legacy systems, as well as organizational issues. From a business perspective customer information has to be stored and managed by using information data structures, models and technology, which affects the development of EIS. Thus, interoperability is essential to exchange information and data by means of services and web services supported by modularized technology.

> 'Our ERP systems are modularized and mutually interconnected to support our processes. We have different modules within F&A and Procure to Pay systems. At the same time IT modules are used to support business functions, both manually and automated. For instance, we have implemented ServiceNow as tooling to support HR services that are interdependent with F&A and P2P.' (Source: Vice President client 11)

In addition, client documentation that was provided illustrated that all clients' EIS are interconnected to vendors' EIS as various business processes are outsourced. Consequently, client architects paid severe attention to develop interoperable systems to manage complexity as technology is provided both in-house and by outsourcing partners.

Table 3. Overview enabling technologies (N = 11)

Client	# of EIS systems deployed	# of EIS instances	EIS solution provider
1	Greater than 10	Greater than 10	SAP
2	Greater than 10	Greater than 10	SAP
3	1	1	SAP
4	1	4–5	Oracle
5	1	1	Oracle
6	1	1	SAP
7	1	2–3	SAP
8	2–3	2–3	SAP
9	1	1	SAP
10	1	1	SAP
11	6–10	6–10	SAP

5 Discussion

5.1 SOE Strategy and Business Services

Our research provides support for the existence of an SOE strategy and related business services. Importantly, the firms' SOE strategy was driven by various business drivers, in which process excellence was recognized to be the most important factor. We find that the firms under study modularized their business services into business components to manage complexity [39]. To manage the interplay between different business services an organizational entity was established to keep oversight. Although employees that form a part of this SOE organizational entity are geographically dispersed, business services are centrally managed and governed (e.g. roles and responsibilities). This finding provide insights that a holistic approach is applied to avoid interdependence issues between business services. [40], who studied business services that are provided in-house, underpins the importance of organizational design of business services. The authors argue that organizational design is a challenge as various design aspects are interrelated (i.e. strategy, collaborative partnerships, shared services processes, policy and regulation). Moreover, firms apply various sourcing modes as our findings demonstrate that all business services to some degree are outsourced to the market. Consequently, the way in which business services are established influence a firm's SOE strategy. We argue that firms develop an SOE strategy that takes modularized business services into account. Thus, an SOE strategy will include strategic decision-making in bundling business services and related sourcing decisions [3]. As such, an SOE strategy contributes to enterprise agility, in which diverse portfolios of strategic sourcing options can be managed to respond to rapid environmental change.

5.2 Business Processes

Interviews revealed that to manage business processes effectively, there is a dependency on the degree in which business services are integrated. We found that to support a firm's aim to respond to changes in an agile way, business services are integrated (e.g. Finance and Accounting and IT) and as a result, business processes are broken down into modular independent services. The latter is consistent with findings of [13] who argue that dynamic processes should be modularized to promote reusability. Based on our findings, business processes are perceived as complex as they span various business services as well as multiples countries. This finding is also reflected by the most ranked business driver by the firms to strengthen their SOE, namely: 'drive process excellence'. The more business processes are established to support both front and back office functions, the higher the degree to manage process interdependencies. However, we found that all firms used a process model to support business services tasks. These process models were predominantly based on supporting EIS (predefined processes and workflows). In addition, SOE employees had the mandate to adapt business processes if necessary to cater to changing circumstances. This finding relate to loosely framed business processes in which firms use a priori defined process model while allowing the execution of the process to deviate from the model [41]. Our findings show that business processes range from central to end-to-end type of configurations. Thus, service-oriented designed business services are needed to establish relationships between dynamic business processes and enabling technology.

5.3   Enabling Technology

The case studies underpin the relevance of enabling technology as a platform to support business processes and corresponding business services. We find that dependent of the scope of enterprises, various business services are increasingly integrated with each other. To a certain extent EIS can integrate data, functions, and processes to support business services functionality. Our findings demonstrate that the firms' EIS are highly modularized (e.g. multiple instances) and interoperable with vendors' EIS. Thus data can be exchanged between firms and their vendors by means of web services and subsequently, reused. The fact that firms EIS are based on loosely coupled modules, implies that the degree of business services complexity can be decreased and may contribute to various sourcing modes. In doing so, business services can be more easily adjusted to respond to endogenous developments [17]. EIS critique in literature argues that large organizations often lead to integration struggles as the degree of interoperability and modularization between EIS is limited [11]. Consequently, business services data is distributed amongst various EIS [42], which is considered as a constraint for business-IT alignment [13].

5.4   Governance

As firms may apply various sourcing modes, in which business services are partially provided in-house and partially outsourced, the degree of complexity to govern these modes will increase. Our findings demonstrate that the firms' SOE organizational entity, which can be seen as a center of expertise, is responsible to develop and establish strategic policies to govern business services holistically. This is related to both business services and supporting business processes. As a result, governance mechanisms were implemented to govern interdependencies. Examples we found concern roles, responsibilities and mandates of senior management to manage business services in practice, which are monitored by the firms' SOE organizational entity. This is consistent with a previous study of [43] that demonstrated that large firms require coordination capabilities when blended modes of delivery are used with regard to business services. On the other hand, we found that operational business services and processes are governed at a decentralized level to cater for changes effectively. As all firms under study apply in-house as well as outsourced sourcing modes, at operational level governance is needed to quickly handle vendors issues. A lack, however, of governance attention may result in strategic SOE issues, such as goal conflicts and goal misalignment [44]. Therefore, both formal (SLAs, KPIs) and relational (trust, commitment) governance include mechanisms to limit the degree of governance issues [45].

5.5   Organizational Readiness

Interviews with the firms' representatives revealed that it is essential to align managerial goals and objectives to manage business services and achieve organizational readiness. As the firms' organization structures are based on business silos (e.g. front, mid and back office), leading senior management per silo is responsible for tactical and operational services. To support these services, tactical strategies on business processes, financial management, and employee roles are formalized and established. Literature shows that organizational readiness is related to both process formalization [46], and IT readiness [47] and as such, is perceived as an important factor that contributes to success. To create a coherent approach on managing business services, however, we found that change management is required to set uniform goals and align fragmented managerial silo-oriented approaches. This finding relates to research of [48] who argues that organizational readiness relates to a firm's transition management capability that strives to effectively integrate business services. Importantly, our findings suggest that the determinant organizational readiness relate to [3] strategic management and organizational issue of 'Redesign and reorganization of activities and orchestration of organizational service flow, p. 45'. Firm's attention and effort to prepare their organization and create a buy-in at management level, and as such become organizationally ready, may overcome this organizational management issue.

5.6 Knowledge and Skills

The business services under study are interwoven which implies that employees have to exchange information continuously. In doing so, employees require in-depth business process knowledge and skills to deal with interdependences as business services span multiple departments. Beyond processes, management and employees need profound business services knowledge and skills to achieve business performance and solve operational issues. This is supported by [49] as knowledge-based business activities have become an increasingly essential component in developing a firm's business strategy. Additionally, firms require specific capabilities, knowledge and skills (e.g. relationship management) as business services are established in-house and provided by vendors. Therefore, firms knowledge and skills is created and transferred within an organizational context and can be divided into firm specific (SOE organizational entity), and general (e.g. departments) knowledge [50]. An SOE strategy, however, is influenced by the ability and willingness of managers and employees of a firm to communicate and transform knowledge on a day-to-day basis [51]. Hence, firms should invest in building knowledge capital to support the exchange of information [52]. We argue that firms that invest in developing specific knowledge and skills are more able to manage operational performance of business services and EIS.

5.7 Summary

Based on the literature background three SOE determinants can be identified: business services, business processes, and enabling technology. The interviews at executive level show three additional determinants, namely: governance, organizational readiness, and knowledge and skills. Our study suggests that executives and SOE managers have to collaborate to create a coherent SOE strategy as business services span multiple departments and changes in one determinant may affect another. For instance, a lack of in-depth knowledge and skills on business services and supporting governance mechanisms may influence the implementation of an SOE strategy negatively. Hence, firms need to establish collaborative processes to cater for changes dynamically. Taking various sourcing modes of business services into account, changes may result in renewed make-or-buy decisions. Moreover, our findings show that firms establish a dedicated SOE entity to manage business services from an integrated perspective. This mechanism may overcome business-IT alignment issues as addressed by [13] as interdependencies between business services, and their impact on the organization, can be managed adequately. Based on the literature review and interviews at executive level we summarize our findings with regard to SOE determinants (see Table 4).

Table 4. Overview influencing SOE determinants

Influencing SOE determinant	Findings based on	Related authors
SOE strategy	Literature	Fremantle (2002), Demirkan and Goul (2006), Vitharana et al. (2007), Chang et al. (2011)
Business services	Literature	Arsanjani (2002), Janssen and Joha (2008)
Business processes	Literature	Fremantle (2002), Cherbakov et al. (2005), Demirkan and Goul (2006), Chang et al. (2011)
Enabling technology	Literature	Fremantle (2002), Demirkan and Goul (2006), Demirkan et al. (2008), Vitharana et al. (2007), Esteves and Pastor (2001), Cherbakov et al. (2005), Chang et al. (2011)
Governance	Empirical	Malone and Crowston (1994), Weill and Ross (2004), Plugge et al. (2013), Huber et al. (2014)
Organizational readiness	Empirical	Ein-Dor and Segev (1978), Janssen and Joha (2008), Chang et al. (2011)
Knowledge and skills	Empirical	Castanias and Helfat (2001), Orlikowski (2002), Rai et al. (2012)

6   Conclusions and Directions for Further Research

In today's rapid changing environment firms are seeking new ways to become more agile to respond to changes adequately. Given the scarce attention to identify SOE determinants this discussion has sought to assist both researchers and practitioners. Based on a literature background we identified three key determinants that implies that an SOE strategy is dependent on the type of business services used, corresponding business processes, and enabling technology. Empirical research shows additional SOE determinants that relate to governance, organizational readiness, and available knowledge and skills. Our findings reveal that a deep understanding of SOE determinants is needed, and they might be dependent on the context in which they are established.

[3] identified that a lack of a clear business and IT strategy and sufficient focus cause strategic issues. Our findings that a more coherent approach is required to manage the identified SOE determinants may explain these strategic SOE issues and by implementing them develop a strategy to overcome these issues. This is our first contribution. When addressing the context of various sourcing modes (e.g. in-house, outsourced), we may conclude that the SOE determinants governance and knowledge and skills becomes

even more important as some business services are provided hierarchally (make), while others operate on arms-lengths (buy). As the boundaries between internal and external sourcing modes may shift regularly, a more network type of organization is used. We argue that clients have to consider both contractual and relational governance to access in-depth knowledge and skills, which may be hindered as the goals of internal and external parties may differ. Therefore, our second contribution relates to practitioners as they become aware of the impact of SOE determinants in their firm.

A limitation is imposed by the limited number of executive management interviews. In future research, a more extensive survey among multiple firms and participants will help us to generalize the results. Another limitation is that SOE determinants are only studied on a generic level. More detailed distinctions between the degree in which business services are provided in-house or outsourced are not made. Research into determinants influencing the sourcing strategy of a firm is needed. In particular, under which conditions are business services provided in-house or outsourced? Additional aspects that can be considered include a firm's ability to manage vendors and their maturity in managing the relationship (e.g. IT governance). Future research may examine these effects.

Appendix A: Short Description of the Questionnaire

General Information				
Participant Name:	<Insert Name Here>	Company Name:	<Insert Name Here>	
Participant eMail:	<Insert eMail Here>	Total number of employees in your company	<Insert number Here>	
Participant Title:	<Insert Title Here>	Industry:	<Insert type Here>	
Participant Area of Responsibility:	<Insert Responsibility Here>	If Other Please Specify	<Specify Here>	
Year Started Service-Oriented Enterprise	<Insert Year Here>	Third Party / Service provider Organization Headcount	<Insert number Here>	
Strategic Value Drivers	Drive Process Excellence	<Insert Yes/No Here>		
	Unlock the Power of Data & Analytics	<Insert Yes/No Here>		
	Mitigate Overall Business Risk & Ensure Compliance	<Insert Yes/No Here>		
	Enhance Sophistication & Collaboration	<Insert Yes/No Here>		
	Achieve Excellence & Consistency in Customer Experience	<Insert Yes/No Here>		
	Increase Effectiveness & Ability to Scale	<Insert Yes/No Here>		
	Build Internal Repository of High Quality Talent	<Insert Yes/No Here>		
	Drive Innovation within the Organization	<Insert Yes/No Here>		
Geographical coverage	North America	<Insert Yes/No Here>		
	South America	<Insert Yes/No Here>		
	Europe	<Insert Yes/No Here>		
	Asia - Pacific	<Insert Yes/No Here>		
	Middle East and Africa	<Insert Yes/No Here>		
Business processes	Decentralized processes	<Insert Yes/No Here>		
	Centralized processes	<Insert Yes/No Here>		
	Business services processes (regional)	<Insert Yes/No Here>		
	Business services processes (global)	<Insert Yes/No Here>		
	End-to-end management processes	<Insert Yes/No Here>		
Functional coverage	Finance & Accounting	<Insert Yes/No Here>	<Insert degree of outsourcing in % Here>	
	Human Resources	<Insert Yes/No Here>	<Insert degree of outsourcing in % Here>	
	Procurement	<Insert Yes/No Here>	<Insert degree of outsourcing in % Here>	
	Supply Chain management	<Insert Yes/No Here>	<Insert degree of outsourcing in % Here>	
	Information Technology	<Insert Yes/No Here>	<Insert degree of outsourcing in % Here>	
	Data analytics	<Insert Yes/No Here>	<Insert degree of outsourcing in % Here>	
	Master Data management	<Insert Yes/No Here>	<Insert degree of outsourcing in % Here>	
	Manufacturing and Operations	<Insert Yes/No Here>	<Insert degree of outsourcing in % Here>	
	Customer Care	<Insert Yes/No Here>	<Insert degree of outsourcing in % Here>	
Enabling Technology	Number of ERP software systems	<Insert number Here>		
	Number of ERP system instance(s)	<Insert number Here>		
	Type of ERP system	<Insert type Here>		

References

1. Cherbakov, L., Galambos, G., Harishankar, R., Kalyana, S., Rackman, G.: Impact of service-orientation at the business level. IBM Syst. J. **44**, 653–668 (2005)
2. Bieberstein, N., Bose, S., Fiammate, M., Jones, K., Shah, R.: Service-Oriented Architecture Compass; Business Value, Planning and Enterprise Roadmap. Pearson, Upper Saddle River (2006)
3. Janssen, M., Joha, A.: Emerging shared service organisations and the service-oriented enterprise: critical management issues. Strat.Out. Int. J. **1**(1), 35–49 (2008)
4. Jetter, M., Satzger, G., Neus, A.: Technological innovation and its impact on business model, organization and corporate culture - IBM's transformation into a globally integrated, service-oriented enterprise. BISE **1**(1), 37–45 (2009)
5. Demirkan, H., Kauffman, R.J., Vayghan, J.A., Fill, H.-G., Karagiannis, D.: Service-oriented technology and management. Elect. Com. Res. App. **7**(4), 356–376 (2008)
6. Conboy, K.: Agility from first principles: reconstructing the concept of agility in information systems development. Inf. Syst. Res. **20**(3), 329–354 (2009)
7. Bernardes, E.S., Hanna, M.D.: A theoretical review of flexibility, agility and responsiveness in the operations management literature: toward a conceptual definition of customer responsiveness. Int. J. Oper. Prod. Mange. **29**(1), 30–53 (2009)
8. Deloitte: GBS study (2016). www2.deloitte.com/us/en/pages/operations/articles/global-business-services-performance-improvement-perspectives.html#
9. KPMG Global insights pulse (2017). http://www.kpmg-institutes.com/institutes/shared-services-outsourcing-institute/articles/campaigns/ssoa-pulse-surveys.html
10. CocaCola. https://vimeo.com/134309216
11. Fremantle, P., Weerawarana, S., Khalaf, R.: Enterprise services: examining the emerging files of web services and how it is integrated into existing enterprise infrastructures. Commun. ACM **45**, 77–82 (2002)
12. Medjahed, B., Benatallah, B., Bouguettaya, A., Elmagarmid, A.: WebBIS: an infrastructure for agile integration of web services. Int. J. Coop. Inf. Syst. **13**(121), 121–158 (2004)
13. Chang, H-L., Hsiao, H-E., Lue, C-P.: Assessing IT-business alignment in service-oriented enterprises. Pac. Asia J. Ass. Inf. Syst. **3**(1), 29–48 (2011)
14. Brown, G., Carpenter, R.: Successful application of service-oriented architecture across the enterprise and beyond. Intel Tech. J. **8**(4), 345–359 (2004)
15. Menor, L., Roth, A.V.: New service development competence in retail banking: construct development and measurement validation. J. Oper. Manage. **25**(4), 825–846 (2007)
16. Gosain, S., Malhotra, A., El Sawy, O.A.: Coordinating for flexibility in e-business supply chains. J. Manage. Inf. Syst. **2193**, 7–46 (2005)
17. Overby, E., Bharadwaj, A., Sambamurty, V.: Enterprise agility and the enabling role of information technology. Eur. J. Inf. Syst. **15**, 120–131 (2006)
18. Davis, T.: Integrating shared services with the strategy and operations of MNEs. J. Gen. Manage. **31**(2), 1–17 (2005)
19. Gulati, R., Lawrence, P.R., Puranam, P.: Adaptation in vertical relationships: beyond incentive conflict. Strat. Manage. J. **26**(5), 415–440 (2005)
20. Heide, J.B.: Plural governance in industrial purchasing. J. Mark. **67**(4), 8–29 (2003)
21. Rai, A., Keil, M., Hornyak, R., Wüllenweber, K.: Hybrid relational-contractual governance for business process outsourcing. J. Manage. Inf. Syst. **29**(2), 213–256 (2012)
22. Demirkan, H., Goul, M., Brown, G.W.: Towards the service-oriented enterprise, Hawaii Conference on System Science, (HICSS-40), Big island, Hawaii (2007)
23. Trepper, C.: Customer care goes end-to-end, Inf. Week, pp. 55–73, 15 May 2000

24. Xu, L.: Enterprise systems: state-of-the-art and future trends. IEEE Trans. Ind. Inf. **7**(4), 630–640 (2011)
25. Zhao, J.L., Tanniru, M., Zhang, L.J.: Services computing as the foundation of enterprise agility: overview of recent advances and introduction to the special issue. Inf. Syst. Front. **9** (8), 1–8 (2007)
26. Ulbrich, F., Borman, M.: Preventing the gradual decline of shared service centers. In: Proceedings of the Eighteenth Americas Conference on Information Systems, Seattle, Washington, 9–12 August 2012
27. Lacity, M.C., Willcocks, L.P.: Advanced Outsourcing Practice: Rethinking ITO, BPO and Cloud services. Palgrave Macmillan, Basingstoke (2012)
28. Oshri, I., Kotlarski, J., Willcocks, L.P.: The Handbook of Global Outsourcing and Offshoring, 3rd edn. Palgrave Macmillan, London (2015)
29. Janssen, M.: Exploring the service-oriented enterprise: drawing lessons from a case study, Hawaii International Conference on Systems Sciences (HICSS-41), Big Island, HI (2008)
30. Davenport, T.: The coming commoditization of processes. Har. Bus. Rev. **77**(1), 101–108 (2005)
31. Markus, M.L., Tanis, C.: The enterprise system experience? from adoption to success, in framing the domains of IT research: projecting the future. In: Through the Past, Zmud, R.W. (ed.) Pinnaflex Educational Resources, Inc., Cincinnati, OH, pp. 173–207 (2000)
32. Sambamurthy, V., Bharadwaj, A., Grover, V.: Shaping agility through digital options: reconceptualizing the role of information technology in contemporary firms. MIS Q. **27**(2), 237–263 (2003)
33. Janssen, M., Wagenaar, R.: From legacy to modularity: a roadmap towards modular architectures using web services technology. In: Traunmüller, R. (ed.) EGOV 2003. LNCS, vol. 2739, pp. 95–100. Springer, Heidelberg (2003). https://doi.org/10.1007/10929179_16
34. Yin, R.K.: Case Study Research: Design and Methods. Sage Publications, London (2009)
35. Miles, M., Huberman A.: Qualitative Data Analysis. Sage, California (1994)
36. Benbasat, I., Goldstein, D., Mead, M.: The case research strategy in studies of information systems. MIS Q. **11**(3), 368–387 (1987)
37. Orlikowski, W.J., Iacono, C.S.: Research commentary: desperately seeking the "IT" in IT research: a call to theorizing the IT artifact. Inf. Syst. Res. **12**(2), 121–134 (2001)
38. Lacity, M.C., Khan, S.A., Yan, A.: Review of the empirical business services sourcing literature: an update and future directions. J. Inf. T. **31**(3), 269–328 (2016)
39. Arsanjani, A.: Developing and integrating enterprise components and services. Commun. ACM **45**(10), 31–34 (2002)
40. Wang, S., Wang, H.: Shared services beyond sourcing the back office: organisational design. Hum. Syst. Manage. **26**, 281–290 (2007)
41. Van Aalst, W.: Business process management: a comprehensive survey. ISRN Soft. Eng., Article ID 507984, 31–37 (2013)
42. Aier, S., Bucher, T., Winter, R.: Critical success factors of service orientation in information systems engineering: deviation ad empirical evaluation of a causal model. BISE **3**(2), 77–88 (2011)
43. Plugge, A., Janssen, M., Joha, A.: Coordinating tensions in orchestrating blended modes of sharing and outsourcing of services. In: Oshri, I., Kotlarsky, J., Willcocks, Leslie P. (eds.) Global Sourcing 2013. LNBIP, vol. 163, pp. 147–162. Springer, Heidelberg (2013). https://doi.org/10.1007/978-3-642-40951-6_9
44. Huber, T., Fischer, T., Dibbern, J. Hirschheim, R.: A process model of complementarity and substitution of contractual and relational governance in IS outsourcing. J. Manage. Inf. Syst. **30**(3), 81–114 (2014)

45. Lioliou, E., Zimmermann, A., Willcocks, L.P., Gao, L.: Formal and relational governance in IT outsourcing: substitution, complementarity and the role of the psychological contract. Inf. Syst. J. **24**, 503–535 (2014)
46. Ein-Dor, P., Segev, E.: Organizational context and the success of management information systems. Manage. Sci. **24**(10), 1064–1077 (1978)
47. Bassellier, G., Benbasat, I.: Business competence of information technology professionals: conceptual development and influence on IT-business partnerships. MIS Q. **28**(4), 673–694 (2004)
48. Luo, Y., Wang, S., Zheng, Q., Jayaraman, V.: Task attributes and process integration in business process offshoring: a perspective of service providers from India and China. J. Int. Bus. Stud. **43**(5), 498–524 (2012)
49. Grant, R.M.: Toward a knowledge-based theory of the firm. Strateg. Manage. **17**(2), 109–122 (1996)
50. Castanias, R.P., Helfat, C.E.: The managerial rents model: theory and empirical analysis. J. Manage. **27**(6), 661–678 (2001)
51. Orlikowski, W.J.: Knowing in practice: enacting a collective capability in distributed organizing. Organ. Sci. **13**(3), 249–273 (2002)
52. Rai, A., Arikan, I., Pye, J.: Fit and misfit of plural sourcing strategies and IT-enabled process integration capabilities: consequences of firm performance in the US electric utility industry. MIS Q. **39**(4), 865–885 (2015)

Automation of Knowledge-Based Shared Services and Centers of Expertise

Vipin K. Suri[1], Marianne D. Elia[1], Pavan Arora[2],
and Jos van Hillegersberg[3(✉)]

[1] Shared Services International Inc., Mississauga, Canada
[2] IBM Watson, New York, USA
[3] Faculty of Behavioural, Management and Social Sciences,
Industrial Engineering and Business Information Systems, University of Twente,
P.O. Box 217, 7500 AE Enschede, The Netherlands
j.vanhillegersberg@utwente.nl

Abstract. Automation of Knowledge-Based services is the natural evolution of Robotic Process Automation (RPA), fueled by new technologies, often categorized as Cognitive Automation (CA). The purposes of this research are to (1) explore the Expertise Shared Services and Centers of Expertise functions where automation of knowledge-based processes is most suitable and (2) understand the value drivers and primary tactical challenges in adopting a strategy for automating Knowledge-Based expertise services. In addition to a literature review conducted, we conducted in-depth interviews with selected executives and experts. We developed case studies to better understand how Software Bots can be deployed for automating Knowledge-Based Expertise Services in organizations when they transition to automation of knowledge-driven processes. Results of our research indicate that the majority of executives and experts are aware of the need for automating Knowledge-Based Expertise Services but most remain unclear regarding its value or how to invest in adoption of this new trend.

Keywords: Expertise Shared Services · Centers of Expertise (COE) ·
Knowledge process automation · Cognitive Automation (CA) ·
Artificial Intelligence (AI) · Intelligent Automation (IA) ·
Intelligent Process Automation (IPA) · Robotic Process Automation (RPA) ·
Software Bots · Big data · Unstructured data

1 Introduction

Automation of Knowledge-Based processes is the natural evolution of Robotic Process Automation (RPA), fueled by technologies often categorized as Cognitive Automation (CA). The CA tools are considered cognitive, in that they 'think', however not necessarily in the same way as a human, but rather leveraging more advanced algorithms that are self-learning in nature. As such, where RPA is a tool that is deterministic (i.e. using pre-defined actions), CA has the ability to render an outcome based on probabilistic evidence. The inherent ability of CA that enables automation of knowledge-based

© Springer Nature Switzerland AG 2019
J. Kotlarsky et al. (Eds.): Global Sourcing 2018, LNBIP 344, pp. 56–75, 2019.
https://doi.org/10.1007/978-3-030-15850-7_4

Expertise Services is the ability to understand context, much like an expert would as a reliable source of advice, having extensive knowledge or ability beyond that of an average person based on experience, occupation or research.

Knowledge Processes concentrate on the identification, acquisition, dissemination and preservation of knowledge in order to drive efficiencies, garner competitive advantage and enhance company value. In general, there are four Knowledge Processes: (a) generating knowledge, (b) sharing knowledge, (c) storing knowledge, and (d) applying knowledge. In today's competitive environment, organizations must have the ability to effectively incorporate all four of these Knowledge Processes into their business.

Using a combination of literature review, in-depth interviews, process classification frameworks and case studies, we address the following research questions:

1. What cognitive tasks are implied in the workflows across common Shared Services functions?
2. What workflows currently are being automated?
3. What is the extent of incremental business value brought by automation of knowledge-based processes?

The number of terms used to describe software tools designed to automate services can be very confusing. These software products are aimed at automating or supplementing different types of human tasks and include Machine Learning (ML), Robotic Process Automation (RPA), Cognitive Automation (CA), Artificial Intelligence (AI) and Intelligent Process Automation (IPA). To develop a common understanding of these terms, we offer the following definitions including those from the IEEE Guide for Terms and Concepts in Intelligent Process Automation [1]:

Machine Learning (ML) - Detection, correlation, and pattern recognition generated through machine-based observation of human operation of software systems along with ongoing self-informing regression algorithms for machine-based determination of successful operation leading to useful predictive analytics or prescriptive analytics capability.

Robotic Process Automation (RPA) - A preconfigured software instance that uses business rules and predefined activity choreography to complete the autonomous execution of a combination of processes, activities, transactions, and tasks in one or more unrelated software systems to deliver a result or service with human exception management.

Cognitive Automation (CA) - The identification, assessment, and application of available machine learning algorithms for the purpose of leveraging domain knowledge and reasoning to further automate the machine learning already present in a manner that may be thought of as cognitive. With cognitive automation, the system performs corrective actions driven by knowledge of the underlying analytics tool itself, iterates its own automation approaches and algorithms for more expansive or more thorough analysis, and is thereby able to fulfill its purpose.

Artificial Intelligence (AI) - The combination of cognitive automation, machine learning, reasoning, hypothesis generation and analysis, natural language processing, and intentional algorithm mutation producing insights and analytics at or above human capability.

Intelligent Process Automation (IPA) - A preconfigured software instance that combines business rules, experience-based context determination logic, and decision criteria to initiate and execute multiple interrelated human and automated processes in a dynamic context. The goal is to complete the execution of a combination of processes, activities, and tasks in one or more unrelated software systems that deliver a result or service with minimal or no human intervention.

Big Data - Big data is data sets that are so voluminous and complex that traditional data-processing application software are inadequate to deal with them. Big data challenges include capturing data, data storage, data analysis, search, sharing, transfer, visualization, querying, updating, information privacy and data source. The term big data tends to refer to the use of predictive analytics, user behavior analytics, or certain other advanced data analytics methods that extract value from data, and seldom to a particular size of data set.

Center of Expertise - A center of expertise or a center of excellence (COE) is a corporate group or team that leads other employees and the organization as a whole in some particular area of focus such as a technology, skill or discipline. It is also known as a competency center or a capability center and is a shared facility or an entity that provides leadership, best practices, research, support and/or training for a focus area. The focus area might be a technology (e.g. SAP), a business concept (e.g. BPM), a skill (e.g. negotiation) or a broad area of study (e.g. knowledge management).

This paper is organized in following sections: Sect. 1 has just provided an introduction to Knowledge Processes and automation terminologies and has set the stage for our study. Section 2 provides a summary of our literature review related to RPA, CA, AI and IPA. Section 3 presents data collection methods. Section 4 provides findings and analysis of data collected and Sect. 5 outlines the conclusions and future research.

2   Literature Review

The business disruption caused by AI and related technologies is already here and more business disruption is on the way. In 1999, the big business disruption was the use of offshoring to create labor arbitrage. The new disruptor is automation arbitrage, a term Gartner is using to describe the recalibration of the amount of human labor that should be used to drive business outcomes. The initial low-hanging fruit in this arena is RPA. It is relatively low cost, quick to implement and unobtrusive; thus, it starts what will likely be one of the most important conversations in the next five years regarding how automation will change the value proposition in all organizations [2].

For more than 130 years, managers have, in effect, been attempting to get humans to act like robots by structuring, routinizing, and measuring work - all under the guise of organizational efficiency. The automation software that is being developed today enables a reversal of this process. We are now able to use software robots to amplify and augment distinctive human strengths, enabling large economic gains and more satisfying work. However, given the widespread skepticism and fears about how many types of employment will fare in the future, managers are in a difficult position. Media headlines such as "Rise of the Robots: Technology and the Threat of a Jobless Future" and "A World without Work" only serve to fuel the anxiety. The plethora of software tools and terms used to describe software designed to automate services can be very confusing. To help make sense of the service automation landscape, it is suggested to avoid the jargon and instead focus on the service characteristics that the tools are designed to help automate. Two broad classes of service automation tools which can be considered are: Robotic Process Automation (RPA) and Cognitive Automation (CA). Each class of tools is designed to deal with specific types of data and processes. A vocabulary needs to be developed for communicating the meaning of various automation approaches. Figure 1 shows how to communicate automation to stakeholders [3]:

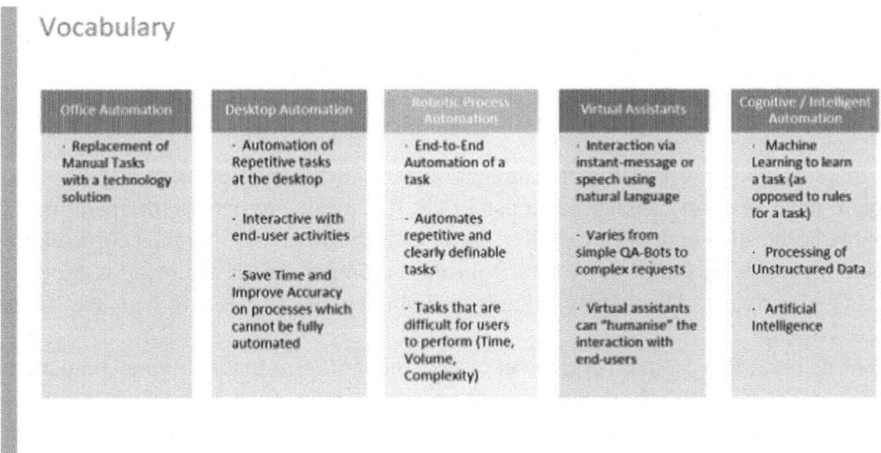

Fig. 1. How to communicate automation to stakeholders [3]

In order to adopt RPA into a stable model for an enterprise, the recommendation is taking a three-stage approach. This focuses on a range of applicable RPA features from the most linear features that deliver the greatest ROI to the most cutting-edge technology that is not yet completely defined. The first is Structured RPA, which can easily automate swivel chair processes, where data currently is manually entered into one system and then the same data is entered into another system; this requires interaction with many applications in order to complete a business process. The next level of automation is Intelligent/Enhanced RPA. With Intelligent/Enhanced RPA (also known as Intelligent Automation (IA) or Intelligent Process Automation (IPA)) intelligent tools use machine learning to build a process related knowledge base in order to automate processes. The last is Cognitive RPA (also known as CA), which provides greater business value by automating processes with the use of advanced machine intelligence, natural language processing, Big Data, and real time analytics. Figure 2 shows a comparison of RPA and Intelligent Automation [4].

RPA vs. Intelligent Automation

	Robotic Process Automation	Intelligent Automation
Automates tasks that are...	Routine: Methodical, repetitive, rules-based	Non-routine: Requiring a thoughtful consideration
Able to...	Follow instructions	Come to conclusions
Application is...	Broader: Can automate any suitable process	Narrower: Application should be targeted to deliver meaningful, insightful outputs
Market offerings are...	Maturing	Emerging
Implementation and ongoing costs are typically...	Lower	Higher
Implementation timeframe are typically of the order of...	Weeks	Months

Fig. 2. Robotic process automation and intelligent automation [4]

In order to apply Intelligent Automation (IA) in the enterprise, it is necessary to explain what IA is and what value it can bring. It is needed to get commitment from the top, break the silos and work together, focus and prioritize, involve the people that will be interacting with the new IA tool from the beginning, involve the right experts on time (e.g., privacy, IT security, cloud) and share your success; it will lead to new initiatives [5].

At its core, IPA is an emerging set of new technologies that combines fundamental process redesign with robotic process automation and machine learning. It is a suite of business process improvements and next-generation tools that assists the knowledge worker by removing repetitive, replicable, and routine tasks. And it can radically improve customer journeys by simplifying interactions and speeding up processes. IPA mimics activities carried out by humans and, over time, learns to do them even better. Traditional levers of rule-based automation are augmented with decision-making capabilities thanks to advances in deep learning and cognitive technology. The promise of IPA is radically enhanced efficiency, increased worker performance, reduction of operational risks, and improved response times and customer journey experiences [6].

New technologies that promise double-digit or even triple-digit same-year returns should rightfully be viewed with skepticism. However, experience shows that the promise of Intelligent Process Automation (IPA) is real if executives carefully consider and understand the drivers of opportunity and incorporate them effectively with other approaches and capabilities that drive a next-generation operating model [6]. A business-led RPA Center of Expertise (COE) is the best way to manage and enhance a virtual workforce - but it does not simply spring into existence. So, the COE processes need to be in place, IT governance agreed, and staff trained to operate robots and continue to enhance processes. Figure 3 below shows the Automation Spectrum and stages of Digital Automation Evolution [4]:

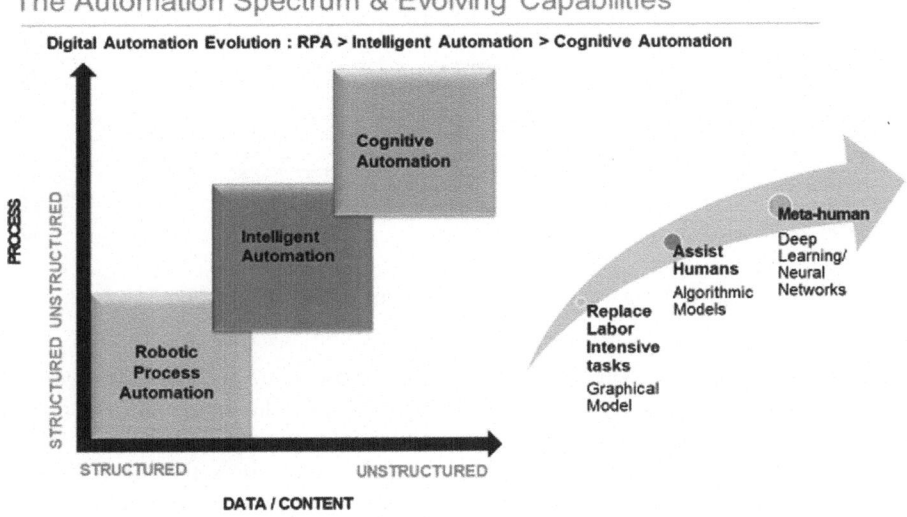

Fig. 3. The automation spectrum and evolving capabilities [4]

Cognitive Automation is defined in the context of a Machine Learning (ML) automation framework. While the proposed properties are found to be critical to such a system, one could arguably relax some of these or expand the notion to include additional desirables. An algorithmic framework will be called cognitive if it has the following properties [7]:

1. It integrates knowledge from (a) various structured or unstructured sources, (b) past experience, and (c) current state, in order to reason with this knowledge as well as to adapt over time;
2. It interacts with the user (e.g., by natural language or visualization) and reasons based on such interactions; and
3. It can generate novel hypotheses and capabilities, and test their effectiveness.

Recently, there have been plenty of predictions about the effects of automation on the nature of human work. Some pundits have predicted that automation will take over more and more functions, leaving very few tasks for humans.

Figure 4 provides characteristics of Core and Non-Core processes [8]. In general, 5% of the processes are Core Differentiating, 15% of processes are Core Competitive and 80% of the processes are Non-Core. Non-Core processes are transactional in nature whereas core processes are knowledge-based.

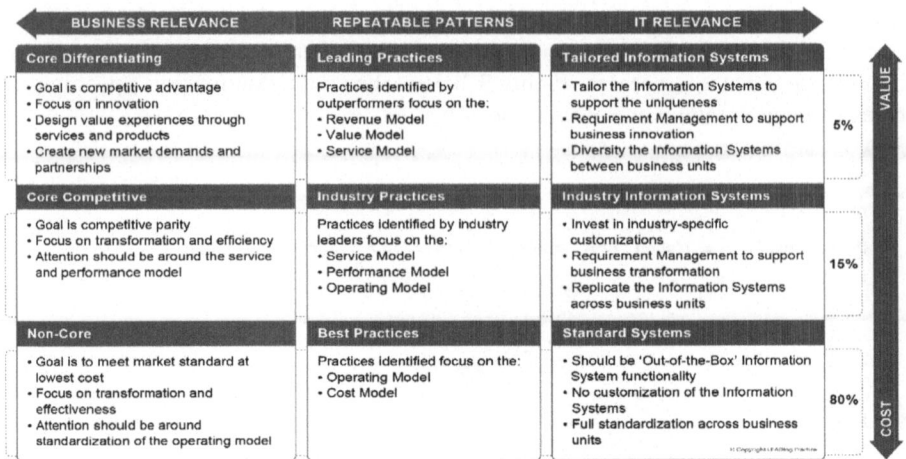

Fig. 4. Characteristics of core and non-core processes [8]

According to [8], the core processes add the most value whereas the non-core processes account for majority of the costs. Figure 4 also classifies requirements for Information Systems as Tailored, Industry and Standard systems.

Reading the headlines and multiple reports, one would think that by mid-2017, most organizations had already automated most of their repetitive, routine activities and processes, and were now well into automating knowledge work - reasoning; natural language processing; probabilistic decision-making; judgment; prediction; under-standing context; converting unstructured data into information; and answering "why?" questions. But this is far from the case. Given this context, it becomes valuable to study, empirically, actual implementations - not least because, in the cognitive automation space especially, we are short of independently researched cases that can provide valuable lessons to those just starting their journeys, or still waiting on the sidelines [9].

RPA and cognitive automation are set to be very big game changers for businesses in the coming years. In the case of RPA, the necessary technology is, in many cases, mature enough to be cheaply, easily and non-invasively, adopted. Immediate benefits can include costs savings, faster and higher quality processing, less error and better regulatory compliance. In practice, the cognitive automation market is still quite immature, despite recent heavy investments made into cognitive automation tools and AI. Studies suggest that more advanced forms of service automation, through software moving into more cognitive non-routine work, are less advanced than the hype suggests and will be mostly small-scale, discrete projects within businesses until the back end of 2018 [9].

In the next five years, it is expected that more and more work groups will be composed of both humans and software robots, each performing tasks for which they are best suited. The robots will very quickly extract, consolidate, and rearrange data for humans to assess and act upon. Humans will deal with new business requirements (which humans may later teach to the software robots), troubleshoot and solve unstructured problems, positively envision services for customers, and build relationships with customers. We are already seeing some of this today, but going forward, robots won't need as much pre-configuration or as much detailed instruction as tools evolve and as robotic process automation moves to the cloud [10].

In some businesses, RPA and CA programs have been managed by different organizational units. RPA is seen as 'today's' tool that could be quickly deployed, whereas CA is seen as more speculative and 'tomorrow's tool. It makes sense to integrate these initiatives going forward as organizations realize that both RPA and CA realms enable business strategies, and together they can complement and magnify value [11].

3   Data Collection Methods

The purposes of this research are to (1) explore where it is most suitable to automate knowledge-based processes within Expertise Shared Services and Centers of Expertise (COE) and (2) understand the value drivers and primary tactical challenges in automating knowledge-based expertise services.

In addition to literature review, in-depth Interviews with executives and experts were conducted. A Process Classification Framework (PCF) published by the American Quality & Productivity Council (AQPC) was used to determine automation scope of Expertise Services and Case Studies were developed for companies where knowledge-based processes are currently being automated.

3.1   In-Depth Interviews

In addition to literature review, in-depth interviews were conducted with 13 executives and experts from 12 industries. In cases where the interviews couldn't be arranged, the questions were emailed to the participants. The demographics of the participants are shown in Table 1 below:

Table 1. In-depth interviews: demographics of participants

S. No.	Industry	Location	Position	No. of participants
1	Engineering services	UK	Head of Analytics	1
2	Consulting	India	Director	1
3	Information technology	China	General Manager - Shared Services	1
4	Innovation practice	UK	Chief Innovation Wizard	1
5	Banking	Canada	Sr. Director, Process Automation & Optimization Vice President, Process Automation	2
6	Telecommunications	The Netherlands	Group SVP - Operations	1

(continued)

Table 1. (*continued*)

S. No.	Industry	Location	Position	No. of participants
7	Banking	UK	Director - IT	1
8	Insurance	USA	Group Head of AI	1
9	Research	UK	Advisory Board Member, Google	1
10	Airlines	USA	Director, Supply Chain Management	1
11	Pharmaceuticals	Sweden	Strategic Development Manager	1
12	Consulting	Spain	Head of Strategy Development	1

The purpose of the in-depth interviews was to seek answers to the following 16 questions:

1. Does your company use Robotic Process Automation (RPA), and if so, for what processes?
2. Have you heard about automation of knowledge-based Expertise Services?
3. Is your company looking to further automate your processes related to Expertise Services?
4. What is your definition of Expertise Services?
5. What are the key success factors for delivering Expertise Services in your Company?
6. How would you describe the value proposition of Expertise Services within your company?
7. Do you see any value in automating knowledge-driven processes (Expertise Services) and if yes, which ones, and what do you expect would be the qualitative incremental value?
8. What business processes are currently being automated in your company?
9. What technologies are currently in use to automate your business processes?
10. Have you heard about Software Bots for automating business processes and if yes, what is your definition of Software Bots?
11. What knowledge-driven processes are candidates for automation using Software Bots?
12. Are you familiar with Cognitive Automation (CA) technology and if yes, what cognitive tasks are included in your internal and external knowledge-driven processes?
13. What are the challenges you've encountered in adopting a strategy for automating knowledge-driven processes using Software Bots?
14. Our research indicates that Robotic Process Automation (RPA) is being used to automate transactional services and that automation of knowledge-driven Expertise Services can also be leveraged using Software Bots. Do you agree?

15. As part of our research, we will be providing data necessary for executives to build a business case for adopting a strategy for automation of knowledge-driven processes. Are your executives open to exploring the business case for automating knowledge-based processes?

16. Knowledge-Based Services are being automated by some companies to increase effectiveness of knowledge-driven processes using Software Bots. In your opinion, what other process automation approaches will be helpful for further value creation in delivering knowledge-driven Expertise Services?

The answers to the questions were summarized and analyzed to develop insights about the trend towards automation of Knowledge-Based Shared Services and Centers of Expertise.

3.2   Process Classification Framework (PCF)

Processes lie at the heart of everything that an organization does to maintain its existence and grow. Most processes involve knowledge to some degree. Improving organizational efficiency and effectiveness inevitably involves process improvements.

APQC's Process Classification Framework (PCF) provides a list of processes that organizations can use to define work processes comprehensively and without redundancies. Beyond being just a list, PCF serves as a tool to support benchmarking, manage content, and perform other important process management activities. APQC's PCF is the most widely used process framework in the world and it creates a common language for organizations to communicate and define work processes. Organizations are using it to support benchmarking and perform other performance management activities. APQC's PCF is a taxonomy of business processes that allows organizations to objectively track and compare their performance internally and externally with organizations from any industry. It also forms the basis for a variety of projects related to business processes [12].

APQC's PCF was developed in the early 1990s by APQC and a group of members from a number of industries and countries throughout the world. Originally envisioned as a tool to aid in performance improvement projects, the framework evolved into the broad taxonomy that it is today. Organizations can use the PCF's common terminology to name, organize, and map their processes. It is also helpful as a tool for explaining a business in terms of horizontal processes rather than vertical functions. AQPC's PCF is designed as a framework and global standard to be customized for use in any organization. Thus, the PCF does not list all processes within a specific organization, and every process listed in the framework does not exist in all organizations.

3.3   Case Studies

Three case studies were developed for companies who have automated Expertise Services using technology-based solutions. These are presented below.

Case#1: Company Industry: Information Technology

According to a study by IDC, "The High Cost of not finding Information", the average knowledge worker spends up to 2.5 h per day searching for or gathering information or data. This includes searches, email queries and other related tasks that all result in a massive amount of time spent trying to find information that already exists. Lucy, by Equals3, offers the next evolution of search, 'reading' through disparate sets of data to find the answer to a specific question posed in natural language. The Expertise Service Automated concerns Market Research.

Business Problems

- Time-consuming to find right information and expensive given resource allocation.
- In many agencies and enterprises, data is locked in silos, either based on access to data or the specialization of resources. Further, businesses invest significantly in data resources that ultimately are poorly used. Too often, important data is not in the hands of the people that need it, as a result they either recreate it, ignore it or waste time trying to procure it through internal channels.
- A global advertising agency experienced this as its employees were spending an inordinate amount of time doing market research, for everything from educating themselves on a competitive market landscape to optimizing audience targeting for a specific campaign.
- The corpus of research included many disparate sources including, the employee's emails, tweets, licensed databases, industry publications and the Internet. Thus, the effort was not only time-consuming, but often incomplete in that only the easiest corpora were searched and read for relevant data.

Solution

- Equals3's Lucy, is an artificially intelligent enterprise solution that can answer questions from all sources of data that she has been integrated with and/or ingested. This means that any team member can ask questions about website analytics, social data, 3rd party research, find information in files, access databases - all through one login and one natural language interface.
- Lucy is trained using IBM Watson's Natural Language Understanding services against the terabytes of unstructured data to analyze text and extract metadata from content such as concepts, entities, keywords, categories, relations and semantic relationships. With internal proprietary services, it integrates and trains external data APIs to be used to answer questions as well. Together, Lucy uncovers insights from unstructured and structured data.
- As artificial intelligence is a shift from deterministic to probabilistic output, Lucy also delivers a confidence interval with each answer. Lucy leverages the confidence interval to get smarter by training on actions when the top answer has a low confidence interval.
- Lucy saved the global agency hundreds of hours of research time on just one account. In just one year, on one account Lucy saved the client 320 h on data collection and mapping, 84 h on basic research question (e.g. how many restaurants are there in NYC), and 720 h on brand specific questions (e.g. how many BMWs were manufactured in the US in 2017).

Benefits

- Enables fewer researchers
- Captures quality research
- Unlocks data in multiple silos
- Savings of $10s of thousands per headcount
- Reduces preliminary research by as much as fifteen times

Case study #2: Company Industry: Professional Services
A large services firm leveraged an automation solution built by Rage Frameworks (recently acquired by Genpact), to cull out more relevant sales lead, as compared to the previous system of manual analysis. Expertise Service Automated: Sales Lead Generation

Business Problems

- The greatest bottleneck hampering growth was lack of visibility into new market opportunities.
- Without timely insights into new opportunities, the company could not align its competitive service offerings with potential sales leads as they arose.

Solution

- Rage Frameworks posited that the problem they faced required understanding the multiple triggers that made for a high value sales lead. If these triggers could be determined and correlated, lead identification could then be automated.
- Rage Frameworks began by acquiring a mass of data that may be indicative of a lead e.g. social media accounts, trade publications, financial statements, news, job postings, and internal CRM data. Following the aggregation of this data, they leveraged their suite of AI tools (Real-Time Intelligence Platform of composable services) to 'read' and analyze the internal and external data. Primarily, natural language services were leveraged and correlated to structured historical data of converted leads.
- The result was immediate. The automated solution discovered two hundred times more high value sales leads in comparison to the manual analysis the company was utilizing. In addition, the ability to rapidly analyze structured and unstructured content offered the company ideas on how to personalize their sales pitch and their future market appetite for new solutions. The professional services company is now leveraging the automation delivered by Rage Frameworks as Intel contributing to sales, product development and market analysis, thereby reassigning labor to more productive tasks.
- Rage Frameworks found that the most important factor to finding high-confidence leads for the client was due to external data, specifically job changes at the lead as well as M&A activity surrounding the target company. The manual process employed before automation did not take these data points into account.

Benefits

- Almost immediately, the automated solution delivered two hundred times more relevant sales leads as compared to the previous system's manual analysis
- The system now also automatically interprets new content to provide instant sales triggers in real-time to ensure sales teams respond quickly to new market opportunities.
- Being able to quickly analyze structured and unstructured content has yielded new ideas for clients and has enabled the predicting of future market appetite for new solutions
- The professional services company can now build product offerings in anticipation of future demand, ahead of market trends enabling capitalization on opportunities.

Case Study #3: Company Industry: Hospitality
The company is a Santa Monica, California, USA based startup that provides an intelligent texting platform for hotels. Founded in 2011, it was built with IBM Watson tools and serves approximately 10 million guests annually through their clients. The Expertise Service Automated is: Customer Service

Business Problems

- Digital disruption and rising competition continues to alter multiple aspects of the hotel industry. For example, hotels are increasingly pressured to control labor costs. From housekeeping to catering to guest services, hotel management is a services business dependent on labor. Thereby, when hotels attempt to cut back on staffing, there is a direct effect on guest experience.
- Given the increased transparency and decision-driving power of guest reviews in social media, along with a new class of competitors (e.g. Airbnb), the correlation of customer satisfaction to revenue has grown significantly.
- Finally, the mobile-first millennial customer base now has expectations of instant response. There is a need to find an innovative way to help hotels improve customer service and satisfaction levels and to automate responses to common guest questions and better anticipate customer needs.
- These intersecting trends put incredible pressure on the very labor force that hotel management is seeking to reduce, particularly guest services. In fact, guest services are the first call for a barrage of frequently asked questions:
  - How do I get on Wi-Fi?
  - Can you send up some fresh towels?
  - What time does the gym close?
  - When is checkout?

These questions take time, and often the busy concierge behind the front desk is forced to put the guest on hold, to check-in the next guest or answer another guest's frequently asked questions.

Solution

It was recognized that the aforementioned pressures within the changing hotel industry required a mobile-first solution to instantly meet guest needs without incremental labor cost. The company found that with text messaging as a universally adopted platform, they could reduce hotel front desk pressures while also meeting guest needs instantly. The company built a virtual concierge service known as Ivy. Ivy answers guests' questions or triggers request through text message. They leveraged the natural language processing (NLP) services offered by IBM Watson to automatically recognize and classify queries as well as respond instantly with answers or actions. Moreover, Watson 'taught' Ivy to detect tone of messages, so if a guest was unhappy, the request could be automatically escalated to a human to speed resolution. The solution is:

- Technology to power a text-based hotel concierge service
- Cloud-based, the company took advantage of application programming interfaces (APIs) and the cloud for its back-end systems so that it can focus on its core competency: customer experience

Benefits

- Guests now engage 10 times more with the new cloud-based service than they do with any other hotel communication channel, leading to improved customer satisfaction levels and reduced problem resolution times

4 Results

The majority of the persons interviewed have been using RPA for automating transactional processes and are looking for solutions to automate their expertise-based processes including decision making based on analysis and judgments. Key success factors for automating Expertise Services include:

- Time saved
- Deep experience and rich knowledge in the function
- Good sense of customer service and responsibility
- Correct root cause analysis

Based on the analysis of data collected, key results are summarized in this section.

4.1 Respondents' Definition of Expertise Services

Literature review and respondents' sentiments can be summarized that Expertise Services are professional services, referring to an organization or individual, requiring professional knowledge and expertise in certain applications, according to customer needs and requirements. Respondents also said that Expertise Services provide advice and help on any domain specific questions, issues and strategic plans. For example, "our HR mobility team has to deal with immigration rules/regulations/options for our 10,000+ employees when they have to travel anywhere in 100+ countries for short term and long term. An expert can be a system/chat bot that can process thousands of immigration related documents and manage multiple websites, synthesize the information and provide specific answers to the questions on behalf of the HR mobility team".

As per the respondents, Expertise Services are classified as "Core Competitive" and "Core Differentiating" Processes which can be automated using Cognitive Automation. The focus of Core Competitive Services is on transformation and efficiency whereas the focus of Core Differentiating Services is on innovation. These Expertise Services are different from Transactional Services which are classified as "Non-Core Processes" which are being automated using Robotic Process Automation (RPA).

Further, Expertise Services provide customers with specialized services in fields where a high level of speciality knowledge is required and in some if not most instances technology content is high. The focus on automation of Expertise Services will continue to be a huge focus in the Shared Services and COE arenas.

4.2 Cognitive Tasks Identified Across the Shared Services Function

Based on our research, in Shared Services, skill-based design organizational structures group services require similar skill sets (competencies) from service providers. The respondents said that the top-recognized cognitive tasks inherent during the delivery of these skill-based Expertise Services are:

- Brokering (procurement, vendor relations and third-party management)
- Business Advice & Counsel
- Communications & External Affairs
- Working capital Management
- Education and Training
- Management Decision Support
- Customer Service
- Research
- Project Management
- Risk Management

Respondents also agreed that leveraging these "like" skill sets across several provided services will create service provider specialists rather than generalists, resulting in individual efficiency and expert delivery, which in turn contributes to overall customer satisfaction.

4.3 Knowledge-Based Processes (Workflows) Currently Being Automated

Based on our research, in addition to automated receipt processes, automated calculation of declaration and payment of VAT etc., legal advice, immigration advice and controlled research, are currently being automated or are being considered for automation within the next two years (see Table 2).

Table 2. Knowledge - based processes: candidates for automation

Finance function	HR function	IT function
Financial systems development & support Portfolio investment management Tax research, planning and advice Financial planning, budgeting and reporting Financial risk management Funding services Financial analysis Decision support	Recruitment consulting HR advice Expatriation services Supplier management Process management HR information systems support Benefits design Complaint handling	Applications development IT strategy development Vendor management IT research and innovation

4.4 Knowledge-Driven Processes that Are Candidates for Automation

Table 3, created from APQC's Process Classification Framework, provides the potential scope of automation of Expertise Services and Activities in Finance, HR, IT, Supply and Marketing functions.

Table 3. Scope of automation of expertise services

Function	Expertise services (based on AQPC's process classification framework)
Finance	Perform planning/budgeting/forecasting Perform cost accounting and control Evaluate and manage financial performance Manage policies and procedures Perform capital planning and project approval Manage treasury policies and procedures Manage debt and investment Manage financial fraud/dispute cases Establish internal controls, policies, and procedures Operate controls and monitor compliance with internal controls policies procedures Develop tax strategy and plan Perform cost accounting and control
HR	Develop human resources strategy Develop and implement workforce strategy and policies Monitor and update strategy, plans, and policies Develop competency management models Manage employee performance Manage employee development Develop and train employees Manage labor relations Manage collective bargaining process Manage labor management partnerships Manage employee grievances Develop and manage reward, recognition, and motivation programs

(*continued*)

Table 3. (*continued*)

Function	Expertise services (based on AQPC's process classification framework)
IT	Develop the enterprise IT strategy
	Define the enterprise architecture
	Manage the IT portfolio
	Perform IT research and innovation
	Evaluate and communicate IT business value and performance
	Develop IT services and solutions strategy
	Perform demand-side management (DSM) for IT services
	Market IT services and solutions
	Establish information security, privacy, and data protection strategies and levels
	Develop information and content management strategies
	Develop the IT development strategy
	Develop the IT deployment strategy
	Plan and implement changes
Supply	Develop production and materials strategies
	Manage demand for products and services
	Establish distribution planning constraints
	Review distribution planning policies
	Develop quality standards and procedures
	Develop sourcing strategies
	Perform quality testing
	Provide logistics governance
Marketing	Perform customer and market intelligence analysis
	Evaluate and prioritize market opportunities
	Develop marketing strategy
	Define pricing strategy
	Define and manage channel strategy
	Develop marketing communication strategy
	Design and manage customer loyalty program
	Establish goals, objectives, and metrics for products/services by channel/segment
	Establish marketing budgets
	Develop and manage pricing
	Develop and manage promotional activities
	Analyze and respond to customer insight
	Develop and manage packaging strategy
	Manage product marketing content
	Develop sales forecast
	Develop sales partner/alliance relationships
	Establish overall sales budgets
	Establish sales goals and measures
	Establish customer management measures
	Manage leads/opportunities
	Develop and manage sales proposals, bids, and quotes
	Manage sales partners and alliances

4.5 Business Value of Automation of Knowledge-Based Expertise Services

The respondents identified the perceived/actual benefits of automating Expertise Services. The value is created at three levels:

1. An expert, AI enabled system is as good, if not better, than what a human can deliver, but costs way less.
2. Scaling an expert system comes at near zero additional cost whereas adding another single human doubles the cost.
3. The expert, AI enabled system can be improved over time and it can be tracked objectively whereas for humans it will be difficult because an employee can exit the organization anytime and a new employee comes with a different expertise level.

The amount of time saved in decision making process and the accuracy of the outcome. One specific respondent's response, paraphrased, reads in part: "Our company cultivates energy and chemical industry, with independent intellectual property rights of crude oil, refined oil, chemicals and other logistics management solutions and an intelligent pipeline software suite of products. We have started automation of Knowledge-Based Services and we can now provide customers with multifaceted large data analysis services and promote customer management and operational service innovation."

Using the value created by automating knowledge-based Expertise Services and the implementation cost of the automation tool, a business case can be easily developed to seek approval of the automation strategy.

4.6 Technologies Currently in Use to Automate Business Processes

Based on our research, RPA is being and has been used fairly predominantly for the past several years to automate primarily transactional-based business processes. Software Bots are being used as an expert system to synthesize information from multiple sources and provide answers to specific questions from users. The largest use of bots is in web-spidering (web crawling), in which an automated script fetches, analyzes and files information from web servers at many times the speed of a human. Literature review suggests that more than half of all web traffic is made up of Software Bots.

Based on our research, the tools and technologies currently in use to automate knowledge-based processes include:

- Artificial Intelligence (AI)
- Intelligent Automation (IA)
- Cognitive Automation (CA) tools

A cognitive robot is an autonomous robot that is capable of inference, perception, and learning based on the imperative, autonomic, and cognitive intelligence levels. The representation and modeling of cognitive robots can be carried out by their architectures and behaviors. It is a framework of a cognitive robot that represents the overall structure, components, and their interrelations and a set of intelligent functions and their interactions with the architecture of the cognitive robots [13].

5 Conclusions and Future Research

5.1 Conclusions

The results of this research clearly indicate that automation of knowledge-based processes and Expertise Services is a recent phenomenon. The automation of knowledge-based processes is here to stay and companies are starting to dip their toes into the cognitive system systems space. The adoption rate for automation technologies in Europe and North America is higher than other countries. In this paper, we have indicated both possibilities and limitations of what automation of Knowledge-Based Services can do in the arena of Shared Services and Centers of expertise. What this means is that in future years, we will see much more transformation in the nature of Shared Services work. It is difficult to assess the impact of automation of Knowledge-Based Services on jobs but as automation into Expertise Services continues, fewer people will be needed in these job categories. A backlash from employees is expected due to increased adoption of Intelligent Automation (IA) and further, Cognitive Automation (CA). With this emergence, new job categories will emerge, and the employees will begin understanding the economics of service delivery and the opportunities to work in higher decision-making environments.

Our research also shows that before a company can begin automating Knowledge-Based Processes the organization must:

- Create Leadership buy-in
- Establish a common understanding of "What is Automation?"
- Leverage existing expertise
- Pilot a strategically selected first process

5.2 Future Research

This research paper introduces the concept of automation of Knowledge-Based Expertise Services and offers the value proposition of automating Expertise Services in Shared Services and Centers of Expertise. The findings and analysis presented here will assist more companies to adopt a strategy to automate knowledge-based processes. Future research is required in the areas of service automation providers and service automation tools. Specifically, future research should focus on answering the following questions:

1. Which service provider organizations are providing services for automation of Knowledge-Based Shared Services?
2. What service automation tools e.g. cognitive automation tools are available for automating Knowledge-Based Shared Services?
3. What industries are adopting the service automation strategy to automate their Expertise Services and what implementation approaches have proven to be effective?

References

1. IEEE 2755: IEEE Guide to Terms and Concepts in Intelligent Process Automation, p. 16, New York (2017)
2. Gartner: Robotic Process Automation (RPA): From Hype to Reality, Gartner Research (2016)
3. King, P.: RPA outlook. In: Robotics & Artificial Intelligence Summit, Amsterdam (2018)
4. Mittal, V.: Successful deployment of RPA. In: Robotics & Artificial Intelligence Summit, Amsterdam, p. 24 (2017)
5. Schepper, M.S.: Common pitfall: how not to implement ai in your business. In: Robotics & Artificial Intelligence Summit, Amsterdam, p. 8 (2017)
6. Berruti, F., Nixon, G., Taglion, G., Whiteman, R.: Intelligent Process Automation: The Engine at the Core of the Next-Generation Operating Model, p. 9. Digital McKinsey (2017)
7. Samulowitz, H., Reddy, C., Sabharwal, A.: Cognitive automation of data science. In: ICML AutoML Workshop: IBM TJ Watson Research Center and Allen Institute for Artificial Intelligence, p. 7, New York (2014)
8. Scheel, H.V.: Robotics and artificial intelligence: the next digital frontier. In: Robotics & Artificial Intelligence Summit, p. 11, Amsterdam (2017)
9. Lacity, M.C., Willcocks, L.P.: Robotic Process and Cognitive Automation: The Next Phase, p. 315. SB Publishing, Stratford-upon-Avon, Warwickshire (2018)
10. Lacity, M.C., Willcocks, M.C.: A New Approach to Automating Services, MIT Sloan Management Review, vol. 58, no. 1, p. 11, Fall (2016)
11. Lacity, M.C., Willcocks, L.P.: Robotic Process Automation and Risk Mitigation: The Definitive Guide. SB Publishing, p. 105 (2017)
12. APQC: APQC Process Classification Frameworks (2016)
13. Wang, Y.: Cognitive robots: a reference model towards intelligent authentification. IEEE Robot. Autom. Mag. **17**(4), 9 (2010)

Knowledge Boundary Spanning Mechanisms in a Shared Services Centre Context

Dragos Vieru[1]([⊠]), Simon Bourdeau[2], and Mélissa Bourdeau[1]

[1] TÉLUQ University of Québec, 5800 rue Saint-Denis,
Montréal, QC H2S 3L5, Canada
dragos.vieru@teluq.ca, bourdeau.melissa@univ.teluq.ca
[2] Université du Québec à Montréal, 405 rue Sainte-Catherine Est,
Montréal, QC H2L 2C4, Canada
bourdeau.simon.2@uqam.ca

Abstract. This study focuses on the roles of knowledge boundary spanning mechanisms and intellectual capital (human, structural, and relational) in managing knowledge sharing in an IT-specialized shared services centre (IT-SSC) context. Although the literature stresses the growing utilization of the SSC as an outsourcing model, there is a lack of studies that examine the dynamic process of knowledge sharing across the organizational boundaries in this specific business model. Drawing on the literatures on SSC and on cross-boundary knowledge sharing we propose a conceptual framework based on four research propositions that were validated with primary and secondary data. The results suggest that IT-SSCs present high human capital, but encounter challenges developing relational and structural capitals. It also appears that IT-SSC management tends to prefer the utilization of boundary spanners and boundary objects instead of boundary discourses and boundary practices as mechanisms for efficient boundary spanning.

Keywords: Shared services centre ·
Knowledge boundary spanning mechanism · Boundary spanner ·
Boundary object · Boundary practice · Boundary discourse · Intellectual capital

1 Introduction

To remain competitive, organizations are transforming the way they deliver their information technology (IT) services through the utilization of different sourcing approaches [24]. Among the different available business models of IT sourcing, some companies choose the Shared Services Centre (SSC) model. According to Schulz et al. [30], a SSC consolidates operational processes in order to reduce redundancies and costs, provide support processes, focus on internal clients, and represents a distinct organizational unit within the organization.

An SSC could be described as an independent, semi-autonomous organizational unit that provides services to various other organizational units, i.e. internal clients [22]. By using this arrangement, companies seek to optimize their processes, to generate value and to improve their services [4, 29]. A shared services centre enables a

© Springer Nature Switzerland AG 2019
J. Kotlarsky et al. (Eds.): Global Sourcing 2018, LNBIP 344, pp. 76–100, 2019.
https://doi.org/10.1007/978-3-030-15850-7_5

company to envisage the benefits of two worlds by using only one business model: (a) the world of outsourced processes and (b) the world of internal-based processes [1]. Nevertheless, combining the advantages of a fusion of different worlds can also result in a combination of the disadvantages of these two realities [17]. For example, Ulbrich and Schulz [35] identify several challenges that managers should overcome when implementing a SSC that delivers IT services (IT-SSC), including the issue of efficient knowledge sharing between IT and non-IT personnel.

It has been shown that knowledge sharing is an essential competence in the delivery of outsourced IT services [26] and that user involvement in defining IT needs is key to ensuring IT projects' success [13, 15]. Nevertheless, little research has been carried out specifically on knowledge sharing in the context of an IT-SSC in the extant literature [36].

To enhance understanding of knowledge sharing in this particular context, the concept of knowledge boundary spanning will be placed at the forefront. In this paper we consider boundary spanning as a process that involves several events and a combined effect of multiple spanning mechanisms [12]. Within an IT-SSC, the IT specialists and the knowledge related to the provided services are centralized in the same place. Therefore, we believe that a knowledge boundary is ubiquitous between the IT-SSC and the rest of the organizational units and that efficient knowledge sharing is important to maximizing the mutual performance of the IT-SSC and the organizational units. It has been shown that knowledge boundaries arise during collaborative efforts to find a solution to a problem [25]. The outcome, nonetheless, is not known in advance; rather, it is shaped by the interaction between the stakeholders during a knowledge-sharing process [6, 14].

The concept of knowledge boundary spanning has already been addressed in the context of IT outsourcing projects [11], as well as in relation to the development of information systems [15], but not in the context of an IT-SSC. Thus, we argue that there is a lack of explanation concerning the role of knowledge boundary spanning mechanisms in this specific organizational context. The work of Hsu et al. [15] lays emphasis on the fact that efficient knowledge boundary spanning, as part of an enterprise information systems development project, would significantly impact the quality of the system and of projects. These results lead us to believe that an IT-SSC would have a hard time optimizing the quality of their information systems and their services if it is not known how to efficiently span the knowledge boundary between the centre and the rest of the organizational units.

In general, spanning mechanisms – boundary object, boundary spanner [25, 37], boundary discourse, and boundary practice [12] – have been found to have an impact on the efficiency of crossing knowledge boundaries. Due to the specificity of the organizational structure of an IT-SSC, the implementation of mechanisms for efficient knowledge boundary spanning might differ from the way they are identified and applied within a traditional internal organizational structure. This assumption leads us to a first research question regarding the process of implementation of such mechanisms within the context of an IT-SSC:

Q1: How are the mechanisms for efficient knowledge boundary spanning used in an IT-SSC?

A recent article concludes that "knowledge boundaries can be effectively spanned when strong intellectual capital exists within the organization" [15, p. 291]. According to Stewart [31], intellectual capital refers to the intellectual content (e.g., experience, knowledge) that has been formalized, captured and extracted, enabling the organization to gain a competitive advantage through the optimization of the value of its assets. It has three dimensions: human capital, structural capital and relational capital [5]. Therefore, if intellectual capital has an impact on the efficient flow of knowledge between different organizational stakeholders, what would be its effect on the process of identifying and implementing the mechanisms for efficient knowledge boundary spanning in an IT-SSC context. Based on this argumentation we advance a second research question:

Q2: How can intellectual capital facilitate effective knowledge boundary spanning in an IT-SSC context?

Our study allows us to better understand the process of knowledge boundary spanning in the context of an IT-SSC. We propose a conceptual framework that serves as an analytical tool to assess the relationship between the mechanisms for effective knowledge boundary spanning and the elements of intellectual capital by using a perspective of knowledge as embedded in practice [7]. Drawing on a systematic literature review that has enabled us to identify the major concepts developed in the context of a SSC and better understand the characteristics and challenges faced by SSCs, we propose a framework based on four research propositions. These research propositions were validated with primary data (semi-structured interviews with two experts in the domain) and with secondary data (published case study). The results our analysis suggest that IT-SSCs present high human capital, but encounter challenges developing relational and structural capitals. Nevertheless, it seems that some shared service centres might have the conditions for efficient development of relational and structural capitals. In addition, it appears that IT-SSC management tends to prefer the utilization of boundary spanners and boundary objects instead of boundary discourses and boundary practices as mechanisms for efficient boundary spanning.

The rest of this paper is organized as follows: In the next section, literature related to SSCs, IT-SSCs, knowledge boundaries, boundary spanning and intellectual capital is reviewed and research propositions are proposed. Next, the research method is introduced. Afterward, data analysis and discussion are presented and followed by conclusions.

2   Theoretical Background

2.1   Shared Services Centres and IT-SSCs

Delivering IT services has always been challenging for organizations [21]. Some organizations have opted for a succession of outsourcing methods via external service providers who combine the services offered to various organizations to generate economies of scale and improve their processes [8, 21]. Other organizations have decided to work independently by creating their own shared service centre (SSC) in which the selected organizational processes are consolidated within an organization, to reduce redundancies and provide support services to the various business units [23, 29, 33].

SSCs, which are service-oriented and focus on internal clients, operate as a separate and accountable semi-autonomous unit within an organization [4, 22]. SSCs represent an "insourcing arrangement" within organizations [22, p. 92] and their implementation is often the preliminary stage of other outsourcing strategies [30]. SSCs represent a collaborative strategy focused on generating organizational value, promoting efficiency, reducing cost and improving service delivery to the rest of the organizational business units [14, 17].

Successfully implementing an IT-specialized SSC to obtain the benefits of shared services may be more arduous than expected [34]. Implementing SSCs, and specifically IT-SSCs, also gives rise to challenges, such as surmounting communication hurdles between IT and non-IT employees; addressing the failure to listen to users' needs; as well as managing the knowledge exchange between the IT-SSC and the organizational units [20, 34, 35]. Moreover, knowledge sharing is an essential skill for delivering IT services since each party, i.e. the organizational units and the IT-SSC, needs to understand the reality of the other to innovate, solve problems and provide adequate IT services. Nevertheless, little work[1] has focused specifically on knowledge sharing in the context of an IT-SSC [36] and efficiently crossing boundaries could play a key role in delivering specific IT services, such as those related to IT development projects [15].

2.2 Knowledge Boundaries

The presence of a knowledge boundary between organizational units makes it difficult to create a joint development of knowledge from several distinct units [12]. This situation prevails where there is an IT-SSC, because knowledge sharing between organizational units (i.e. the IT-SSC expert and the users in the business units) can represent a major challenge since knowledge has to cross the boundaries between these different entities. It is therefore imperative to better understand the basic concepts related to effective knowledge boundary spanning (EKBS). Adapting Hsu et al.'s [15] definition of EKBS to the context of an IT-SSC, EKBS can be defined as the interactions between IT-SSC staff and employees in organizational units aimed at achieving "effective syntactic knowledge transfer, semantic knowledge translation and pragmatic knowledge transformation" [15, p. 286].

We adopt the perspective which sees knowledge as localized, embedded, and invested in practice [6, 25]. Given the tacit and sticky nature of knowledge [7], the problems related to knowledge boundaries can be defined as "the knowledge delivery problems in which the tacit and sticky nature of localized knowledge may actually hinder problem solving

---

[1] The authors conducted a systematic review of the literature on SSCs and IT-SSCs in the Elsevier and ABI/INFORMS databases following Templier and Paré's [32] recommendations. The review focused on peer-review articles on the topics of SSCs and IT-SSCs. A total of 52 articles (30 journal articles, 18 conference papers and 4 book chapters) were identified. Seventeen articles focused on IT-SSCs and none of them were in the AIS basket of eight. Only five articles cover the topic of knowledge management in SSCs and one slightly touches on this topic in relation to IT-SSCs [35].

and knowledge creation across functions. In practice, this specialization of knowledge increases the difficulty of collaborating across functional boundaries and accommodating knowledge developed in other practices" [15, p. 283]. Thus, knowledge boundaries are not static and they adjust to environmental learning structures and to the social and material interactions of individuals [12].

2.3 Boundary Spanning and Its Mechanisms

To further understanding of knowledge sharing in IT-SSCs, it is appropriate to place the boundary spanning concept at the forefront. In such a context, effective knowledge sharing becomes essential to maximizing the mutual performance of both the organizational units and the IT-SSC [15]. As mentioned by Ulbrich and Schulz [35], one key challenge related to IT-SSCs is tied to the nature of the communication between IT and non-IT employees. Although communication problems seem to be distinct from those of knowledge sharing, there is a link between communication and knowledge management challenges because, as reported by Ulbrich and Schulz [35], sometimes IT-SSC staff hide behind their technical jargon during exchanges with organizational units.

To effectively manage knowledge across boundaries, Hawkins and Rezazade [12] propose a spanning process, characterized by multiple actors and the adoption of four complementary spanning mechanisms: (1) *boundary spanners*, i.e. "human agents who translate and frame information from one community to another in an effort to promote coordination (p. 1803)"; (2) *boundary objects*, i.e. "physical, abstract, or mental object that serves as a focal point in collaboration enabling parties to represent, transform and share knowledge (p. 1805)"; (3) *boundary practices*, i.e. "a boundary spanning mechanism that overcomes a knowledge boundary by engaging agents from different knowledge communities in collective activities (p. 1806)", and; (4) *boundary discourse*, i.e. "the content of knowledge that shapes the dialogue among the experts from distinct domains" (p. 1807).

More specifically, boundary spanners could use their competence and their social capital, to translate knowledge, frame it and provide legitimization to EKBS [37]. Boundary objects such as, standardized forms, narratives or routines, could help develop shared meaning across boundaries, as well as reinforcing and objectifying knowledge that is crossing boundaries [25]. Boundary practices are novel activities which provide a context where individuals can engage in learning, understanding, internalizing and co-creating tacit and situated knowledge [36]. Finally, boundary discourses focus on the domains of knowledge exchanged across boundaries, and how explicit knowledge is transferred and translated across boundaries to fill knowledge gaps [12]. Thus, as knowledge boundaries arise during collaborative work, the final results of such work are shaped by the interactions of individuals. The integration of the four spanning mechanisms could be used to analyze and clarify how knowledge crosses boundaries between an IT-SSC and organizational units. However, because the relationship between IT-SSCs and organizational units can be knowledge intensive and knowledge is considered a key resource [33, 35], the concept of intellectual capital [31] could also enhance understanding of EKBS in the context of an IT-SSC.

2.4 Intellectual Capital

Intellectual capital can be defined as the "intellectual material that has been formalized, captured, and leveraged to create wealth by producing a higher-valued asset" [5, p. 440] and encompasses three types of sub-capital: (1) *human capital*, i.e. the "tacit knowledge embedded in the minds of the employees"; (2) *structural capital*, i.e. "the organizational routines of the business"; and (3) *relational capital*, i.e. the knowledge embedded in the relationships established with the outside environment (p. 444). Hsu et al. [15] argue that, in IT development projects, users and developers must cope with knowledge boundaries. The authors argue that intellectual capital, expressed through (1) mutual understanding, i.e. relational capital; (2) participative decision-making, i.e. structural capital; and (3) mutual user-IT understanding, i.e. human capital, can bridge knowledge boundaries between users and IT developers. Their study shows that intellectual capital can facilitate knowledge boundary spanning because "it can effectively promote syntactic knowledge transfer, semantic knowledge translation, and pragmatic knowledge transformation (p. 293)." Because effectively crossing knowledge boundaries is paramount to organizational structures that deliver IT services and because IT-SSCs are isolated from other organizational units, adopting an intellectual capital lens to explore knowledge sharing in the specific context of IT-SSCs could be illuminating.

3   Conceptual Framework and Research Propositions

Because IT-SSCs deliver various IT-based services to other organizational units [35], the IT-SSC is therefore expected to be able to carry out effective knowledge boundary spanning as optimally as possible. Yet, due to the nature of the knowledge integral to the IT-SSC's practices, the EKBS process becomes more complex. Thus, several EKBS mechanisms can be mobilized intermittently over time. Moreover, it has been suggested that intellectual capital can facilitate EKBS [15].

As IT-SSCs have specific characteristics, we have developed a conceptual framework (see Fig. 1) that will enhance understanding of the relationships between the intellectual capital components and the boundary spanning mechanisms involved in the knowledge sharing between an IT-SSC and organizational units. We suggest that the process of cross-boundary knowledge sharing is mediated by boundary spanning mechanisms and the utilization of a specific mechanism or a mix of mechanisms will be influenced by the existing levels of the three intellectual sub-capitals (human, structural, and relational) within the IT-SSC.

Thus, given a context of low intellectual capital, an organization could more actively mobilize its boundary spanning mechanisms to promote EKBS. On the other hand, the use of boundary spanning mechanisms could promote the development of intellectual capital during EKBS. Since IT-SSCs have specific characteristics, structures and roles [e.g., 33, 35], as compared with other organizational units, we can conjecture that the dynamics of intellectual capital within IT-SSCs differs from that within other organizational units. Thus, given that such dynamics can impact EKBS [15], the research propositions developed hereafter will focus on how the intellectual capital within IT-SSCs relates to the effective crossing of knowledge boundaries.

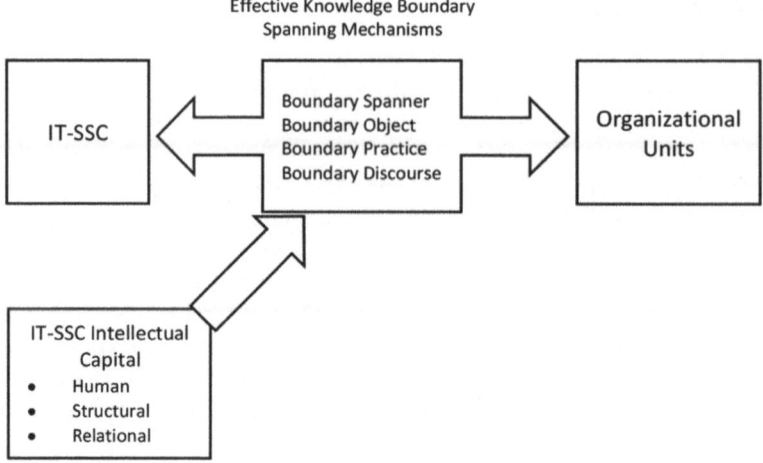

Fig. 1. Conceptual framework: knowledge sharing process in SSC context

3.1   Proposition #1 – The Human Capital of IT-SSCs

Given the idiosyncrasies of IT-SSC, it can be argued that IT human capital will be more prevalent among the IT-SSC developers than among the other organizational unit users. Since they focus primarily on internal clients, it is highly likely that IT-SSC developers will learn, and be particularly aware of, their clients' business needs. Thus, as pointed out by Schulz et al. [29], the IT-SSC developer will develop business knowledge about the organization, its units and its processes. This characteristic will help IT-SSC developers deliver IT services adapted to internal clients' realities and needs. Although the work of IT-SSC developers should be mainly oriented towards developing solutions for internal clients, some developers might, in fact, know little about the client's real needs. It appears that conflicts between an IT-SSC and organizational units can emerge due to the failure of IT-SSC developers to listen to users' needs [17].

One organizational motive for implementing an IT-SSC is the fact that, with such SSCs in place, organizational units can concentrate on their specific roles and functions [16]. Once organizational units can focus on their primary mission, users from these units have less opportunity to develop their IT-related knowledge.

Thus, we propose an initial research proposal:

P1: *Given that the primary role of an IT-SSC is to deliver IT services to internal organizational units, the IT-SSC will tend to have higher IT-related human capital than the other organizational units.*

3.2   Proposition #2 – The Structural Capital of IT-SSCs

Several indications may lead us to conclude that, by its nature, an IT-SSC would have a negative impact on the participation and the perceived authority of users in decision-making related to IT developments. Indeed, with the implementation of an IT-SSC, the power and responsibilities of the organizational units relative to IT would be decreased because of its transfer to the IT-SSC. Formerly located within each organizational unit, the IT developers would now reside within a single organizational unit, i.e. the IT-SSC. Such staff transfer could result in a loss of control and influence for the organizational units relative to IT decision-making. Moreover, the principal-agent relationship [9] within an IT-SSC is particular as: (1) the principal and the agent operate within the same organization, and (2) the relationship, which exists between several clients and a single vendor, creates a sort of monopoly. Thus, since the IT-SSC becomes the only IT service provider for several organizational units, the IT-SSC is placed in an advantageous position relative to IT decision-making.

Nevertheless, structural capital could possibly vary within an organization depending on the degree of customization of the services provided by the IT-SSC [20]. For example, IT-SSCs which have business value based on knowledge and are business-oriented would have more customization and provide a business model customized to the reality of each organizational unit. Such a high level of customization is associated with a more decentralized IT governance structure [19].

Thus, we believe that structural capital and the participation of organizational unit users in IT decision-making could be more prominent in IT-SSCs where the governance structure is decentralized and where the level of customization of the IT services is higher. Inversely, IT-SSCs characterized by a low level of IT services customization and a more centralized governance structure will have low structural capital. Based on the above argument, the second research proposition we are advancing is the following:

P2: *The monopoly position of an IT-SSC with respect to the other organizational units diminishes the influence of the organizational units on IT decision-making, which would have a negative impact on structural capital.*

3.3 Proposition #3 – The Relational Capital of IT-SSCs

Several indications suggest that IT-SSCs may face some challenges linked to relational capital. For example, the lack of trust and the frustration of internal clients with respect to IT-SSCs that Janssen and Wagenaar [18] have pointed out suggest the interactions between IT-SSC developers and organizational units' users, as well as their levels of mutual trust, would tend to be very low. Indeed, mutual trust is not automatically present when an IT-SSC is implemented. It must be developed over time through interactions. Having lost part of their IT staff to the IT-SSC, organizational units may hesitate to trust a new and separate organization that does not have a proven track record. This situation could undermine the basis for mutual trust between users and IT-SSC developers.

In addition, IT-SSCs have management controls which differ from those of other organizational units: they have internal hierarchical controls as well as controls related to the market mechanisms active within the organizational units [27]. We believe that these market-related controls could impede the quality of relationships between IT-SSC members and the organizational units by placing additional pressure on the IT developers' work. The user-pays principle may also reduce the quality of relationships between organizational units and the IT-SSC. Indeed, to minimize costs, organizational units may be tempted to minimize interactions with the IT-SSC and undermine a mutual and trusting relationship. Thus, we propose a third research proposition:

P3: *The user-pays principle would have a negative impact on relational capital. This would put additional pressure on the IT-SSC to minimize prices.*

3.4   Proposition #4 – Effective Knowledge Boundary Spanning Mechanisms in IT-SSCs

According to Hawkins and Rezazade [12], there are four categories of mechanisms for effectively crossing knowledge boundaries. We consider, as proposed by these authors [12], knowledge crossing between boundaries to be a process that involves and integrates complementary EKBS mechanisms: spanners, objects, practices and discourse. As the nature and structure of IT-SSCs makes it challenging to develop strong intellectual capital and since intellectual capital is a factor that favours EKBS [15], IT-SSCs should benefit from optimizing EKBS mechanisms. Thus, because the nature and structure of IT-SSCs differ from those of other organizational units, we argue that the way EKBS mechanisms are deployed in an IT-SSC will differ from the way they are deployed in other organizational units.

EKBS mechanisms include, firstly, *boundary spanners*. These are individuals who translate and reformulate information passing from one group to another to facilitate coordination and problem solving [25]. Such individuals are knowledgeable about both the business context and the IT services. In the case of IT-SSCs, as all IT specialists are centralized under the same roof, IT developers might sometimes find it difficult to express themselves in simple, understandable language during exchanges with organizational units. Boundary spanners could possibly better translate IT knowledge passing to and from organizational units and IT developers. Alternatively, boundary spanners could facilitate domain-specific communication from organizational units' users to IT-SSC developers. In this way, boundary spanners could increase users' confidence in the IT-SSC and lead to an increase in relational capital.

The second mechanism is *boundary objects*, which are common objects shared by different groups that allow them to represent, transform and share knowledge [25]. These boundary objects could be particularly relevant in the context of IT-SSCs. Because their services are intangible, it can be challenging for IT-SSC developers to describe the IT services they offer and deliver to organizational units. Thus, boundary objects could allow both stakeholders, i.e. developers and users, to better understand and become aware of this intangible IT knowledge. For example, detailed service level agreements between IT-SSCs and organizational units would be beneficial for facilitating dialogue between parties. The use of a boundary object facilitates the description of services by enabling IT-SSCs and organizational units to communicate their needs and constraints related to services rendered via a familiar object common to all.

Boundary practices, the third mechanism, allow for the creation of new knowledge through the collective commitment of parties to the practice of common activities [15]. Working together facilitates the sharing and modification of knowledge across borders. Faced with practical problems, participants in each group modify their knowledge collectively. However, this EKBS mechanism might be more complex and challenging to introduce in the context of IT-SSCs. Indeed, as the main objective of IT-SSCs is to centralize IT activities, standardize them and pool expertise under one roof, merging the practices of IT users and developers might distort the very nature of IT-SSCs. By working in conjunction with organizational units, an IT-SSC could integrate boundary practices as a method of sharing knowledge.

Boundary discourses, the fourth mechanism, refers to the content of knowledge that characterizes exchanges between experts in different groups. This relates to the way language itself is used to allow knowledge to cross borders. Boundary discourse is a mechanism that can be challenging for IT-SSCs. Centralizing IT expertise under one roof, may encourage IT specialists to develop specialized jargon which they can use to communicate among themselves. However, such a context might render the interactions with organizational units more difficult and complicated [35]. Nevertheless, it seems that the developers in IT-SSCs would benefit from taking stock of the boundary discourses of organizational units to develop solutions which reflect the organizational unit's discourse. Thus, IT developers should express themselves using terms that are easier for organizational units to understand. Based on the above argument, we propose a fourth and final research proposition:

P4: *To promote EKBS, IT-SSCs should mobilize boundary spanners and boundary objects and, to a lesser extent, promote boundary practices and boundary discourse.*

4 Methodology

As little research has been done on knowledge sharing in IT-SSCs [36], the four research propositions, which juxtapose the concepts of intellectual capital and EKBS mechanisms, have been analyzed using two different sources of data: 1. Secondary data (an existing case study); 2. Interviews with experts.

The case study, which focuses on an IT-SSC, is a doctoral thesis titled "Realizing Shared Services - A Punctuated Process Analysis of a Public IT Department" [28]. Using a process case analysis approach and a punctuated socio-technical IS change model, this thesis was developed to enhance understanding of how an IT department can be transformed into an IT-SSC. Based on an ethnographic field study, it provides a rich set of primary data as well as "a narrative account of the process of realizing IT-SSs, a normative process model grounded in empirical data, and lessons for practitioners" [28, p. 19]. The case study focuses on an IT department (Uni-IT) in a large American university, with approximately 210 employees, which was facing "pressure from the many university departments and colleges to show cost accountability and provide visibility regarding how IT funds were being used" [28, p. 13]. The transformation from an IT department to an IT-SSC took place over a period of 24 months. To provide external validity to the case study, interviews with IT-SSC experts were conducted to triangulate the data [10].

In the first phase of reviewing this study, Olsen's [28] thesis was read several times to ensure familiarity with the case study's content. Then, for each research proposition, citations and explanations providing support were identified, with focus being confined to one proposition at a time. Throughout this iterative process, keywords were identified as a way to help circumscribe citations for each proposition (see Table 1). Reviewing the case study one proposition at a time allowed us to identify common points, redundancies and contradictions.

In the second phase of the review, to evaluate the relevance of our research propositions and the results of the case study, two semi-structured interviews with two IT-SSC specialists were conducted. These interviews enabled us to compare the research propositions and the chain of evidence extracted from Olsen's [28] case study with the experience and knowledge of two IT-SSC experts[2].

5   Data Analysis

5.1   Secondary Data – Case Study

Proposition #1 – Human Capital
In IT development, human capital represents, in large part, the developers' knowledge of the clients' context and business needs [3]. In the Uni-IT case study, some IT-SSC employees worked daily and directly with the various organizational units because they needed to understand their reality and needs to guide them and "educate" them, in particular, about the implications and the cost of IT. As explained by one facilitator:

> *"I was just going to say that I think the dilemma is trying to scope the project right up front. Most of our customers have a champagne and caviar appetite and they have a hamburger and Coke checkbook.[…] So the thing is you have to educate them right up front" [28, p. 161–162].*

It seems that organizational units have little IT knowledge and are more focused on their primary mission. It is the IT-SSC employees who are responsible for informing their clients of the value of their various services and what may best suit their needs. At Uni-IT, some individuals are more likely to guide organizational units on a day-to-day basis, i.e. consultants and principals, since they work in conjunction with the organizational units and bridge the gap between the organizational units and the IT-SSC. In particular, their knowledge regarding the organizational units' functional needs highlights the importance of Uni-IT's intellectual capital to EKBS between the IT-SSC and the organizational units. Indeed, since the role of consultants and principals is to support the organizational units, they acquire a clear knowledge of the administrative and functional reality of each unit.

Thus, human capital seems to be paramount at Uni-IT and is reflected in the valorization of the service culture which underscores the need for the IT-SSC to understand the needs of the organizational units: "The result of service-thinking was a

---

[2] One respondent was an IT vice-president with 15 years of IT-SSC experience and the other one was an assistant vice-president with 20 years of experience in IT-SSC.

Table 1. Coding list

Proposition	Keywords used	References
1#	Knowledge; Competency; Customer; Business unit; Services	[15]
2#	Meeting; Business unit; Decision; Influence; Dependency; Monopoly	[15]
3#	Customer relationship; Working relationship; Cost	[15]
4# – Spanner	Consultant; Principal; Politics and power relations	[12, 25]
4# – Object	E-mail; Quote; Shared Meanings	[6, 12]
4# – Discourse	Lexicon; Vocabulary; Description	[12]
4# – Practice	Do together; Collective activities; Co-creation	[12]

paradigm shift from task performance – "what I do" – to service provision – "what I deliver"" [28, p. 106]. Such a paradigm shift requires that Uni-IT must no longer work in silos, that IT-SSC employees become familiar with their clients' characteristics and that this knowledge be developed by Unit-IT managers:

> *"In addition to learning their own individual roles, managers had to learn new skills such as presenting quotes to customers, answering customer inquiries about cost, conducting detailed internal budgeting, and buying and selling internal services" [28, p. 122].*

Knowledge of the IT-SSC clients' needs also influences how work is organized at Uni-IT: "Prior to this, managers would often only sell the services that they provided; thereby the organization would lose the opportunity to meet the needs of the customer with other services" [28, p. 68–69]. The paradigm shift helped the IT-SSC better understand and guide its clients:

> *"We really have to train our people to take that lexicon out of their vocabulary. We have to train them to say that, 'Morgan now does that,' not, 'I don't do that.' Or, 'Let me transfer you now' or, 'I can take that request to them for you,' or something to help it get there, but 'I don't do that anymore,' can't be an acceptable response"[28, p. 87).*

In order to properly guide the organizational units, the IT-SSC's human capital must be expanded as much through knowledge of the customer's reality as through knowledge of the different specialties of the organization. As the case study states, "several times managers expressed the importance of knowing the others' roles to allow for lead passing" [28, p. 88]. Thus, the secondary data seems to provide support for the first research proposition, since the IT-SSC at Uni-IT seems to have higher IT-related human capital than the other organizational units.

Proposition #2 – Structural Capital

Structural capital relates to organizational routines which promote interactions between individuals such as, for example, the active participation of stakeholders in decision-making. At Uni-IT, the SSC is a monopoly as there is only one IT supplier, namely, the IT-SSC, which has several clients, namely, the organizational units. Thus, this situation has created greater interdependence between the IT-SSC and the organizational units, and requires more interaction between them. With the introduction of the IT-SSC at Uni-IT, redundant services were eliminated and each service offered by the IT-SSC became distinct because the IT-SSC structure "was designed to allow each manager to develop expertise and provide services within specialized domains" [28, p. 95]. For instance, weekly meetings, called "walkthroughs," between different IT-SSC managers were conducted:

> "Walkthroughs were described as communicating understanding of "who will be doing what, for whom, in relation to the delivery of products and services. By rehearsing key business processes by conducting dozens of walkthroughs, Uni-IT had a smoother transition from task to service-oriented delivery" [28, p. 107].

This structural mechanism was also used to coordinate and identify which services provided by internal managers would need to be pooled to meet the demands of an organizational unit. Such mechanisms "reinforced manager responsibility and enabled each manager to be aware of how their services might be able to be bundled to meet the needs of a client" [28 p. 120). However, walkthroughs did not include any organizational units' representatives and no meetings were held at Uni-IT to promote the influence of clients on decision-making. As a result of dealing with the IT-SSC monopoly, organizational units' managers appear to feel threatened or inferior, as one manager pointed out:

> "I think there are some folks around campus who are threatened by the whole process: Uni-IT is starting to know what it costs to run their shop, and I have no idea how much it costs to run my shop or where my money goes" [28, p. 108].

However, the IT-SSC seems to have been sensitive to its monopoly position and responded to the clients' criticisms by taking necessary actions to meet their needs. For instance, following an iPad implementation project that would allow new students to enroll in the classroom, the CIO and other IT-SSC managers received an email from the organizational unit manager client complaining about the cumbersome nature of the estimates and the "wasted" time spent establishing estimates that were neither revealing nor helpful to the client. The following day, the head of the IT-SSC contacted all IT-SSC managers and told them:

> "We would like to use the next leadership team meeting to walk through the initiation of this project and determine any lessons that can be learned in order to improve the process for future project requests from customers" [28, p. 80].

Although, Uni-IT clients do not seem to have a particular role to play in the major decision making process and are not part of the walkthroughs, it seems that their criticisms of the IT-SSC are taken seriously as actions have been taken to meets the clients' needs. Thus, the secondary data seems to provide support for the second research proposition, since the monopoly position of the IT-SSC with respect to the Uni-IT organizational units seems to diminished the latter's influence in the IT decision-making process and simultaneously have a negative impact on Uni-IT's structural capital.

Proposition #3 – Relational Capital

Relational capital refers to interactions, respect and mutual trust with the external environment. The fact that the IT-SSC at Uni-IT billed organizational units for their services allowed units to compare the price paid with similar services on the market. Many organizational unit managers did not understand why they should now have to pay for services that had cost them nothing in the past. The constant price justification and the comparison with services offered on the market created tension during inter-actions. In addition, several IT-SSC managers suspected that the imposition of service billing could alter their relations with the organizational units, as reported by one IT-SSC manager:

> *"If we want to ruin our PR related to our restructuring, the best thing for us to do is to go out there and relate it to doing fee for service. We've all kind of jumped on this bandwagon like we're ready to go out there and start charging for things where we haven't charged for them in the past"* [28, p. 157].

However, IT-SSC managers' hands-on experience with the process of estimating quotes has enabled them to develop interpersonal skills that reduce the tensions created, as outlined by one manager:

> *"It was six months (after announcement day) before I felt like I owned my business enough to actually be an entrepreneur. Because, I'm trying to understand my business and what my role is in the organization and how I interact with customers and with my coworkers"* [28, p. 89].

Nevertheless, to respond to this threat of altering their relationships with organi-zational units, IT-SSC managers made undeniable efforts to minimize costs and simultaneously minimize the amounts billed to customers: "I think we underestimated the finesse that it takes, you learn that every time I quote a price to someone there is a little dance that happens" [28]. Managers are anxious about the idea of proposing a costly estimate higher than the client's budget or higher than comparable services on the market [28].

Thus, Olsen's [28] case study supports the third research proposition, since the ubiquitous user-pays principle in the IT-SSC seems to have negatively impacted Uni-IT's relational capital, and put pressure on the IT-SSC to minimize its prices.

Proposition #4 – Effective Knowledge Boundary Spanning Mechanisms in IT-SSCs

In the Uni-IT case study, consultants and principals acted as *boundary spanners* for clients:

> *"The consultant was charged with being the public face of the organization, meeting with customers to determine their needs before bringing these needs back to the leadership team where managers would then identify who would be the "prime" (e.g. prime contractor) on the project and the individual managers whose services were requisite to complete the project"* [28, p. 68].

After the deployment of the IT-SSC at Uni-IT, it was no longer the first randomly selected individual from the IT department who took the initiative to help and serve an organizational unit, but rather a consultant specialized in the analysis of the client's needs was appointed to this role. Therefore, consultants were generalists who had global knowledge of the IT-SSC's services and who would guide organizational units according to their particular needs. The IT-SSC became a one-stop shop, facilitating communication and knowledge transfer between organizational units and the IT-SSC. Thus, the secondary data supports the first part of the fourth research proposition, which asserts that IT-SSCs should mobilize boundary spanners to promote EKBS.

One *boundary object* used at Uni-IT was the emails used to communicate between the IT-SSC and organizational units. For instance, the administrator of the student orientation service wrote an email to the CIO and other IT-SSC managers informing them of the poor quality of the costing process. The next day, the CIO sent an email to the IT-SSC managers asking them to identify solutions that would improve the process for future client requests [28]. This email served as a trigger to sensitize managers to this reality and, as reported by one IT-SSC manager, the email: "stated a few ground rules for the meeting: The customers' perception is reality. The focus of the discussion will be on those items that Uni-IT can control" [28]. A second boundary object used by the IT-SSC was the service quotations which were used to communicate the detailed cost description for an IT service. The quotations allowed organizational units to clearly identify the nature and scope of IT services and their costs. It helped the two entities to work on shared concerns because it provided a detailed description of the IT services and helped the IT-SSC managers explain those services. The quotations helped IT-SSC managers refine their interventions and adapt the IT services offered to the organizational units' needs and budgets, because the clients could accept, negotiate, amend or refuse the service conditions. This tool facilitated discussion by using a common focal point that everyone could adjust as they saw fit:

"On several occasions debates between meeting facilitators and engineers arose on the subject of costing. Engineers favored taking time to gather requirements while facilitators favored getting a rough estimate back to the customer as soon as possible. Both had strong arguments" [28, p. 84]

The CIO argued that the role of the quotations was to show the organizational units the importance of IT services and clarify the options available and the associated costs. Thus, the second part of proposition #4 seems to be supported by the case study, given that the IT-SSC at Uni-IT mobilized boundary objects to facilitate EKBS.

Boundary discourses refer to the content of knowledge that shapes the dialogue between experts in different fields. In the case study [28], IT-SSC employees seemed to make an effort to adapt their approaches and vocabulary during their exchanges with the organizational units. For instance, IT-SSC employees realized that their approaches and vocabulary could create confusion among organizational units:

"We really have to train our people to take that lexicon out of their vocabulary. We have to train them to say that, 'Morgan now does that,' not, 'I don't do that.' Or, 'Let me transfer you now' or, 'I can take that request to them for you,' or something to help it get there, but 'I don't do that anymore,' can't be an acceptable response" [28, p. 84]

Thus, based on the case study, the third part of research proposition #4 seems to be upheld, given that the IT-SSC tended to promote boundary discourse.

Finally, *boundary practices* favor engagement in collective activities that allow the generation of common knowledge. In the Uni-IT case study, the IT-SSC does not seem to have developed boundary practices with organizational units. Indeed, the thesis analysis does not allow us to identify any mechanisms that promoted EKBS through specific practices, since the study focuses on the transformation of an IT department into an IT-SSC rather than on boundary practices.

On the other hand, it would not be surprising to find there were no boundary practices at Uni-IT since the main objective of an IT-SSC is to centralize IT services by standardizing processes and developing IT expertise in a common organization. Implementing boundary practices would distort the goal of consolidating similar activities within one organization and streamlining organizational units so that they can concentrate on their primary missions. Thus, no support for the fourth part of the proposition was identified.

5.2   Primary Data – Expert Interviews

Proposition #1 – Human Capital

Proposition #1 implies that, since the main function of an IT-SSC is to deliver IT services to its customers, it must have highly competent employees, demonstrating leadership and intellectual agility [15]. Generally, the experts interviewed agreed with the first research proposition and mentioned that recurrently conducting business with the same client (i.e. organizational units) allows IT-SSC employees to develop and acquire strong human capital.

Nevertheless, Expert #1 mentioned that, one key factor that helps optimize human capital development is to have a low turnover rate in the IT-SSC. He argues that relying on employees that have been around for a long time in the IT-SSC helps to optimize its human capital. Thus, an IT-SSC does not automatically have a high level of human capital and the presence of "senior" employees could favor more human capital:

"In general, we have people who are very familiar with it [the IT-SSC] and this makes a big difference. [...] Because they are able to make the connection with what is happening in the business, not just the systems" [translation from French] (Expert #1).

In addition, Expert #2 indicated that the way in which IT-SSCs are structured could impact their human capital: some are organized along technological lines, while others develop teams based on the clients' business needs:

"Often the structure of IT-SSCs is oriented towards the technology [that they service]. I would say that the most effective [teams] are those that are oriented toward business units, but again, it depends on the context. This is not always feasible or desirable" [translation from French] (Expert #2).

Such IT-SSCs would be classified as decentralized rather than balanced and, in such a context, it would be easier to develop human capital. Thus, the interviews support the first research proposition since the IT-SSCs that do business with the same clients, on a recurring basis, have a high level of human capital. However, the turnover rate and the organizational structure of an IT-SSC can affect its level of human capital.

Proposition #2 – Structural Capital

This proposition posits that the monopoly position of an IT-SSC vis-a-vis organizational units could reduce the influence of organizational units on decision-making and negatively impact structural capital. Expert #1 argued that IT-SSCs must be monopolies to avoid duplication, to prevent the development of separate technological platforms that cannot communicate, and to prevent incrementally increasing the operational cost of IT (through the presence of multiple platforms):

> *"Yes, this limits the client's influence. It limits their decision-making, they do not have the same freedom, because they are "forced" to do business with us because we want to ensure cohesion and avoid IT chaos" [translation from French] (Expert #1).*

Further, Expert #1 mentioned that, in the long run, the IT-SSC monopoly tends to eliminate information silos and promote information flow. It also limits client decision-making for the purpose of "reducing costs and ensuring the sustainability of all systems" (Expert #1). Expert #2 provided a more nuanced explanation, arguing that the client's difficulties in making decisions in the context of an IT-SSC structure is not necessarily related to the monopoly itself but to the fact that there is often more than one organizational unit involved in an IT project:

> *"Even if they had their choice of IT provider, they would have to choose an IT provider for a particular problem, except that the business expertise required to perform the query is in several organizational units; the complexity is there, it isn't the monopolistic position that is the problem" [translation from French] (Expert #2).*

Thus, the second research proposition seems to be partially confirmed as it was referred to from two complementary perspectives by the IT-SSC experts. Thus, the explanation proposed by Expert #1 seems to relate to underscores the fact that the SSC must play a key role in managing the decisions of organizational units to optimize global processes and systems, as well as to ensure the IT-SSC's effectiveness. On the other hand, Expert #2's explanation seems to stress the importance of less a process standardization and a greater flexibility, allowing for more focus on clients' needs and simultaneously creating more room for shared decision-making.

Proposition #3 – Relational Capital

This proposition posits that the user-pays principle could have a negative impact on the relational capital as it would put additional pressure on the IT-SSC to minimize prices. The two experts agreed with this proposition. Nevertheless, they stressed that not all IT-SSCs necessarily had to integrate the user-pays principle. Indeed, they mentioned that, when the user-pays principle is present, relationships are more difficult to maintain. For instance, Expert #1 highlights the fact that some of the IT-SSC's clients complained about the high pricing of services delivered and mentioned that they could be delivered at a lower price by an external provider. However, clients forgot to compare the quality of the service rendered:

> *"[Clients] compare this with one of their competitors who has a system that they have purchased, but it is local. Thus, if they lose their local server, the competitor can no longer serve its clients. We are centralized. We have an infrastructure in place, we have high availability centres, that means that all the data are copied to the second in two centres that are in two different physical places. So the system is practically never down" [translation from French] (Expert #1).*

These altercations with the different organizational units undoubtedly put pressure on the IT-SSC to minimize its prices: *"We have to be very careful about our costs because they never stop telling us: "You are expensive! You are expensive!" (Expert #1)*.

On the other hand, the two experts interviewed also highlighted the possibility, for some IT-SSCs, of not using the "bill back" or user-pays principle. For instance, there are some organizations in which *"there is a budget, it is the IT budget [of the IT-SSC] and…according to established priorities by the IT-SSC and the organizational units, the money is spent" (Expert #2)*. Thus, by not exploiting the user-pays principle with its clients the IT-SSC will enhance the quality of its relationships.

Thus, the third research proposition seems to be partially confirmed since relational capital is not automatically minimized by the application of the user-pays principle. Based on the interviews, it seems that IT-SSCs that rely on a user-pays approach have more difficult relationships with organizational units and such IT-SSCs could be observed to make efforts to minimize costs. Nevertheless, since SSCs that are some-what decentralized tend to place less emphasis on costs, it seems that they might not automatically apply the user-pays principle. This approach could favor a less conflictual relationship between the IT-SSC and the organizational units. However, it could create an impression among clients that IT services are free and the effort to ensure a return on investment would be minimized.

Proposition #4 – EKBS Mechanisms

The presence of *boundary spanners* between IT-SSCs and organizational units facili-tates EKBS according to the two experts, who tend to mobilize liaison officers on both sides of the knowledge border, – one business liaison officer and one IT liaison officer:

> *"We work hard to ensure that IT analysts working with business units have business expertise in the sector they work with […] and on the other hand, organizational units have a so-called "business unit representative." This is the person who initiates the requests" [translation from French] (Expert #2)*.

According to the experts, the boundary spanners should be senior analysts who must be able to understand the discourse of organizational units and to see beyond the discourse to truly understand the client's needs and translate these for their IT-SSC colleagues:

> *"Someone can say something and the other person interprets it according to his experience, but the speaker, with his experience, did not mean the same thing. So you have to be able to get past that and really listen [to the customer]" [translation from French] (Expert #1)*.

Thus, the experts highlighted the fact that IT-SSCs tend to mobilize liaison officers to promote EKBS, which supports the first element the fourth research proposition.

The use of *boundary objects* by IT-SSCs to promote EKBS was highlighted in the interviews. The two experts proposed the use of a COBIT-based development methodology to structure the way IT-SSCs can do business with organizational units during the stages of the IS development process. Organizational units must be familiar with the boundary objects, which would include statements of work, functional anal-yses, etc., and these must be approved by them:

"All business units have been trained in this to understand the methodology, but also to understand what documents will be used to accurately exchange information and ensure that business units are able to approve their content" [translation from French] (Expert #2).

These documents are the backbone of the IT development methodology, and they make it possible to ensure that the organizational units' needs and the IT-SSC's constraints are well understood on both sides. In addition, the IT-SSC may use prototypes:

"Depending on the complexity of the request we will make prototypes that we will work on with the users, saying there are new systems, new screens to be added, here is how it would work, so that they can visualize it" [translation from French] (Expert #1).

Thus, to promote EKBS, the interviewed experts indicated that IT-SSCs mobilize boundary objects, and this supports the second element of the fourth research proposition.

Boundary discourse seems to be a pervasive challenge in the IT-SSC context. Although boundary objects can use a simple and vulgarized vocabulary to ensure everyone's understanding, it seems that the vulgarization of discourse by IT-SSC employees is more complex than this would imply, as pointed out by Expert #2:

"Yes, this is a constant challenge, it is more challenging in some places than in others. It depends on people. Some are more technical than others." [translation from French]

Nevertheless, the fact that some IT-SSCs use the same representative to interact with a given business unit allows the business unit to become more familiar with the IT vocabulary and concepts and thereby promotes understanding of the IT-SSC discourse. Moreover, the fact that boundary spanners must develop expertise related to the business unit enables them to develop a boundary discourse adapted to the needs of their clients. Thus, the interviewed experts supported the third element of the fourth research proposition, by pointing out that, to promote EKBS, IT-SSCs tend to favor liaison officers and objects over discourses.

According to the two experts interviewed, *boundary practices* could be used by IT-SSCs to promote EKBS. Nevertheless, this mechanism is used in specific cases: major and complex IT projects. For instance, in large and complex IT projects, IT-SSCs could encourage organizational units affected by the project to release one or more of their full-time employees so that they can come to work in the IT-SSC during the project. However, this strategy does incur costs for the organizational units:

"Of course, when you release someone full-time, you have to "back staff" as we say, meaning hire someone temporarily who is going to do the job, and there are costs related to that, and this is not always well received [by organizational units]" [translation from French] (Expert #2).

However, this mechanism is not used in small projects as it is complex and unproductive to release staff for a short period, and the IT-SSC may be faced with the need to intermittently "share" this resource with the organizational unit (Expert #2).

Because IT-SSCs centralize and focus on IT activities and because organizational units primarily focus on their core activities, introducing boundary practices can be complex and challenging. However, the interviewed experts stressed that it is extremely beneficial to use such EKBS mechanisms in large and complex IT projects. Thus, the interviews partially support the fourth element of the last research proposition.

6   Discussion

Based on the case study analysis and the interviews with IT-SSC experts, it seems that human capital is particularly strong and plays a key role in IT-SSCs, whereas relational capital and structural capital are less developed because of the monopolistic position IT-SSCs tend to hold and the user-pays principle they tend to apply. As proposed in the conceptual framework and the research propositions, IT-SSCs mobilize liaison officers (e.g., consultants and principals) and use boundary objects to allow EKBS. On the other hand, boundary discourses and boundary practices, although imperfect, seem to be of interest and are being developed to improve EKBS. Table 2 summarizes the main findings resulted from the case study analysis and the interviews with IT-SSC experts.

Analysis of the case study and the interviews suggests that IT-SSCs have strong human capital. In particular, the case study highlights the fact that organizational units seem to have limited IT knowledge. Therefore, it seems to be the business knowledge developed by consultants and principals in IT-SSCs which builds human capital [3]. Thus, by promoting a service culture, the IT-SSC at Uni-IT also developed its human capital as it worked with organizational units on a daily basis to guide them through the IT development process. The interviews with the two experts underscore the fact that IT-SSCs with low employee turnover rates can optimize human capital by developing solid and concrete knowledge of their clients' business needs and contexts.

The data analysis shows that the monopoly position of IT-SSCs seems to diminish the influence of organizational units on decision-making and negatively impact structural capital. However, the experts revealed a more nuanced perspective on this matter. However, they stated that this would not be the case for IT-SSCs where processes are less standardized and more flexible, which facilitates the participation of organizational units in decision-making.

According to the case study, the use of "quotes" to transparently show the costs of a project had a negative impact on the relationship between the IT-SSC and its clients. Organizational units were able to compare prices with the external market. The IT-SSC therefore had to constantly justify its prices in response to its customers' complaints. The interviews with the two experts also highlighted the fact that the user-pays principle undeniably had a negative impact on relational capital and that it put pressure on IT-SSCs to minimize their costs. Nevertheless, the user-pays principle is not automatically applied by all IT-SSCs. Some IT-SSCs do not use the user-pays principle in order to optimize the quality of the relationship between the IT-SSC and other organizational units. Yet such a situation would convey to the organizational units the idea that services are free. To overcome this impression that services are free, experts advise that, at the least, a "show back" principle should be applied, to educate clients.

In the case study, consultants and principals were mobilized to bridge the gap between the IT-SSC and the organizational units. They translated the client's needs for the IT-SSC and the IT-SSC's specifications and constraints for the organizational units. The two experts not only highlighted the importance of selecting senior analysts as liaison officers, but also discussed using a liaison officer who comes directly from the organizational unit receiving services. Representatives of the organizational units who worked with the IT-SSC on a recurring basis developed the capacity to translate the discourse of the IT-SSC for other users.

Table 2. Synthesis of findings

Propositions	From the case study analysis	From the interviews with experts
#1 – Human Capital	- HC is paramount at Uni-IT and is reflected in the valorization of the service culture which underscores the need for the IT-SSC to understand the needs of the organizational units	- IT-SSCs have strong human capital - A low turnover rate for employees of IT-SSCs can promote a high level of human capital - A decentralized IT-SSC would facilitate the development of strong human capital
#2 – Structural Capital	- The monopoly position of the IT-SSC with respect to organizational units has a negative impact on structural capital	- The monopoly position of the IT-SSC with respect to organizational units has a negative impact on structural capital only when the IT-SSC is "balanced." -The monopoly position of the IT-SSC with respect to organizational units would not have a negative impact on the structural capital when the IT-SSC is decentralized
#3 – Relational Capital	- The user-pays principle had a negative impact on relational capital. The constant price justification and the comparison with services offered on the market created tension (lack of trust) during interactions. This principle put additional pressure on an IT-SSC to minimize the prices of services offered	- The user-pays principle is not automatically used in all IT-SSCs - When the user pays principle is used in an IT-SSC, it is true that this principle has a negative impact on relational capital and places additional pressure on the IT-SSC to minimize prices
#4a – Boundary Spanner	- IT-SSC tends to mobilize liaison officers (consultants) to promote EKBS	- IT- SSCs tend to mobilize liaison officers and organizational units can also mobilize liaison officers to represent them
#4b – Boundary Object	- IT-SSCs tend to mobilize boundary objects (service quotations) to promote EKBS	- IT-SSCs tend to mobilize boundary objects to promote EKBS. IT-SSCs can use an IS development methodology to structure the use of boundary objects
#4c – Boundary Discourse	- IT professionals made the effort to eliminate IT jargon when communicating with users	- IT-SSCs tend to favor boundary discourse less as a mechanism for optimizing EKBS - It is less critical to develop an effective boundary discourse when the IT-SSC deals with the same representatives of organizational units on a recurring basis
#4d – Boundary Practice	- no boundary practices at Uni-IT since the main objective of an IT-SSC was to centralize IT services by standardizing processes and developing IT expertise	- IT-SSCs tend to favor boundary practices only in the context of major projects

IT-SSCs tend to mobilize boundary objects to promote EKBS. In the case study, we found that quotes and e-mails were used as boundary objects. During the interviews with experts, several boundary objects were mentioned, including statements of work, functional analyses and prototypes.

According to the case study and the interviews, using boundary discourses to promote EKBS seems to be challenging. In the case study, the IT-SSC realized how difficult it was to promote an effective boundary discourse. The experts also highlighted this challenge but relativized its importance by indicating that certain strategies, such as dealing with the same representatives from organizational units, would allow representatives to better understand IT jargon and would minimize the need to develop the IT-SSC's capacity to "vulgarize" its discourse.

The two experts agreed that IT-SSCs should make little use of border practices, as such practices are relatively costly and can create inconveniences for some organizational units (hiring new staff for a specific time period). However, it appears that such practices have been efficiently used in major projects. For example, the cost of releasing employees so they can work directly in the IT-SSC during a major project may be smaller than the inconvenience experienced by organizational units trying to fulfill their primary responsibilities.

7 Further Empirical Validation of the Conceptual Framework

The next step in our study is to empirically validate our conceptual framework by using a multi-case study method. We will adopt an explanatory theory-building-from-cases approach [10]. An explanatory approach seeks to find relationships between an "observed state of a phenomenon and conditions that influence its development" [2, p. 428]. Following Eisenhardt's [10] methodological recommendations, we will anchor our preliminary construct specification in the extant literature and we will craft our data collection instruments and protocols on the basis of this literature, following a deductive pattern. This will be followed, after our entry in the field, by a "flexible and opportunistic" [10, p. 533] data collection approach, and a within-case and cross-case data analysis, which are inductive in nature.

We will use a multiple-case design and will select the cases applying a logic of replication, maximizing variation, thus predicting "contrasting results but for predictable reasons" [38, p. 47], yet allowing comparison. Interviews will be the main method of data collection. In line with our theory building approach, we will remain open to the exploration of new topics and themes during data collection [10]. Following our theory building approach, we will triangulate the interview with archival sources, including project documentation and other organization documents. We will perform within-case and cross-case analyses. Cross-case analysis will be conducted by using methods suggested by Eisenhardt [10], as the cases will be compared to identify similarities and differences between them.

8 Conclusion

This paper contributes first to the breadth of the scientific literature on SSCs. In particular, it has helped deepen understanding of concepts related to knowledge management in the context of IT-SSCs. A conceptual framework and research propositions related to EKBS and intellectual capital within the context of IT-SSCs are proposed. The study also shows how EKBS mechanisms and the components of intellectual capital could affect IT-SSCs. A second contribution is made to the field of knowledge management. This study analyses several concepts within the context of an IT-SSC using the perspective of knowledge being embedded integrated into practice [25]. Our data analysis suggests that there is mutual interaction between intellectual capital and EKBS mechanisms.

Concerning practitioners, this study is undeniably a resource for IT managers working in the world of IT-SSCs. Our analysis suggests that it is essential that practitioners understand EKBS mechanisms and the components of intellectual capital that characterize their organization. The results of this study will guide them in the evaluation of these mechanisms. Their assessment will allow them to optimize EKBS between their SSC and organizational units and to simultaneously encourage innovation in the development of new systems by optimizing the level of users' involvement in the development process.

Although this paper makes a contribution to the fields of IT and knowledge management, it also has limitations. First, the study's results cannot be generalized because it relies on an illustrative case study and two interviews. As emphasized by Eisenhardt [10], case-building theory can result in narrow and idiosyncratic theory. Nevertheless, this illustrative case study has allowed us to better understand certain phenomena that have not been studied in the context of an IT-SSC. A second limitation of this study is that the case study data had previously been collected for different research purposes.

References

1. Amiruddin, R., Aman, A., Sofiah, Auzair, M., Hamzah, N., Maelah, R.: Mitigating risks in a shared service relationship: the case of a Malaysian bank. Qual. Res. Acc. Manag. **10**(1), 78–93 (2013)
2. Avgerou, C.: Explaining trust in IT-mediated elections: a case study of e-Voting in Brazil. J. Assoc. Inf. Syst. **14**(8), 420–451 (2013)
3. Bassellier, G., Benbasat, I.: Business competence of it professionals: conceptual development and influence on IT-business partnerships. MIS Q. **28**(4), 673–694 (2004)
4. Bergeron, B.: Essentials of Shared Services. Wiley, Hoboken (2003)
5. Bontis, N.: Managing Organizational Knowledge by Diagnosing Intellectual Capital: Framing and Advancing the State of the Field. Int. J. Technol. Manage. **18**(5–8), 433–462 (1999)
6. Carlile, P.R.: Transferring, translating, and transforming: an integrative framework for managing knowledge across boundaries. Organ. Sci. **15**(5), 555–568 (2004)
7. Cook, S.D., Brown, J.S.: Bridging epistemologies: the generative dance between organizational knowledge and organizational knowing. Organ. Sci. **10**(4), 381–400 (1999)

8. Dibbern, J., Goles, T., Hirschheim, R., Jayatilaka, B.: Information systems outsourcing: a survey and analysis of the literature. ACM Sigmis Database **35**(4), 6–102 (2004)
9. Eisenhardt, K.M.: Agency theory: an assessment and review. Acad. Manag. Rev. **14**, 57–74 (1989)
10. Eisenhardt, K.M.: Building theories from case study research. Acad. Manag. Rev. **14**(4), 532–550 (1989)
11. Feng, Y., Ye, H., Pan, S.L.: Delivering knowledge across boundaries: a process model of knowledge delivery in offshoring projects. In: Proceedings of the 14th Pacific Asia Conference on Information Systems, Taipei, Taiwan (2010)
12. Hawkins, M.A., Rezazade, M.H.: Knowledge boundary spanning process: synthesizing four spanning mechanisms. Manage. Decis. **50**(10), 1800–1815 (2012)
13. He, J., King, W.R.: The role of user participation in information systems development: implication from a meta-analysis. J. Manage. Inf. Syst. **25**(1), 301–331 (2008)
14. Herbert, I., Seal, W.: A knowledge management perspective to shared service centers: a case study of a finance SSC. In: Shared Services as a New Organizational Form, pp. 133–151. Emerald Publishing, Bingley (2014)
15. Hsu, J.S.-C., Chu, T.-H., Lin, T.-C., Lo, C.-F.: Coping knowledge boundaries between information system and business disciplines: an intellectual capital perspective. Inf. Manage. **51**(2), 283–295 (2014)
16. Janssen, M., Joha, A.: Issues in relationship management for obtaining the benefits of a shared service center. In: Proceedings of the 6th International Conference on Electronic Commerce, pp. 219–228. ACM (2004)
17. Janssen, M., Joha, A.: Motives for establishing shared service centers in public administrations. Int. J. Inf. Manage. **26**(2), 102–115 (2006)
18. Janssen, M., Wagenaar, R.: An analysis of a shared services centre in e-government. In: Proceedings of the 37th Hawaii International Conference on System Sciences, HI (2004)
19. Joha, A., Janssen, M.: Types of shared services business models in public administration. In: Proceedings of the 12th Annual International Digital Government Research Conference: Digital Government Innovation in Challenging Times, pp. 26–35. ACM (2011)
20. Joha, A., Janssen, M.: Factors influencing the shaping of shared services business models: balancing customization and standardization. Strateg. Outsourcing Int. J. **7**(1), 47–65 (2014)
21. Kern, T., Willcocks, L.: Exploring relationships in information technology outsourcing: the interaction approach. Eur. J. Inf. Syst. **11**(1), 3–19 (2002)
22. Knol, A., Janssen, M., Sol, H.: A taxonomy of management challenges for developing shared services arrangements. Eur. Manag. J. **32**(1), 91–103 (2014)
23. Lacity, M., Fox, J.: Creating Global Shared Services: Lessons from Reuters. MIS Q. Executive **7**(1), 17–32 (2008)
24. Lacity, M., Yan, A., Khan, S.: Review of 23 years of empirical research on information technology outsourcing decisions and outcomes. In: Proceedings of the 50th Hawaii International Conference on System Sciences, HI (2017)
25. Levina, N., Vaast, E.: The emergence of boundary spanning competence in practice: implications for information systems' implementation and use. MIS Q. **29**(2), 335–363 (2005)
26. Levina, N., Vaast, E.: Innovating or doing as told? status differences and overlapping boundaries in offshore collaboration. MIS Q. **32**(2), 307–324 (2008)
27. Minnaar, R.A., Vosselman, E.G.: Shared service centres and management control structure change: exploring the scope and limitations of a transaction cost economics approach. J. Acc. Organ. Change **9**(1), 74–98 (2013)
28. Olsen, T.J.: Realizing Shared Services – A Punctuated Process Analysis of a Public IT Department. Dissertation, Georgia State University (2012)

29. Schulz, V., Herz, T., Rothenberger, M.A., Brenner, W.: It shared service center and external market activities. In: Proceedings of the 16th Americas Conference on Information Systems, Lima, Peru (2010)
30. Schulz, V., Hochstein, A., Ubernickel, F., Brenner, W.: Definition and classification of it-shared-service-center. In: Proceedings of the 16th Americas Conference on Information Systems, San Francisco (2009)
31. Stewart, T.: Intellectual Capital: The New Wealth of Organizations. Doubleday Business, p. 304 (1997)
32. Templier, M., Paré, G.: A framework for guiding and evaluating literature reviews. Commun. AIS **37**, 113–137 (2015)
33. Tomasino, A.P., Fedorowicz, J., Williams, C.B., Gentner, A.A., Hughes, T.T.: Embracing system complexity in a shared service center collaboration. MIS Q. Executive **13**(2), 63–75 (2014)
34. Ulbrich, F.: Improving shared service implementation: adopting lessons from the BPR movement. Bus. Process Manage. J. **12**(2), 191–205 (2006)
35. Ulbrich, F., Schulz, V.: Seven challenges management must overcome when implementing IT-shared services. Strateg. Outsourcing Int. J. **7**(2), 94–106 (2014)
36. Vieru, D., Arduin, P.-E.: Sharing knowledge in a shared services center context: an explanatory case study of the dialectics of formal and informal practices. In: Kotlarsky, J., Oshri, I., Willcocks, Leslie P. (eds.) Global Sourcing 2016. LNBIP, vol. 266, pp. 19–39. Springer, Cham (2016). https://doi.org/10.1007/978-3-319-47009-2_2
37. Vieru, D., Rivard, S.: Knowledge sharing challenges during post-merger integration: the role of boundary spanners and of organizational identity. Int. J. Bus. Manage. **10**(11), 1–12 (2015)
38. Yin, R.: Case Study Research: Design and Methods. Sage Publications Inc, Thousand Oaks (2003)

The Role of Willingness and Motivation in the Art of Start: A Case Study of IT SME Supplier Selection and Development

Toan C. Nguyen[1(✉)], Erik Wende[2], and Gerhard Schwabe[2]

[1] EWERK GmbH, Brühl 24, 04109 Leipzig, Germany
t.nguyen@ewerk.com
[2] University of Zurich, Rämistrasse 71, 8006 Zürich, Switzerland
{wende,schwabe}@ifi.uzh.ch

Abstract. To successfully start cooperation with suppliers is challenging. This case study analyzes how a Germany-based IT client cooperates with its suppliers. Both the client and its suppliers are SMEs in IT outsourcing sector. The case explores (1) the role of supplier's willingness in client's supplier selection decision, (2) motivations of suppliers to join the client's supplier development programs and (3) what activities are used in ITO sector to develop suppliers. The results show that besides supplier capabilities, supplier willingness also plays an important role in supplier selection. The selection is not a one-way decision from clients, but a negotiation between the client and suppliers. To come to the cooperation, both parties have to be aligned with their partner's strategy, show the willingness to cooperate and the commitment on top management level. The motivations of suppliers to join the client are fourfold. They are because the suppliers (1) want to win the contract, (2) to improve their capabilities by learning new skills from the client, especially (3) when the cooperation is aligned with their development strategy and (4) when they realize the commitment and the potential of the client to cooperate and develop the suppliers. In ITO sector, a wide range of supplier development activities are implemented by clients and suppliers including direct supplier activities (finance and human) and indirect activities (incentive, evaluation, competitive pressure). However, it depends on (1) the perceived client-supplier relationship, (2) the supplier absorptive capacity and (3) the supplier developing capability of the client.

Keywords: ITO sector · SME · Supplier selection · Willingness of supplier · Supplier development · Supplier perspective

1 Introduction

In IT outsourcing (ITO), it is challenging to successfully start cooperation with external suppliers [1]. Liang et al. [2] identify several major themes in ITO research, which warrant further investigation. These include: (1) ITO decisions, (2) client-supplier relationship in ITO and (3) the supplier's perspective in ITO research [2]. These gaps motivated this research.

© Springer Nature Switzerland AG 2019
J. Kotlarsky et al. (Eds.): Global Sourcing 2018, LNBIP 344, pp. 101–123, 2019.
https://doi.org/10.1007/978-3-030-15850-7_6

ITO decisions include (1) the decision to outsource or not, (2) the selection of suppliers and (3) re-outsourcing decisions [2]. When a client is willing to outsource, the selection of suitable suppliers is the most important step to ensure the success of the venture, because the right choice of an outsourcing supplier has a positive impact on the productivity and performance of the client company, and probably on market reaction to increased or decreased market returns [3]. There are various measurements which assist clients to select the right suppliers. e.g. In their book, Oshri, Kotlarsky and Willcocks [4] summarize three classes of suppliers' capabilities provided by Levina and Ross [5], including client-specific capabilities, process capabilities and human resource capabilities. They also suggest three core competencies of suppliers, including delivery competencies, transformation competencies and relationship competencies [6]. Many other researchers focus on the capabilities or competencies of suppliers as the key measurements for selecting the right suppliers (e.g. Chang et al. [3]). However, researchers rarely consider factors other than suppliers' capabilities (e.g. willingness, adaptability) in supplier selection criteria. Whether those factors play an important role in supplier selection, therefore, calls for further investigation.

Regarding the latter themes, there has been significant research on the impact of client-supplier relationship on ITO success [2]. There is general consensus among ITO researchers that the client-supplier relationship plays a crucial role in determining ITO success [7]. The intersection of relational governance and contractual governance appears to be a significant predictor of ITO results [2]. Both parties must be involved and invest in the client-supplier relationship to benefit from the arrangement. However, most researchers have focused solely on the interest of clients, and the concerns of suppliers have rarely been explored [2].

An important function of the client-supplier relationship is supplier development (SD). SD is any effort of a firm with its supplier(s) to increase the performance or capabilities of the supplier and meet the firm's short- and/or long-term supply needs" [8]. SD includes direct SD activities (e.g. training, human investment, capital investment) and indirect SD activities (e.g. incentive, supplier evaluation and feedback) [9]. Those activities are considered relationship-specific investment. Motivations to invest in SD from the client perspective are widely discussed in the literature [9]. However, factors that drive suppliers to invest in a client-supplier relationship or to join a SD program are still under-studied [9, 10]. Based on those arguments, we set out to answer the following questions:

RQ1:   What factors other than supplier capabilities can influence the client decision on supplier selection in ITO sector?

RQ2:   What factors influence suppliers to invest in a client-supplier relationship or to join an SD program?

RQ3:   What supplier development activities are the client and suppliers using in IT outsourcing sector?

To answer these questions, we analyze a case study in the ITO sector. The case study explores the relationship between a Germany-based ITO client and its suppliers in Vietnam, with a particular focus on the contribution of both parties and relationship specific investment.

The paper is structured as follows. After identifying the research questions, we reviewed the theoretical background with relevant concepts and issues. Next we explained the methodology used in the research as a case study. The detail descriptions of the case are also presented afterward. Then we discussed the results that we found in the case, reflecting the research questions and gaps. The research implications and contributions for theory and practice are presented, as well as limitations and suggested future research.

2 Theoretical Background

2.1 Supplier Selection in ITO Sector

In outsourcing management, supplier selection has a significant influence on business outcomes [11]. This decision is complicated because various criteria must be considered [12]. Thus, there have been numerous studies exploring the supplier selection process. Dickson [13] explores 23 criteria ranging from "extreme", "considerable", "average" and "slight" importance for supplier selection. Weber et al. [12], based on Dickson's [13] paper, reviews of 74 papers from 1967 to 1990 in which those criteria have also been used. In line with Dickson [13], their review shows that the most frequently used criteria include: net price, delivery, quality, production capacity and technology capability. Among them, depending on the research context, some authors just focus on some criteria, or even only one criterion in the supplier selection process [12]. Mukherjee [14] makes a review on supplier selection criteria and methods. His review shows that previous authors used a wide range of criteria to evaluate and select suppliers. The most frequently used criteria include: cost, quality, delivery, supplier profiles, technology and capability of suppliers. However, other criteria such as the relationship with suppliers, supplier willingness are usually under-estimated and rarely discussed in supplier selection [14].

In the ITO sector, most authors also use the supplier capabilities as the main criteria to evaluate the suppliers. Those capabilities can be categorized differently depending on the author's point of view. For example, Oshri et al. [4] summarize twelve key capabilities that ITO suppliers should obtain to be competitive including: leadership, business management, domain expertise, behavior management, sourcing, process improvement, technology exploitation, program management, customer development, planning and contracting, organization design and governance. Those capabilities are categorized into three key competences: (1) delivery competency, (2) transformation competency and (3) relationship competency [4]. Chang et al. [3] suggest that SME clients can use a simplified model with four key criteria to evaluate the suppliers, they includes (1) capability of professional skills, (2) capacity of service, (3) capacity of operation and (4) external evaluation. Nevertheless, researchers rarely consider factors other than suppliers' capabilities (e.g. cooperation willingness, adaptability of suppliers) in the supplier selection criteria. Whether those factors play an important role in client supplier selection, therefore, calls for further investigation.

2.2   Client-Supplier Relationship in ITO

Firms are not competing individually in the market, but they compete in a supply chain, which they are a part of [15]. Buyer firms always need the cooperation of suppliers. When buyers have problems regarding the supplier's quality, cost or delivery, they have certainly three options: (1) switch to another supplier, (2) internalize the function or (3) improve the current supplier's capabilities to meet their demands. The third option is increasingly favored by a significant number of enterprises [16].

The fast-changing IT environment creates desirable conditions for clients and their suppliers to form strategic alliances [2]. This has led to increased research interest in the area of inter-organizational relationships in the ITO sector. Research papers mostly examine client-supplier relationship characteristics and the impact of client-supplier relationship on ITO success [2]. The client-supplier relationship is a social exchange relationship characterized by the tension of trust and control [17]. ITO clients and suppliers are both contractually and socially related to each other, thus their relationship has economic, contractual and social characteristics [2]. Clients and suppliers need not only trust from each other to achieve efficient cooperation, but also control mechanisms to monitor ITO performance. Various measurements that clients use to regulate ITO results have been investigated. The outcome-based control is dominant in ITO contracts, especially in the early stages of projects [18]. However, when the projects encounter problems, behavior and relational control are often added to mitigate the situations [18]. Research on the impact of ITO relationships on the ITO success usually takes two approaches. One attempts to identify ITO relationship characteristics that predict ITO success, and the other focuses on the complementary nature of relational governance and contractual governance [2]. The balance between trust (relational) and structure control (contractual) is likely to result in a better ITO performance [19, 20].

Mirani [21] proposes the two phases of relationship between clients and suppliers including (1) transactional stage and (2) relational stage. The transactional stage is an initial stage in a relationship building between a supplier and a client. This stage is characterized by a short-term contract, free price market mechanisms, a small-sized and simple project, and a contractual relationship. The relationship will reach relational stage if both parties are satisfied by each other in the previous stage. The features of this stage are a long-term relationship, ongoing interactions, a large and complex project or a series of small-sized projects.

2.3   Supplier Segmentation and Development

Clients usually choose not only one supplier, but a portfolio of suppliers as a backup strategy. Those suppliers in the portfolio are usually different in their capabilities and attitude. Rezaei, Wang and Tavasszy [22] examine a framework which combines the two concepts of supplier segmentation and supplier development (SD) into one research to propose the so-called Best Worst Method to employ SD in practice. According to them, after selecting the portfolio of suppliers, buyer firms must classify suppliers to enable implementation of effective SD initiatives. Suppliers are evaluated based on their capabilities and willingness to join the SD. There are eight main criteria of capabilities and four criteria of willingness of supplier which are illustrated in the table below (Table 1):

Table 1. Capabilities and willingness as criteria for supplier segmentation

Dimension	Main criteria
Capability	Technical capability
	Design capability
	Product quality capability
	Delivery capability
	Intangible capability
	Service capability
	Financial/cost capability
	Organizational capability
Willingness	To improve performance
	To share information
	To rely on each other
	To get involved in long-term relationship

Source: Extracted from Rezaei et al. [22]

Based on the two dimensions, suppliers are categorized into four groups: (1) low capability and low willingness, (2) low capability and high willingness, (3) high capability and low willingness and (4) high capability and high willingness. Each group is suggested to be treated with specific SD activities or programs which can leverage supplier capabilities and willingness respectively.

2.3.1 Supplier Development Activities

Prior to Krause and Ellram [8], Watts and Hahn [23] also define SD as *"a long-term cooperative effort between a buying firm and its suppliers to upgrade the suppliers' technical, quality, delivery, and cost capabilities and to foster ongoing improvements"*. SD is vital for firms not only from a purchasing perspective, but also from a corporate perspective [24]. The key objective of a purchasing department is to develop effective and reliable sources of supply. The collaborative effort of buyer and supplier could ensure that: (1) suppliers remain economically viable, (2) buyer firms remain competitive and (3) the customer-supplier relationship remains intact. Thus the purchasing units which lead in supplier development could also increase the stature of their functions within their respective organizations [8]. Regarding the second perspective, SD can help firms meet their strategic objectives. As purchasing departments have the primary responsibility of linking supplier's capabilities with the internal requirements specified by corporate and manufacturing strategies, a proactive SD effort may advance the competitive strategies of the firms [8].

Previous studies classify SD activities in many different ways. A general tendency to classify SD activities based on the level of activity of the customer is perceptible [9]. Other criteria used to distinguish by customer (human versus financial resources), the circumstances within which the activities are conducted (reactive or proactive). Notwithstanding, the distinction between direct and indirect activities [25] is a simple example of this principle and mostly used by researchers (Table 2).

Table 2. Frequency of SD activities are used in manufacturing sectors

Types of SD	Frequency (percentage of publications that list the activities in their questionnaire)		
	Often (>30%)	*Sometimes (10–30%)*	*Occasionally (<10%)*
Indirect	• Supplier evaluation/feedback • Supplier awards • Certification of supplier • Creation/increase of competitive pressure on suppliers	• Increase of objectives for suppliers • Provision of incentives (e.g. current/future business) • Supplier audits • Precise specifications	• Communication of the customer's strategic objectives • Supplier days • Quality as criterion for supplier selection
Direct (human resources)	• Training of supplier staff • Supplier visits • Transfer of staff to the supplier • Technical support for the supplier • Invitation of the supplier to the customer's premises	• Involvement of the supplier in the customer's product development process • Joint process optimization • Providing consulting services to the supplier	• Involvement of the customer in the supplier's product development process • Support of the supplier during market entry • Dedicated supplier development team
Direct (financial resources)	• Financial support of the supplier, e.g. joint investments	• Financing of tools, etc.	• Investment in the supplier company

Source: Sucky and Durst [9]

2.3.2   Impacts of SD Activities

According to Sucky and Durst [9], SD activities can impact not only the supplier performance, but also the client performance and the relationship between clients and the suppliers. The Table 3 below summarizes the potential impacts of SD:

Table 3. Impacts of SD on suppliers and clients

SD Impacts on suppliers	SD Impacts on clients
The supplier's performance in operations such as improvement in quality, cost, lead times, service and reliability	The buyer firm's performance in operations such as improvement in quality, cost, lead times, service and reliability
The supplier's capabilities, e.g. the enhancement of methodological knowledge in production (lean manufacturing, Six Sigma, Kaizen, etc.)	The buyer firm's overall business performance, e.g. higher revenues or greater responsiveness to changes in the marketplace
The supplier-customer relationship, e.g. in the sense of a better working climate between customer and supplier	The buyer-supplier relationship, e.g. in the sense of a better working climate between buyers and suppliers

Source: Extracted from Sucky and Durst [9]

Most empirical studies agree that SD has a positive impact on supplier's performance [9]. However, there are also some researches shows the no positive correlation between SD and supplier performance [16, 26] or even negative impact of SD initiatives on actual supplier's development [26]. Furthermore, although the outcomes of SD are considered positive, there is still room for improvement (e.g. [23]).

There are only a few research papers that explicitly examine the relationship between SD and improvement in supplier's capabilities. In general, these showed a positive correlation between SD and the capabilities of suppliers [26, 27].

Some studies investigate the link between SD and supplier-customer relationship. Here, there are also contradictory findings. Humphreys, Li and Chan [28] confirm a positive correlation, while Blonska et al. [29] indicate that SD has no direct influence on the supplier adaptation or a supplier's preference for the buyer investing in its development. [16] indicates there is no positive correlation between direct SD and the relationship between customers and suppliers.

Overalls, the majority of studies identified positive correlation between SD and buyer firm's performance [9]. One exception is a paper by Li et al. [30] who note a negative correlation between greater expectations on the part of buyers (as a result of prescribed targets and supplier awards) and the buyers own operating performance.

2.3.3 SD Activities in ITO Sector

There has been a great deal of research into SD activities in manufacturing sector. This rages from motivation of SD, determinants of SD, success factors of SD and impacts of SD [9]. However, there is a lack of research into SD in the service sectors, especially the ITO sector. A reason for this is that SD has long been considered as pertaining primarily to industrial production. Conversely, companies in the service sector rarely participate in SD programs, especially in SD activities [27]. However, we have observed that there has been a change in what clients and suppliers in the service sectors regarding SD practice. Thus, we set out to explore to what extent SD activities have been implemented by clients and suppliers in ITO.

3 Methodology

Since the research questions of this study are "What" and "Why", a case study is selected to analyze the working process between an IT client and its suppliers [31]. In this case study, data were collected via three sources including direct observation, internal documents and in-depth interviews with relevant informants (Table 6).

To ensure the validity and the reliability of measurements in the case study, each source of evidence was reviewed carefully by two researchers and relevant participants. For example, the internal documents were reviewed by both researchers and employees of the company; the direct observation of interaction between the client and suppliers were undertaken and recorded via written diaries and reviewed by the project manager; and the interviews with participants were recorded. Written transcripts were also sent to the interviewees to ensure that all information was interpreted properly and aligned with what the interviewees said.

3.1   Case Description

The case study focused on a successful 21-year old Germany-based IT company. The company has many customers but struggles to maintain service standards due to the lack of internal resources. Thus, the company chose to consider software development suppliers in Vietnam, a growing destination for IT outsourcing in Asia. After searching and evaluating a number of suppliers, the company decided to visit seven potential IT suppliers. All suppliers were small & medium-sized enterprises (SMEs) in Vietnam. After that, there was a period of time in which the company has been working with the suppliers to select the right one for further steps of cooperation. Those included further communications to explore the suppliers, sending request for proposals, invitation to external training from a third party and joining a pilot project. Finally, the client selected one supplier for a pilot project using a platform which is completely new to the supplier. The case study could also be described as a working process between the client and its suppliers as Fig. 1 below:

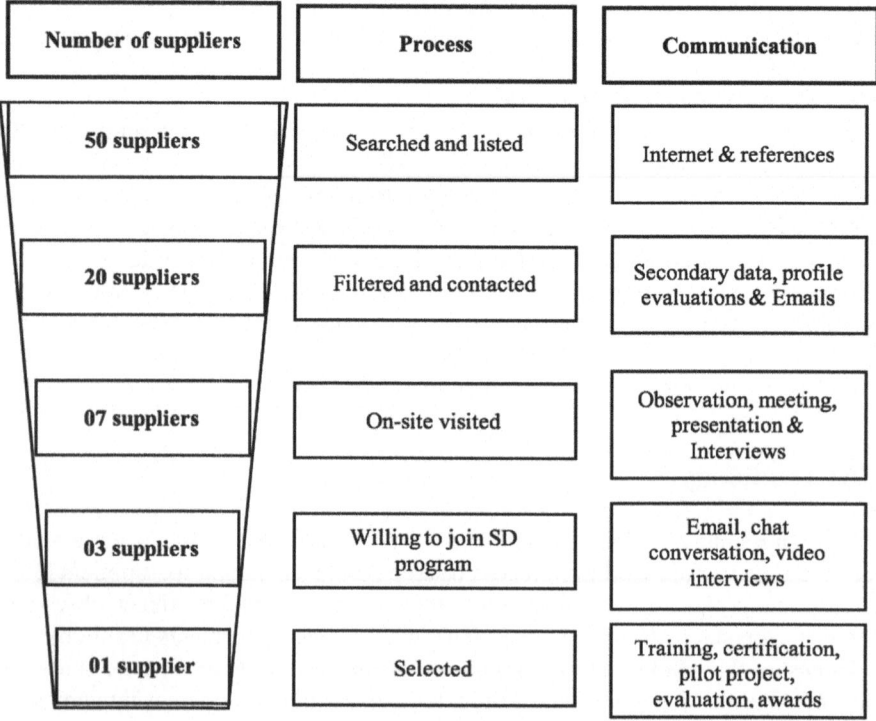

Fig. 1. The working process and communication between the client and its suppliers

In this case study, the method for selecting suppliers was different from typical ITO supplier selection. The client usually, after screening profiles and historical performance of the suppliers, invites suppliers to undertake a pilot project to test capability. In this case, after visiting suppliers on-site, the client required the suppliers to invest in a new technology, which is used by the client. The suppliers were also required to pay for themselves to be trained by a third party to be able to use the new platform. Then they can come to the client. Surprisingly, out of seven suppliers, three were willing to join the program and agreed to the client's requirements. However, only one of the three suppliers showed high willingness and proactively contacted the client and the third party for the training. The client finally chose only that supplier due to its commitment to the project (Table 4).

Table 4. The summary of suppliers' profiles

Supplier[a]	A	B	C	D	E	F	G
Firm structure	Joint venture (Norway + Vietnam)	100% Japanese capital	Vietnam	Vietnam	Joint venture (Japan + Vietnam)	Vietnam	Vietnam
Number of employees	120	130	125	35	80	30	67
Year of establishment	2005	2003	2003	2015	2013	2010	2011
Main market	Europe, Australia, Japan, New Zealand	Japan, Australia, Singapore	US, Japan, Australia, Europe	US, Japan, Korea	US, Europe, Singapore, Japan	Singapore, France, Vietnam	US, Singapore, Australia, Europe
Hourly rate of developer (*)	12–22 USD/h	14–18 USD/h	16–25 USD/h	12–20 USD/h	14–16 USD/h	12–20 USD/h	14–20 USD/h

[a]For confidential reason, names of suppliers are replaced by A, B, C, D, E, F and G.
(*): Hourly rate varies depending on developer experience. No significant difference between suppliers.

During the working process with suppliers, there was intensive communication between the client and suppliers. These include emails, chat conversation, requests for proposal and video calls. Those sources of evidence were reviewed by researchers to analyze the context and the working processes of the client and its suppliers (Table 5).

Table 5. Summary of the communication frequency between the client and its suppliers

Communication	A	B	C	D	E	F	G
Number of emails before visiting	10	13	4	8	6	8	15
Number of emails after visiting	16	18	17	20	15	6	22
Number of chats	2 times	0 time	2 times	4 times	2 times	1 time	2 times
Amount of chat texts	5 pages	0 page	5 pages	13 pages	1 page	1 page	6 pages
Number of video calls	2 times	0	0	3 times	0	0	1 time
Number of emails after training accepted	N/A	N/A	N/A	97	N/A	N/A	N/A
Number of calls after training accepted	N/A	N/A	N/A	14	N/A	N/A	N/A

3.2   Data Collection Techniques and Participants

Regarding the above research questions, each question requires its suitable data collection techniques. The table below illustrates how each question was answered. Those include data from (1) observations in the client firm and (2) in-depth interviews with relevant informants.

Table 6. Summary of the research questions and data collection techniques

Research question	Participants	Sources of evidence
RQ 1: Factors other than capabilities of suppliers can influence selecting decision	**Client:** CEO, project manager, sourcing coordinator	In-depth interview Observation
RQ 2: Motivations of suppliers to join the client and SD activities	**Client:** CEO, project manager, sourcing coordinator	In-depth interview
	Supplier: CEO, project manager, business development manager	In-depth interview
RQ 3: SD activities in ITO sector	**Client:** CEO, project manager, sourcing coordinator	In-depth interview Observation
	Supplier: CEO, project manager, business development manager	In-depth interview

11 interviews with both client and supplier representatives were conducted with an average duration of 44 min per interview. The total 480 min of interview were audio-recorded and transferred (Table 7).

Table 7. Summary of informants for the interviews from both client and suppliers

	Interviewees	Working experience	Duration of interview
Client	CEO (co-founder)	21 years	43'
	Project manager	5 years	55'
	Sourcing coordinator	2 years	47'
Supplier A	Project manager	6 years	45'
Supplier B	Business development manager	8 years	45'
Supplier C	Business development manager	7 years	40'
Supplier D	CEO	15 years	45'
	Project manager	5 years	52'
Supplier E	CEO	15 years	50'
Supplier F	CEO	12 years	35'
Supplier G	CEO	11 years	38'

3.3 Data Analysis Techniques

The analysis of case study evidence is one of the least developed and most difficult aspects of doing case study because the strategies and techniques have not been well defined [31]. We follow Yin's [31] and Miles and Huberman's [32] procedures for analyzing case study evidences as follows:

- *Putting information into different arrays*
- *Making a matrix of categories and placing the evidence within such categories*
- *Creating data displays (flowcharts and other graphics) for examining the data*
- *Tabulating the frequency of different events or important information*
- *Examining the complexity of such tabulations and their relationships by calculating second-order numbers such as means and variances (if any)*
- *Putting information in chronological order or using other temporal scheme.*

There are three general strategies to analyze case studies: (1) relying on theoretical propositions, (2) considering rival explanations and (3) developing a case description [31]. The first one is the most preferred strategy [31]. We chose that strategy to follow the theoretical propositions that led to our case study. We also combined with developing a case description when the theoretical background does not support well the research context. For example, supplier selection criteria in the first question have been very well studied, thus we based on the previous theoretical background to explore further if another factor (willingness of the suppliers in this case) plays an important role in the selection process of the client in ITO sector. For the second question, basing on the motivations of client to implement SD which have been well defined, we analyzed what are the motivations (or reasons) why a supplier wants (or does not want) to join the client and SD programs. Therefore, the answers for the second question are sometimes expressed as a case description. Regarding the third question, the SD activities in manufacturing sectors have been clearly defined, and we used those references to determine if those activities are also applied in ITO sector.

The final step was pattern matching, in which we compared empirical data with the predicted pattern (from theoretical propositions or questions). This enabled us to determine if the patterns coincide, thereby strengthening internal validity of the case study and helping to answer the research questions [31].

4 Results and Discussion

4.1 Supplier Selection and Segmentation in ITO Sector

4.1.1 The Criteria Go Beyond Supplier Capabilities

It is not necessary to have all criteria in the supplier selection process, it is really dependent on the business contexts [4]. In this case investigated, most of the key criteria identified in the literature review were used by the client to select suppliers. Interviews with the client's CEO, project manager and sourcing coordinator showed that important selection criteria include: skillset of supplier's developers, price, international experience of suppliers, English capability, service and business processes.

- **Skills:** The skillset that the vendor needs to work in client projects. *"Specifically, I also consider how many developers for specific skills that the vendors obtain, how* *experience they are, and the historical successful projects they have done"*, said the sourcing coordinator.

- **Price:** Price is an important selection criterion, since the goal of projects is finally to optimize the resources and reduce costs. However, the price is always viewed in parallel with other relevant perspectives such as quality of the service, capability and experience of the suppliers and the specific context of an ITO project.

"We consider the price of the suppliers. It is not sole the hour rate or man month price, but we also evaluate the quality, delivery and other aspects of the suppliers. Regarding those 7 suppliers, their hour rates are quite similar. There is no significant different in hour rate of developers, varying around 14–22 USD, depending on experience of the developers", said the project manager.

- **Market:** It is a good indicator to evaluate the vendors' experience in international relationship with clients.

"It is very important, especially when we have experienced some unexpected results of the previous projects with external vendors due to the cultural differences and lack of international experience of the vendors. When a vendor has good experience in working with international clients (especially in Europe, where we are working), it would be more highly evaluated", said the sourcing coordinator.

- **English Communication**: *"it is really a fundamental requirement for ITO vendors to work with international clients. However, most of vendors have a certain level of English which is enough for them to communicate with the client. Furthermore, in our case, we have two Vietnamese who can support in communicating with the vendors"*, the sourcing coordinator said.
- **Service and Business Processes:** How the vendor performs business, undertakes work and communicates with clients. It is quite difficult to evaluate exactly how good a supplier is because it requires time working with them in real projects.

"I can only evaluate partly that of the vendors as I just worked with them for a short period of time. For better understanding of vendors' service and business process, we have to work with them in real projects in which we give them time to perform and then explore their behaviors", the project manager added.

Beyond these capabilities, all three interviewees from client firm emphasized the **"willingness"** of the suppliers to cooperate with the client.

"Besides those criteria above, we also consider if the vendors are willing to invest in this specific relationship with us. It is not only the willingness to work with or to sell some services to us, but also the willingness of the vendor to adapt its structure or process to fit with our requirements for a better cooperation", said the client's CEO.

The sourcing coordinator also added:

"We are really impressed by a vendor that always shows its eagerness to work with us during the communication in Vietnam and also via Email, Chat with us when we are in Germany. That vendor is completely willing and ready to make everything to cooperate with us."

Willingness of suppliers is not just to get the project from the client, but also to (1) improve performance, (2) share information, (3) rely on each other and (4) get involved in long-term relationship [22].

> *"During the communication with vendors, I honestly could not evaluate exactly how good suppliers' capabilities are, because we have never worked with them in real projects. But one important thing I considered is the willingness of the supplier to cooperate with us. One supplier always shares us information about their company that they want to improve the skills of developers and learning new skills to focus on the new market, and always ask us for the opportunity of long-term cooperation"*, said the project manager.

Thus, besides supplier capabilities, the willingness of suppliers to adapt to client requirements and priorities is an important influence on supplier selection decision, especially in the initial stages of selection, before the client has worked in real projects with suppliers.

4.1.2 Tough to Find a Suitable Supplier in the Portfolio of Suppliers

Following the model from Rezaei et al. [22], we analyzed the suppliers regarding their capability and willingness, ranging from low, middle to high level. Capability includes skills required from the client, service and business processes, international market experience, cost competency (price), and English communication. Willingness can be understood as the adaptability of the vendor with respect to the client's requirements and the willingness to cooperate with the client. Interviewees were asked to assess vendors by evaluating capability and willingness. The Fig. 2 below illustrates perceived level of capability and willingness, based on the average evaluation of three interviewees from the client:

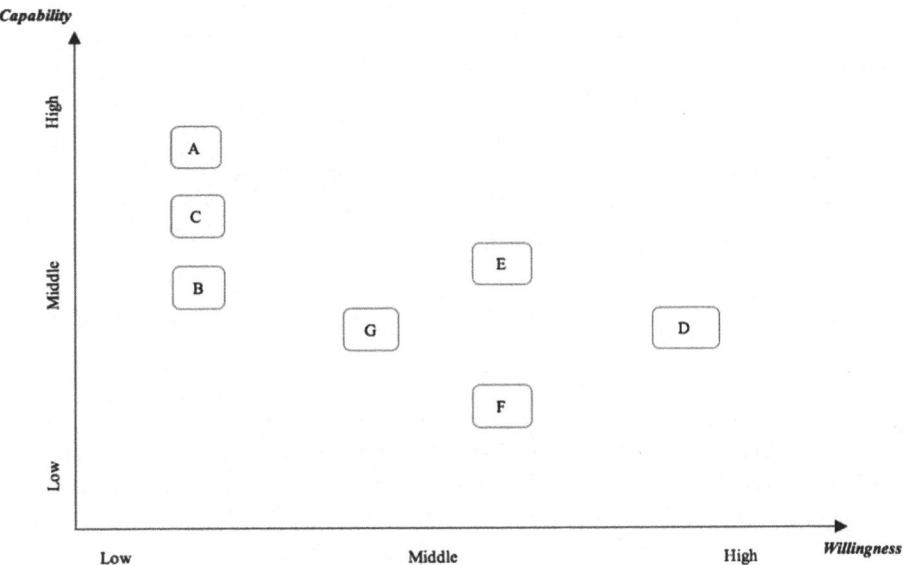

Fig. 2. Perceived supplier capabilities and willingness

As shown in the Fig. 2, Supplier A is evaluated as the most capable.

"This supplier has shown a very professional business process working with us, the company's profile is really impressive, their staffs speak English very good", expressed the sourcing coordinator.

The CEO also said:

"Besides its good profile, I am also interested in their organizational culture, it is quite similar to us; we are a medium firm too, with about 150 employees. They also communicate the company's values, missions, visions very clearly to the client and internal staffs."

Thus, if only the capabilities are considered, supplier A would be the preferred choice. *"We really want to invite them to join our project, because they are simply the best one among suppliers"*, said the project manager.

However, this supplier was regarded as having low willingness. Despite its professional working process, the supplier also showed a skeptical attitude towards the client and did not share much their information with the client. *"Supplier A is very skeptical with our invitation to training and the project afterward. Maybe they have many big projects and we are not their priority"*, said the project manager.

The two other suppliers, B and C, also exhibited low willingness to join the client and SD programs, although their capabilities are middle and high respectively, according to client's evaluation.

"I think supplier C is also a good vendor, although not as good as Supplier A. It is a 100% Japanese Capital Company and has some big projects with other clients in Japan. Thus they do not want to invest in the training programs. Regarding supplier B, I do not think that they are really good. They are just in middle of capabilities, this vendor was also not really interested in the training with us", said the project manager.

In contrast, the three other suppliers D, E and F were very willing to join the program. Among them, supplier D has a medium capability level and highest willingness to join the client SD program. The client decided to engage firstly with supplier D, to implement the training and pilot project.

"Supplier D is a young Vietnamese company. Their CEO and developers are also very young. However, they are full of energy and eager to learn. I am really impressed with its willingness and the way they show us that they really want to cooperate with us", the client CEO said.

The project manager also added:

"I think supplier E's capabilities, skills and experience are surely higher than supplier D and supplier F seems to be the weakest, but supplier D's attitude towards us is unbelievable. They not only agreed to join the training like the two others, but also proactively contacted the third party, registered for the training and informed us immediately."

In ITO context, it is not always possible to achieve the optimal solution, in which a supplier has both high capabilities and high willingness towards the clients. Thus, the supplier selection is not just a one-way decision which the client can make, but a negotiation and evaluation process from both sides to come to the cooperation.

4.1.3   The Supplier Perspective Should Be Taken into Account

Most extant ITO research papers consider the supplier selection solely from client perspective, with little consideration supplier priorities (see the review of Weber et al. [12], Mukherjee [14]). However, in practice, suppliers also "select" the client, especially when both the client and suppliers are all SMEs, and the client does not really dominate over the suppliers.

In this case study, the client really wants to work with a supplier. However, this supplier did not "select" the client as it did not agree to join the training program with the client.

"At that time, we had some other projects to fulfill. Thus, we did not have enough resource to invest in the training with that client. Honestly, our managers are also not sure if it is a potential opportunity for us. So we'd better focus on our core current projects", said the project manager of supplier A.

Supplier B and C also had an unfavorable view for the client and training programs.

"Currently, we have big clients and do not have resources to invest in such a training program which cannot ensure any projects afterward. Furthermore, our company only considers projects more than 25.000 USD, and now most of our projects with clients are from 40.000 USD or more. Thus, at that time we honestly thought that this client is not really potential and worth our investments", added the business development manager from supplier C.

The business development manager from supplier B also expressed:

"We are a 100% Japanese Capital Company, so we have our main clients in Japan. Some other clients are in Singapore and Australia, but not many. Thus we are focusing on the Japanese market. Europe is not really our target. However, if there are some projects which are suitable with our skills and capacity, we are also open to handle those projects. In case of this client, we would surely not involve in because that is not aligned with our development strategy and we do not have resource to invest in this program."

4.2   Motivations of the Supplier to Join the Client and SD Programs

4.2.1   Win the Client and Get the Business First

As might be expected, all suppliers showed initial interest in the business opportunity presented by the client. *"Our company always welcomes new clients. If there are new projects from the client, we are willing to take them"*, expressed the CEO of supplier G. Furthermore, the suppliers that were willing to join the training program also wanted to enter the European market, and viewed working with this client is an opportunity to gain insight into the market, style of working and cultural differences.

"We would like to invest in this training program and the client because we are planning to expand to European market. Thus, having a project with this client is the first step for us to be familiar with the market and also to explore further opportunities", said the CEO of supplier E.

The CEO of supplier D also expressed: *"actually, we are small and new company. So we are looking for new clients all over the world. We have not had any clients in Europe, so it is a good opportunity for us to try ourselves in a new market"*.

The suppliers that did not agree to join the training program were reluctant to proceed due to the investment requited.

4.2.2   Opportunities to Improve Supplier Capabilities

Besides gaining the client and entering a new market, the two suppliers were also motivated by the opportunity to gain new skills. *"If we join the training with this client, more or less we will learn new skills which are necessary for us in the future"*, the CEO of supplier E said. For the supplier D, they expected not only to obtain this specific skill through the training, but also to get further skills and capabilities from the client afterward.

> *"We are learning and improving our technical and management skills every day. That is a good opportunity to serve a client other than our traditional clients in Japan, in which we can get more experience and learn from this client during the projects"*, said the CEO of supplier D.

A majority of IT suppliers in Vietnam are quite new and have low levels of expertise, compared with more established ITO destinations [33]. Therefore, many Vietnamese suppliers are motivated to improve their capabilities. Working with international clients in Europe or the USA is seen by many as an opportunity to gain valuable experience.

4.2.3   Client's Commitment Is Important to Convince Suppliers

Besides the business opportunity and the opportunity to improve capabilities, suppliers also would like to see the commitment of the client to the cooperation. When the client shows its commitment for a long-term relationship, it can convince the supplier not only to be its supplier, but also to join SD activities.

> *"I can see that the client really commits to the cooperation with vendors in Vietnam. They also have Vietnamese staffs to facilitate the working with us. During the pilot project, they have given us feedback and evaluation to improve. That is really helpful for us. Their CEO will visit us the second time, that is a good chance for me to talk with him about our cooperation in future. We are trying to serve this client the best"*, said the CEO of supplier D.

The Table 8 below summarizes motivations of suppliers to join the client and SD programs:

Table 8. Motivations of suppliers to join the client and the SD programs

Motivations to join the client or SD programs	A	B	C	D	E	F	G
Win the contract[a]	X	X	X	X	X	X	X
Enter new market (Europe)				X	X		
Align with supplier's development strategy				X	X		
Obtain new capabilities				X	X	X	
Apparent opportunities to be trained for new capabilities				X	X	X	
Build long-term relationship				X	X	X	
Apparent commitment and willingness of the client				X	X		

[a]All suppliers wanted to get the project, although some did not agree to join the training program.

We also explored the reasons why some suppliers were not willing to join the client and training program. These suppliers all perceived investment in the training program risky because there was no guarantee that they would subsequently win the contract. Secondly, some suppliers did not have enough resources for the program. Some did not perceive that the client aligned with their development strategy (e.g. targeting market, core capabilities to develop). Finally, when suppliers did not perceive the client as showing sufficient commitment or potential, they did not "select" the client to invest their resources.

"That is quite risky for us to invest in such a training when we are not sure if the project comes. Honestly, our managers could not find the potential of this client in this project. When we work with the client for several projects and see the commitment from them, it is easier for us to invest in this client", said the business development manager of supplier C (Table 9).

Table 9. Reasons why suppliers do not join the client and SD programs

Reasons not to join the client or SD programs	A	B	C	D	E	F	G
Risky for supplier[a]	X	X	X	X	X	X	X
Not enough resources to join	X	X	X				X
Did not align with supplier's development strategy	X	X	X				
Did not perceive sufficient commitment of client		X	X				
Did not perceive sufficient client potential	X	X	X				

[a]When a supplier agreed to join the training, it still felt risky for their investment.

4.3   SD Activities in ITO Sector

4.3.1   SD Activities Are also Popular in ITO Sector

During this case study, a wide range of SD activities are explored. The assumption that SD activities are only for the manufacturing sector and not for service sectors [27] may be correct in many cases, but not in the ITO sector. The suppliers in this case study have received or participated in many SD programs including both direct and indirect activities.

The most frequent SD activity is training. Training programs for suppliers in ITO are various, including on-site training in supplier firms, online training via video conferences, training in the client firm and training with a third party.

"Two or three times a year, our client in Japan came to train our developers for one or two weeks, especially before projects start and there are some new platforms, templates or technologies which we will use for more effective working process", said CEO of supplier D.

Besides training, visits to suppliers and invitations to clients are also very common in ITO sector. *"Our clients usually come to visit us. When we have worked with the client for long time, even top managers of the client visit us at least once a year. That is to make both parties understand one another better and be more communicative. And we also get invited from our clients to visit their companies. Sometimes we actively visit our client too. It is not only strengthening the relationship, but also for our developers to experience new working environment and motivate them to work more effectively"*, the CEO of supplier A said.

From client perspective, the client in this case also implements various activities for its suppliers. *"Of course, we usually visited our suppliers. Our CEO comes to Vietnam, Czech Republic very often to visit our partners there. We also invited top managers and key developers of suppliers who have worked in projects with us to visit our company. It is to improve the relationship with suppliers, and also to train the supplier's developers as a type of on-the-job training in our company"*, said the sourcing coordinator of the client.

> *"In some projects, to qualify the vendor, we offered them training from the third party; of course we paid for suppliers' developers to learn that new platform. The requirement is that after the training they have to work for us in relevant projects in which the new platform will be used. Some of our vendors have joined the program like this and we continue doing so to have more resources"*, said the client CEO.

During the project, suppliers also received technological supports from the client's developers when necessary. *"It is very often and easy because now we can work via video calls, chats, emails… even 24/7 or in real time because of the modern technology to support the communication"*, said the CEO of supplier D.

Other indirect SD activities such as feedback, evaluation and incentives for suppliers are also very common.

> *"During the projects, we received the feedback from the clients so often. That is to control the progress and the quality of the project. We also received evaluation at the end of projects whether we have done good jobs or deliver satisfactory outcomes to the clients. Usually, we will get further projects if our performance is ok"*, said the CEO of supplier F.

Other indirect activities such as supplier auditing, supplier awarding or supplier days are not popular, because they are simple not suitable for ITO sector. *"Clients usually visit us, train us, give us feedback, but auditing us is not really as we are usually working in project-based setting or offer them dedicated teams. After finishing projects, if the client is satisfied, they may continue with us further projects. It is more like incentive than awards for us. And the supplier days, I think, are not existing in ITO sector because the clients usually separate their vendors in different projects"*, said the CEO of supplier E.

Regarding direct financial investment, in ITO sector clients sometimes invest capital in the supplier, especially after they have been working for long period or many projects. *"Our client not only gives us direct training, but also invest some money for us to upgrade our infrastructure and develop our staffs who worked in their dedicated team through the third organization"*, said the CEO of supplier C.

> *"There is a client from Australia; they want to invest in our company. But I have not agreed because I want to keep the control of my company. It will be complicated if we are influenced by other people when they invest in our company"*, the CEO of supplier G expressed.

SD activities are also very frequently undertaken in the ITO sector. Both clients and suppliers are willing to implement those SD programs as long as they are necessary for their business processes.

4.3.2 SD Activities Do not Come Automatically

Although clients and suppliers in the ITO sector undertake a variety of SD activities, those activities do not occur automatically. There are some determinants for an SD program.

Firstly, it depends on the relationship between client and vendors. When the relationship is in the transactional stage [21], there are mostly no SD activities. *"When we started a project with new clients, there are rarely such activities to develop our developers, because the client only wants the job get done by us with our owned capabilities"*, said the CEO of supplier E. However, when the relationship reaches the relational stage, SD activities are implemented as both parties need to improve the quality of the service and the capabilities of the supplier. *"After several successful projects with us, the client visits us more frequently, gives us some training for new technologies or platforms, or even invites us to their firm as a traveling chance for our developers and top managers"*, said the business development manager of supplier B.

The relationship is also reflected through the commitment of top managers on both sides. When both the client and the supplier are committed to the cooperation, they are more willing to invest in SD activities. *"It is important to realize the commitment of the clients, especially from the top manager to the relationship and the SD activities. When we see our client's commitment, we will be more willing to join the SD programs. It is because joining those programs is sometimes only useful for this specific client. We cannot use those skills or technologies for another client"*, explained the CEO of supplier E.

Secondly, direct SD activities can only occur when clients are capable of developing suppliers. For example, a supplier serves another small IT client, they are very close and have cooperated for a long time, although the small client really wants to improve the supplier's service, but unfortunately it cannot do so due to its lack of capability to develop the supplier. The same situation occurs when an IT supplier has a client which is a non-IT firm. Thus, the only opportunity is to implement indirect SD activities such as incentives, feedback, visits to influence the suppliers.

"Our clients include both IT companies and non-IT companies. Working with other IT companies is quite easy because we are all IT technicians. We can communicate more effective with our IT clients than with some non-IT clients. We receive technical supports or training mostly from IT partners. With non-It ones, there are rarely any activities to support us, we even have to train them to use our products, how to maintain the server and websites and so on", said the project manager of supplier A.

Thirdly, SD activities also depend on the absorptive capacity of the supplier. Absorptive capacity is the ability of suppliers to (1) acquire external knowledge, (2) assimilate the knowledge, (3) transform the knowledge and (4) exploit the knowledge in the real product/service or working process [34]. In this case study, the client had a range of in-house training resources, which the client intended to utilize to train the supplier. However, it was found in some instances that the supplier was simply not capable of gaining the required knowledge.

There are available resources of the supplier to get trained, developed by the client. Sometimes, the client really wants to develop the supplier through some training programs, but the supplier is simply not able to get that knowledge.

5 Conclusions

5.1 Contributions of the Research

From a dyadic perspective, the research explored three issues: (1) the role of supplier willingness in supplier selection process of the client, (2) the motivations of suppliers to join the client (training programs, pilot projects) and (3) supplier development activities in ITO sector. The results show that besides supplier capabilities, the client also considers the willingness of the suppliers. It is the willingness, as viewed by Rezaei et al. [22], to share information, to improve the capabilities, to rely on each other and to be involved in a long-term relationship. Furthermore, supplier selection is not a one-way decision of the client, but a negotiation and evaluation of both parties. Regarding the motivations of suppliers to join the client, they depend on how both parties view the relationship. The perceived commitment and willingness to cooperation of both client and suppliers is a significant influence on the supplier decision to join the client and SD programs. Furthermore, it depends on the capability of the client to develop its suppliers. When the client and suppliers are willing and able to invest in the suppliers, it is possible to implement together a variety of activities that are comparable to SD activities in the manufacturing sector. Both direct and indirect activities are implemented to develop or motivate the suppliers to improve capabilities, performance and the relationship between the client and suppliers.

The results from this case study make a theoretical contribution to the knowledge in ITO sector, with respect to the influence of supplier willingness in supplier selection, SD practice in ITO sector and the motivations of suppliers to join such activities. Based on research findings, further implications for managers and future research directions are also proposed.

5.2 Managerial Implications of the Research

It is quite interesting to view the supplier selection in ITO sector from dyadic perspective in this case study. It is apparent to client managers that the decision whether to collaborate is not uniquely theirs. Suppliers also have a significant role in the decision process. In this situation, the client has minimal control over the supplier and the client is required to make an appealing offer to suppliers to show that cooperation investment is worthwhile.

For the ITO suppliers, especially for smaller suppliers, showing high willingness to cooperate and eagerness to develop can overcome capability shortcoming, and improve the chance of winning contracts. A client who seeks long-term cooperation with offshore suppliers considers not only current skills and capabilities, but also the supplier plans and ambitions.

For a successful cooperation in the ITO sector, both clients and vendors should align their strategies and show the commitment to the cooperation. This can be achieved only through significant effort in communication, supports from both parties during negotiation and initial projects.

Regarding SD programs, there is a wide range of activities that have been implemented in the ITO sector. Thus, clients and suppliers should consider which activities are suitable in their specific situations and can bring the best outcomes for the cooperation. Obviously, those activities should be aligned with both parties' development strategies because most of SD activities in the ITO sectors are considered relationship-specific investments which may not be adopted with other clients or projects.

5.3   Limitations and Future Research

In case study research, it is always difficult to assess the generalizability of results. Furthermore, in this case study, research was conducted only during the initial phases of collaboration, before any real projects were commenced. Thus, it was not possible to accurately evaluate the capabilities of each supplier.

In future, quantitative research with a significant sample size on (1) the influence of supplier's willingness on the supplier selection process and (2) determinants or motivations for suppliers joining the SD programs would be interesting and useful for managers and academia. Another direction is to explore the impact of SD activities on the supplier performance in the ITO sector. For example, further studies could compare the impact of direct and indirect SD programs on the supplier performance and the relationship between client and supplier. This would help ITO managers decide which SD activities should be implemented for improving the overall performance and the relationship between clients and suppliers.

References

1. Niazi, M., Mahmood, S., Alshayeb, M., et al.: Challenges of project management in global software development: a client-vendor analysis. Inf. Softw. Technol. **80**, 1–19 (2016). https://doi.org/10.1016/j.infsof.2016.08.002
2. Liang, H., Wang, J.-J., Xue, Y., et al.: IT outsourcing research from 1992 to 2013: a literature review based on main path analysis. Inf. Manag. **53**(2), 227–251 (2016). https://doi.org/10.1016/j.im.2015.10.001
3. Chang, S.-I., Yen, D.C., Ng, C.S.-P., et al.: An analysis of IT/IS outsourcing provider selection for small- and medium-sized enterprises in Taiwan. Inf. Manag. **49**(5), 199–209 (2012). https://doi.org/10.1016/j.im.2012.03.001
4. Oshri, I., Kotlarsky, J., Willcocks, L.: The handbook of global outsourcing and offshoring. Palgrave Macmillan, Basingstoke (2010)
5. Levina, N., Ross, J.: From the vendor's perspective: exploring the value proposition in IT outsourcing. MIS Q. **27**(3), 331–364 (2003)
6. Willcocks, L.P., Lacity, M.C.: Global sourcing of business and IT services. Palgrave Macmillan UK, London (2006)
7. Lacity, M.C., Khan, S., Yan, A., et al.: A review of the IT outsourcing empirical literature and future research directions. J Inf Technol. **25**(4), 395–433 (2010). https://doi.org/10.1057/jit.2010.21
8. Krause, D.R., Ellram, L.M.: Critical elements of supplier development the buying-firm perspective. Eur. J. Purch. Supply Manage. **3**(1), 21–31 (1997). https://doi.org/10.1016/S0969-7012(96)00003-2
9. Sucky, E., Durst, S.M.: Supplier development: current status of empirical research. IJPM **6**(1), 92 (2013). https://doi.org/10.1504/IJPM.2013.050612

10. Ahmed, M., Hendry, L.: Supplier development literature review and key future research areas. Int. J. Eng. Technol. Innov. **2**(4), 1293–1303 (2012)
11. Dominic, P.D.D., Whab, A.A., Kannabiran, G., et al.: A new hybrid model for the supplier selection decision. IJBIS **5**(3), 230 (2010). https://doi.org/10.1504/IJBIS.2010.031928
12. Weber, C.A., Current, J.R., Benton, W.C.: Vendor selection criteria and methods. Eur. J. Oper. Res. **50**(1), 2–18 (1991). https://doi.org/10.1016/0377-2217(91)90033-R
13. Dickson, G.W.: An analysis of vendor selection systems and decisions. J. Purch. **2**(1), 5–17 (1966)
14. Mukherjee, K.: Supplier selection criteria and methods: Past, present and future. Int. J. Oper. Res. **27**(1/2), 356–373 (2014)
15. Lambert, D.M.: Supply chain management – processes, partnerships, performance. In: Schönberger, R. (ed.) Dimensionen der Logistik: Funktionen, Institutionen und Handlungsebenen, 1st edn, pp. 553–572. Gabler, Wiesbaden (2010)
16. Wagner, S.M.: Supplier development practices: an exploratory study. Eur. J. Mark. **40**(5/6), 554–571 (2006). https://doi.org/10.1108/03090560610657831
17. Mao, J.-Y., Lee, J.-N., Deng, C.-P.: Vendors' perspectives on trust and control in offshore information systems outsourcing. Inf. Manag. **45**(7), 482–492 (2008). https://doi.org/10.1016/j.im.2008.07.003
18. Choudhury, V., Sabherwal, R.: Portfolios of control in outsourced software development projects. Inf. Syst. Res. **14**(3), 291–314 (2003). https://doi.org/10.1287/isre.14.3.291.16563
19. Goo, J., Kishore, R., Rao, H.R., et al.: The role of service level agreements in relational management of information technology outsourcing: an empirical study. MIS Q. 119–145 (2009)
20. Sabherwal, R.: The role of trust in outsourced IS development projects. Commun. ACM **42** (2), 80–86 (1999). https://doi.org/10.1145/293411.293485
21. Mirani, R.: Client-vendor relationships in offshore applications development. Inf. Res. Manage. J. **19**(4), 72–86 (2006). https://doi.org/10.4018/irmj.2006100105
22. Rezaei, J., Wang, J., Tavasszy, L.: Linking supplier development to supplier segmentation using best worst method. Expert Syst. Appl. **42**(23), 9152–9164 (2015). https://doi.org/10.1016/j.eswa.2015.07.073
23. Watts, C.A., Hahn, C.K.: Supplier development programs: an empirical analysis. Int. J. Purch. Mater. Manage. **29**(1), 10–17 (1993). https://doi.org/10.1111/j.1745-493X.1993.tb00002.x
24. Krause, D.R., Handfield, R.B., Scannell, T.V.: An empirical investigation of supplier development: reactive and strategic processes. J. Oper. Manage. **17**(1), 39–58 (1998). https://doi.org/10.1016/S0272-6963(98)00030-8
25. Wagner, S.M.: Indirect and direct supplier development: performance implications of individual and combined effects. IEEE Trans. Eng. Manage. **57**(4), 536–546 (2010). https://doi.org/10.1109/TEM.2009.2013839
26. Wagner, S.M.: The relationship between a firm's efforts to develop deficient suppliers and competitive advantage: paper presented at the 14th annual IPSERA conference. Archamps, France (2005)
27. Krause, D.R., Scannell, T.V.: Supplier development practices: product- and service-based industry comparisons. J. Supply Chain Manage. **38**(2), 13–21 (2002). https://doi.org/10.1111/j.1745-493X.2002.tb00125.x
28. Humphreys, P.K., Li, W.L., Chan, L.Y.: The impact of supplier development on buyer–supplier performance. Omega **32**(2), 131–143 (2004). https://doi.org/10.1016/j.omega.2003.09.016

29. Blonska, A., Rozemeijer, F., Wetzels, M.: The influence of supplier development on gaining a preferential buyer status, supplier adaptation and supplier relational embeddedness, Paper presented at the 24th IMP Conference (2008)
30. Li, W., Humphreys, P.K., Yeung, A.C.L., et al.: The impact of specific supplier development efforts on buyer competitive advantage: an empirical model. Int. J. Prod. Econ. **106**(1), 230–247 (2007). https://doi.org/10.1016/j.ijpe.2006.06.005
31. Yin, R.K.: Case study research: design and methods. In: Yin, R.K., 3rd edn. Applied Social Research Methods Series, vol. 5. Sage, Thousand Oaks (2003)
32. Miles, M.B., Huberman, A.M.: Qualitative data analysis: an expanded sourcebook, 2nd edn. Sage, Thousand Oaks (1994)
33. Vinasa: Vietnam's 30 Leading IT Companies (2014). http://vinasa.org.vn/Portals/0/Document/Top30%20Web.pdf
34. Cohen, W.M., Levinthal, D.A.: Absorptive capacity: a new perspective on learning and innovation. Adm. Sci. Q. **35**(1), 128 (1990). https://doi.org/10.2307/2393553

Implementing and Contracting Agile and DevOps: A Survey in the Netherlands

Erik Beulen[✉]

TIAS School for Business and Society,
Warandelaan 2, PO Box 90153, 5000 LE Tilburg, The Netherlands
e.beulen@tias.edu

Abstract. Digital transformations facilitate the need for speed. Continuous deployment is becoming the norm. Organizations need to change their service delivery and are increasingly adopting agile software development and DevOps. This requires different capabilities in IT delivery as well as in the business. A lot of organizations struggle in identifying, retaining and recruiting accountable executives, product owners and scrum masters. Organizations operating in dynamic markets have started earlier with the implementation of agile and DevOps and the delivery percentage of agile and DevOps is higher than for organizations operating in less dynamic markets. Furthermore, the market is anticipating on a decrease of the onshore percentage in delivering agile and DevOps in 2020. The market is also anticipating on an increase of output based contracting for agile and DevOps in 2020. In the current contracts, there are hardly clauses protecting organization for poor service provisioning. Technical debt is predominantly not a service provider risk. Also, most service providers are fully compensated for contracted but cancelled sprints and releases. Both technical debt and cancelled sprints and releases impact the cost efficiency of agile and DevOps significantly. Finally, organizations struggle with re-negotiating their infrastructure contracts to facilitate the agile and DevOps delivery. This all requires attention of Chief Information Officers and procurement departures. They must anticipate on delivery and contracting issues and promote and orchestrate agile and DevOps.

Keywords: Agile · DevOps · Fixed price · Offshore outsourcing ·
Onshore outsourcing · Price per function point · Price per story point

1 Introduction

In this day and age digital transformation is very much into fashion, but access to capabilities and contracting are major concerns for many organizations. Digital transformations dominate the agenda of most of business executives. Digital transformation can be described best as using mobile devices, social media, analytics, Internet of Things, and the cloud to improve the topline by enriching existing products and services, and creating new services, by making smart use data [1–4]. Digital transformations are a combine business and IT effort and are performed by joint teams. Digital transformations create new business models [5].

© Springer Nature Switzerland AG 2019
J. Kotlarsky et al. (Eds.): Global Sourcing 2018, LNBIP 344, pp. 124–146, 2019.
https://doi.org/10.1007/978-3-030-15850-7_7

Digital transformation is also necessary in an increasingly competitive and dynamic market. Organizations require speed and innovation to keep up with market dynamics [6–9]. Agile software development, often in combination with DevOps, are adopted by many organizations to implement digital transformation. Digital transformation adoption according to market research is high: enterprise wide (41%), working on strategy (27%), in individual business units (22%) and only 10% has not adopted digitization [10]. For executives, it is important to understand the need for agile and DevOps better. Are market dynamics enforcing digital transformations and as a consequence agile software development and DevOps delivery are required? Also identifying, retaining and recruiting agile and DevOps talent is the number one challenge for most organization in implementing digital transformations successful [3]. However, currently most of the agile and DevOps delivery is performed onshore. This leaves an untapped potential in terms for availability of capabilities in countries like China, India, Philippines, Eastern European and Latin American countries and in terms of cost efficiencies (labor arbitrage).

Finally, most of the agile and DevOps services are currently contracted based on input obligations. The risk of successful implementations of digital transformations is fully with organizations instead of shared or transferred risks with service providers. The research objective is to explore agile and DevOps delivery and contracting.

2   Agile and DevOps

DevOps is a set of practices intended to reduce the time between committing a change to a system and the change being placed into normal production while ensuring quality [11]. Successful introduction of DevOps requires "organizational rewiring" [12]. This is much more fundamental and includes significant change management on top of the implementation of a toolset.

Agile is embedded in Dev(elopement) (Agile Manifesto - 2001). Small development teams focus on continuous delivery of software in short sprints. This requires also an increased deployment frequency, which requires tooling.

Combining development and operations in a single DevOps team requires segregation of duties. The control needs to be separated from operations. The replacement of manual deployments by fully automated deployments reduces the risk level of deployments significantly [13].

The biggest challenge of DevOps is in finding the right resources, organizations need digital natives [14]. This is a bigger challenge is Dev(elopement) than in Op (eration)s. In Dev(elopement) the product owner role is equally pivotal as hard to fulfill. This role has to align the bottom up prioritization (team level) and the top down enterprise strategic themes [15], also stakeholder management is important [12]. Agile@scale is a learning curve for most organizations. Frameworks like SAFe and LeSS are challenged by agile purist. But for larger organizations top down structure, governance and process & tooling standard are required to implement desirable functionality [16]. Priorities need to be set, functional requirements as well as non-functional requirements. Not prioritizing non-functional requirements will create technical debt [17–19].

Market dynamics are related to the number of clients and suppliers overtime [20, 21]. Also, variance in sales volumes, frequency of service or product innovations and rise of substitutes contribute to market dynamics. Management need to prepare for adapting to market dynamics [22–24].

Maturity of professionals is related to the number of years of experience in a role and in relevant other roles, level of education and training, number of years with the company [25–27]. Furthermore, leadership capabilities are contributing to the maturity of processionals [28, 29].

3   Hypotheses

Digital transformations require agile and DevOps adoption. This research explores the Pearson correlation between the percentage of Agile software development and the percentage of operation in DevOps 2017 and in 2020 (Pearson correlation – [30–33]. The hypotheses test if the market dynamics are a predictor for the adoption of Agile software development and operations in DevOps 2017 and in 2020. The survey respondents provide their insight and understanding for both 2017 and 2020. The 2020 insights are obviously the survey respondent's vision on the future.

For organizations with high market dynamics the expectation is that the experience with agile and DevOps is expected to be higher as there is a bigger need for agile and DevOps adoption. For organizations with high market dynamics the expectation is that the percentage of Agile software development and the percentage of operation in DevOps 2017 and in 2020 is higher, as there is a bigger need for agile and DevOps adoption. The 95% critical values of the correlation coefficients decide if r is significant or not. This will provide insides in the expected impact of market dynamics on agile and DevOps adoptions.

$$\rho = \text{the degree of market dynamics versus \% of delivery}$$

$$H_{0 \text{ (market dynamics – agile delivery - 2017)}} : \rho = 0$$
$$H_{A \text{(market dynamics – agile delivery - 2017)}} : \rho > 0$$

$$H_{0 \text{ (market dynamics – agile delivery - 2020)}} : \rho = 0$$
$$H_{A \text{(market dynamics – agile delivery - 2020)}} : \rho > 0$$

$$H_{0 \text{ (market dynamics – DevOps delivery - 2017)}} : \rho = 0$$
$$H_{A \text{(market dynamics – DevOps delivery - 2017)}} : \rho > 0$$

$$H_{0 \text{ (market dynamics – DevOps delivery - 2020)}} : \rho = 0$$
$$H_{A \text{(market dynamics – DevOps delivery - 2020)}} : \rho > 0$$

This research also explores the difference between the % onshore delivery with agile and DevOps 2017 and in 2020. The hypotheses test if the 2017 % onshore delivery is higher than the % onshore delivery in 2020 (two sample t test with paired samples). The 5% Student t values (one tail) decide if r is significant or not. This will provide insides in the expected developments in % onshore delivery for agile and DevOps.

ρ = % onshore delivery 2017 versus % onshore delivery 2020

$H_{0 \text{ (agile 2017 – agile 2020)}}$: $\rho = 0$
$H_{A \text{ (agile 2017 – agile 2020)}}$: $\rho < 0$

$H_{0 \text{ (DevOps 2017 – DevOps 2020)}}$: $\rho = 0$
$H_{A \text{ (DevOps 2017 – DevOps 2020)}}$: $\rho < 0$

This research finally explores the difference between the % input based contracting with agile and DevOps 2017 and in 2020. The hypotheses test if the 2017 % input based contracting are higher than the % input based contracting in 2020. The 5% student t values (one tail) decide if r is significant or not. This will provide insides in the expected developments in % input based contracting for agile and DevOps.

ρ = % input based contract 2017 versus % input based contracting 2020

$H_{0 \text{ (agile 2017 – agile 2020)}}$: $\rho = 0$
$H_{A \text{ (agile 2017 – agile 2020)}}$: $\rho < 0$

$H_{0 \text{ (DevOps 2017 – DevOps 2020)}}$: $\rho = 0$
$H_{A \text{ (DevOps 2017 – DevOps 2020)}}$: $\rho < 0$

4   Data Collection

The data for this research is collected by a survey. The survey was submitted to ICT Media, a Dutch organization that facilities IT decision makers in the Netherlands. The members of this community are Chief Information Officers and their direct reports. The response rate was 6.2% (217 responses to 3,500 invitations). However, some respondents provided inconsistent responses. Other respondents didn't complete the survey. The number of responses that has been taken into account is 89, which reduced the response rate from 6.2% to 2.5%. The survey was an anonymous survey; therefore, it is not possible to conclude the representativeness of the sample (89 responses versus total community of 3,500 members). However, the spread over the different sectors and spread of the size of the organizations the respondents represent do not indicate that the respondents are not representative for the community, which was also confirmed by ICT Media.

The survey was conducted in Dutch. The participants completed their response via a portal. The responses were collected from 23 October to 8 November 2017. The potential participants received one friendly reminder the second week the survey was introduced.

5 Survey Population Characteristics

The participating organizations include national and international organizations. Over 25% of the participating organizations generate over 25% of their revenues outside the Netherlands (see Fig. 1). As expected the larger organization are predominantly the international organization. Nearly half of the organizations operate in financial services (20 of the 89 respondents), government (11 of the 89 respondents) and manufacturing (10 of the 89 respondents).

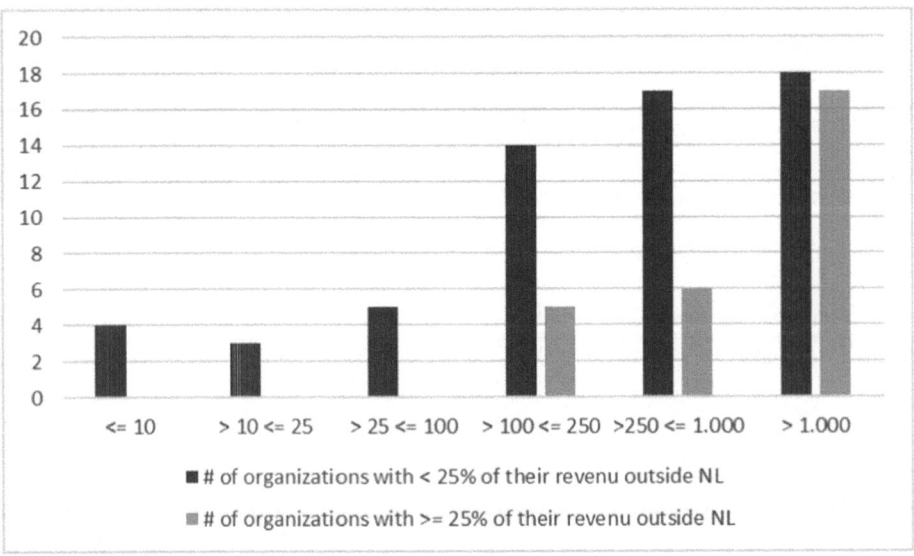

Fig. 1. Participating organizations by annual revenue in 1.000m Euro – split in national and international organizations – N = 89.

Nearly half of the organizations have an IT spend of +5% of their revenue (41 of the 89 respondents). One third of the organizations spend 50% or more of their IT-budget with service providers (31 of the 89 respondents) The application management budget ranges from less than 1m Euro to +50m per annum (see Fig. 2).

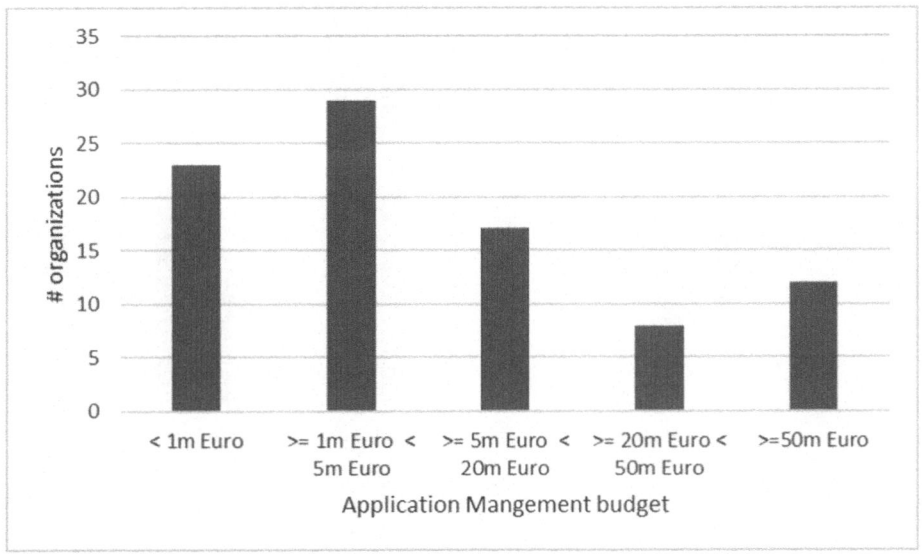

Fig. 2. Number of organizations by application management budget (N = 89).

Most organizations characterize their market condition as very dynamic (65% of 89 respondents score 4 or higher on market dynamics). Two third of the organizations facing dynamic market conditions are large organizations (>=250m annual revenue), see Fig. 3. The participating organizations of the sectors Manufacturing, Real estate & Construction and Utilities & Telecom face less dynamic market conditions than the organizations of other sectors, see Fig. 4.

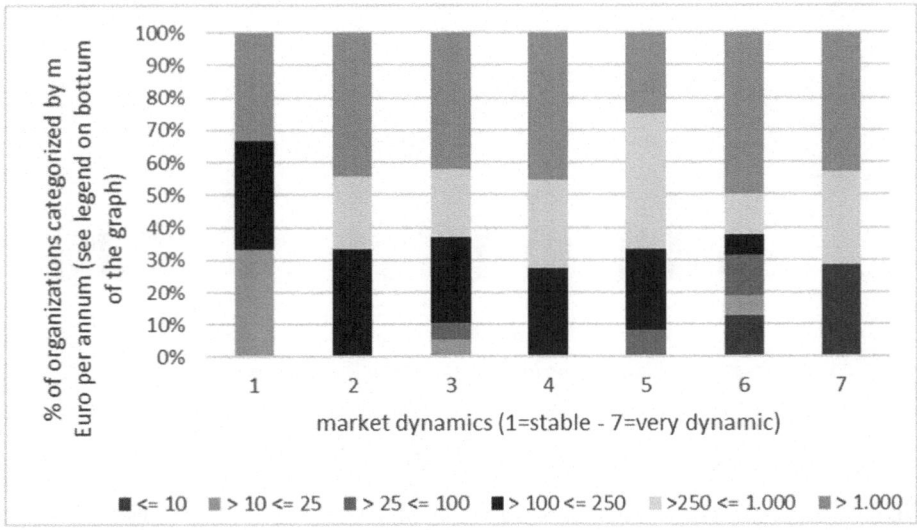

Fig. 3. Percentage of organizations categorized by m Euro revenue per annum by market dynamics (1 = stable – 7 = very dynamic) (N = 89).

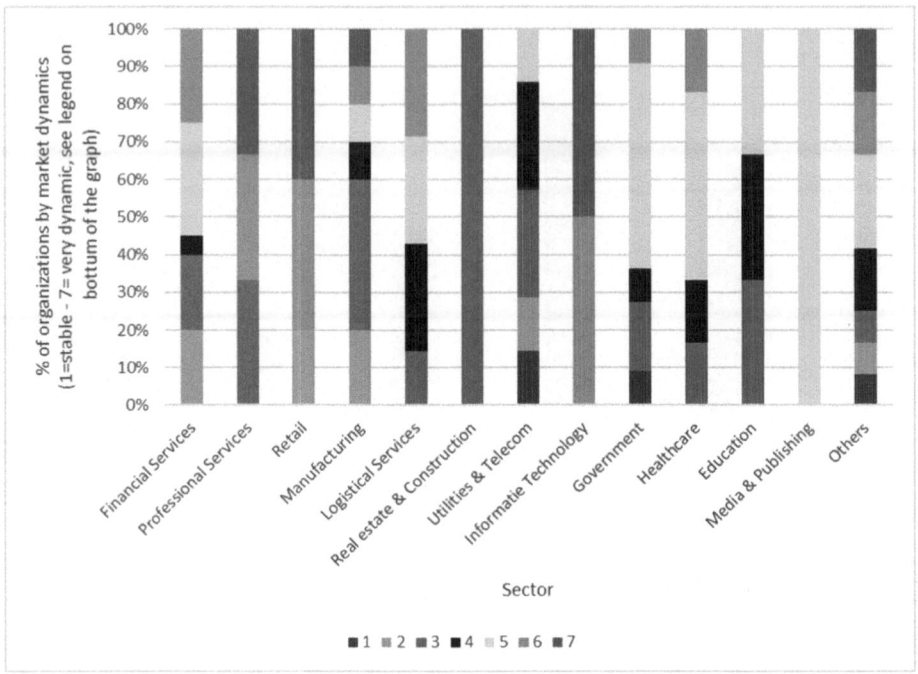

Fig. 4. Percentage of organizations categorized by sector and by market dynamics (1 = stable – 7 = very dynamic) (N = 89).

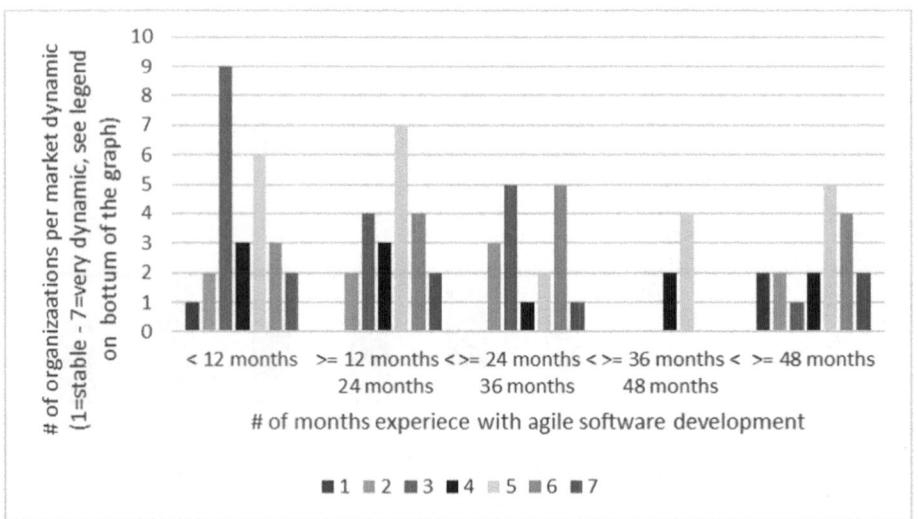

Fig. 5. Number of organizations categorized by market dynamics (1 = stable – 7 = very dynamic) per number of months of experience in agile software development (N = 89).

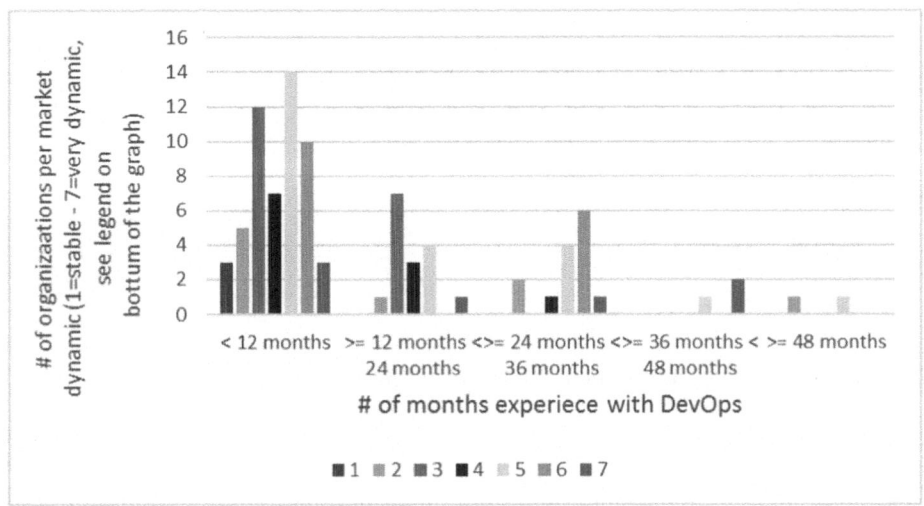

Fig. 6. Number of organizations categorized by market dynamics (1 = stable – 7 = very dynamic) per number of months of experience in DevOps (N = 89).

Organizations operating in very dynamic markets have started earlier with agile and DevOps adaption (see Fig. 5). This can be explained by the increased need for agile and DevOps enabling speed and flexibility required by market dynamics. Also, the experience with DevOps is less than the experience with agile, see Fig. 6. This can be explained by the need to have agile software development to successfully implement DevOps.

The respondents score for different roles in agile software development and DevOps were much higher than expected, especially the scores for the Product Owner (average 3,72 - 2017, in a 1–7 Likert scale), Accountable Executive (average 3,18 - 2017), and Scrum Master (average 4,01). Most of the respondents also expect significant improvements for all roles in 2020. The expected lowest score in 2020 is for the Accountable Executive role (average 4,31). The scores are discussed in more detail in Sect. 7 and require further investigation.

6   Data Analyses

The number of responding organizations taken into account was 89 organizations (N = 89). The preferred minimal number of responses is 25 [30]. The number of responses is sufficient for reliable testing.

The impact of market dynamics was tested for agile software development and DevOps. The hypotheses are tested for both 2017 and 2020. The 95% critical values of the correlation coefficients decide if r is significant or not. Only the market dynamics and percentage DevOps in 2017 is significant, although the market dynamics and percentage agile in 2017 is nearly significant (see below text boxes).

ρ = the degree of market dynamics versus % of delivery

$H_{0\ (market\ dynamics\ –\ agile\ delivery\ -\ 2017)} : \rho = 0$
$H_{A(market\ dynamics\ –\ agile\ delivery\ -\ 2017)} : \rho > 0$

$y = 0{,}0376x + 0{,}2651$

$R^2 = 0{,}0383$ and $r = 0{,}1957$

The calculated r indicates a uphill (positive) linear relationship.

df=n−1=89−1=88

The critical values associated with df=88 are ±0,2074. If r is r is greater than the positive critical value, then r is significant. Since r=0,1957 and 0,1957<0,2074, r is not significant and the line cannot be used for prediction.

ρ = the degree of market dynamics versus % of delivery

$H_{0\ (market\ dynamics\ –\ agile\ delivery\ -\ 2020)} : \rho = 0$
$H_{A(market\ dynamics\ –\ agile\ delivery\ -\ 2020)} : \rho > 0$

$y = 0{,}0188x + 0{,}5377$

$R^2 = 0{,}0128$ and $r = 0{,}1132$

The calculated r indicates an uphill (positive) linear relationship.

df=n−1=89−1=88

The critical values associated with df=88 are ±0,2074. If r is r is greater than the positive critical value, then r is significant. Since r=0,1132 and 0,1132<0,2074, r is not significant and the line cannot be used for prediction.

ρ = the degree of market dynamics versus % of delivery

$H_{0 \text{ (market dynamics – DevOps delivery - 2017)}}$: $\rho = 0$
$H_{A \text{(market dynamics – DevOps delivery - 2017)}}$: $\rho > 0$

$y = 0{,}0337x + 0{,}0515$

$R^2 = 0{,}0801$ and $r = 0{,}2829$

The calculated r indicates a uphill (positive) linear relationship.

df=n−1=89−1=88

The critical values associated with df=88 are ±0,2074. If r is r is greater than the positive critical value, then r is significant. Since r=0,2829 and 0,2829>0,2074, r is significant and the line can be used for prediction.

ρ = the degree of market dynamics versus % of delivery

$H_{0 \text{ (market dynamics – DevOps delivery - 2020)}}$: $\rho = 0$
$H_{A \text{(market dynamics – DevOps delivery - 2020)}}$: $\rho > 0$

$y = 0{,}0232x + 0{,}3414$

$R^2 = 0{,}0214$ and $r = 0{,}1463$

The calculated r indicates a uphill (positive) linear relationship.

df=n−1=89−1=88

The critical values associated with df=88 are ±0,2074. If r is r is greater than the positive critical value, then r is significant. Since r=0,1463 and 0,1463<0,2074, r is not significant and the line cannot be used for prediction.

The delivery percentage for onshore delivery in 2020 will be significantly lower than in 2017 for both agile and DevOps (see below text boxes).

$\rho = \%$ delivery onshore 2017 versus $\%$ delivery onshore 2020

$H_{0 \text{ (agile 2017 – agile 2020)}} : \rho <= 0$
$H_{A \text{ (agile 2017 – agile 2020)}} : \rho < 0$

$\text{Mean}_{\text{(agile 2017 – agile 2020)}} = 7.1556$
$\text{Std dev}_{\text{(agile 2017 – agile 2020)}} = 40.0825$
$N = 89$
Degrees of freedom $= 88$

t Stat $= 1.6842$
t Critical one-tail (.05) $= 1.6624$

The critical values associated with df=88 is 1.6624. If t Stat is larger than the critical value, then we can reject H_0.

Since t Stat = 1.6842 and 1.6842 > 1.6624, t Stat is significant and we can expect with 95% confidence a decrease in onshore agile software development in 2020 compared to 2017 onshore software development.

$\rho = \%$ delivery onshore 2017 versus $\%$ delivery onshore 2020

$H_{0 \text{ (DevOps 2017 – DevOps 2020)}} : \rho >= 0$
$H_{A \text{ (DevOps 2017 – DevOps 2020)}} : \rho < 0$

$\text{Mean}_{\text{(DevOps 2017 – DevOps 2020)}} = 4.8989$
$\text{Std dev}_{\text{(DevOps 2017 – DevOps 2020)}} = 23.3112$
$N = 89$
Degrees of freedom $= 88$

t Stat $= 1.9826$
t Critical one-tail (.05) $= 1.6624$

The critical values associated with df=88 is 1.6624. If t Stat is larger than the critical value, then we can reject H_0.

Since t Stat = 1.9826 and 1.9826 > 1.6624, t Stat is significant and we can expect with 95% confidence a decrease in onshore DevOps in 2020 compared to 2017 onshore DevOps.

Input based contracting in 2020 will be significantly lower than in 2017 for both agile and DevOps (see below text boxes).

ρ = % input based contracting 2017 versus % input based contracting 2020

$H_{0 \text{ (agile 2017 – agile 2020)}} : \rho = 0$
$H_{A \text{ (agile 2017 – agile 2020)}} : \rho < 0$

Mean $_{\text{(agile 2017 – agile 2020)}}$ = 9.9213
Std dev $_{\text{(agile 2017 – agile 2020)}}$ = 27.3239
N = 89
Degrees of freedom = 88

t Stat = 3.4255
t Critical one-tail (.05) = 1.6624

The critical values associated with df=88 is 1.6624. If t Stat is larger than the critical value, then we can reject H_0.

Since t Stat = 3.4255 and 3.4255 > 1.6624, t Stat is significant and we can expect with 95% confidence a decrease in input based agile contracting in 2020 compared to 2017 input agile contracting.

ρ = % input based contracting 2017 versus % input based contracting 2020

$H_{0 \text{ (DevOps 2017 – DevOps 2020)}} : \rho = 0$
$H_{A \text{ (DevOps 2017 – DevOps 2020)}} : \rho < 0$

Mean $_{\text{(DevOps 2017 – DevOps 2020)}}$ = 4.8876
Std dev $_{\text{(DevOps 2017 – DevOps 2020)}}$ = 17.4671
N = 89
Degrees of freedom = 88

t Stat = 2.6398
t Critical one-tail (.05) = 1.6624

The critical values associated with df=88 is 1.6624. If t Stat is larger than the critical value, then we can reject H_0.

Since t Stat = 4.8876 and 4.8876 > 1.6624, t Stat is significant and we can expect with 95% confidence a decrease in input based DevOps contracting in 2020 compared to 2017 input DevOps contracting.

7 Discussion

Three topics for agile and DevOps require a discussion: a. The maturity of roles b. changes in onshore/nearshore/offshore profile and c. changes in input/output contracting obligations profile. Also, additional contracting issue including the costs of technical debt, compensation for contracted but cancelled sprints and releases and implications of adjusting current infrastructure contracts.

a. The maturity of roles

The maturity of the roles as scores for different roles in agile software development and DevOps were much higher than expected. In this section, the focus is on the 2017 maturity scores of the product owner, accountable executive and scrum master. There is not a real difference in the maturity score for small organizations (<250m Euro revenue) and large organizations (>=250m Euro revenue), see Fig. 7. Especially for the Accountable Executive this is remarkable. The Accountable Executive is more important in large organization as coordination across multiple Product Owners is required. Larger organizations were expected to have more mature Accountable Executives. One of the respondents also labelled the role of Accountable Executive as Servant Leader, supporting the Agile and DevOps teams in accomplishing their objectives.

There is a difference in the maturity score for less experienced organizations (<24 months) and experienced organizations (>=24 months), see Fig. 8. This difference is predominantly for the Product Owner and Scrum Master role and less for the Accountable Executive role.

b. Changes in onshore/nearshore/offshore profile

Furthermore, some of the respondents mentioned the role of agile coaches in addition to the role of Product Owners. Agile coaches potentially can improve the business involvement. As mentioned by some of the respondents also technology alignment is required. Introducing Product Manager roles might be helpful and ensures an IT-architectural alignment and enables managing technical debt.

Secondly the split in onshore, nearshore and offshore delivery is explored in more detail. For both agile and DevOps the size of organizations has little impact on the delivery split. Larger organizations are slightly more aggressive, for both agile and DevOps, by having a larger part of the service delivery in offshore locations instead of nearshore locations (see Figs. 9 and 10). Currently global service providers are able to deal with smaller contact volumes. Scale is no longer a pre-requisite for nearshore and offshore delivery. The difference between organizations with revenue pre-dominantly in the Netherlands versus organizations with revenue pre-dominantly outside the Netherlands is bigger. Organizations with revenue pre-dominantly outside the Netherlands more aggressively ramp up offshore delivery. These organizations are used to engaging with global service providers and are considering the risks associated with nearshore and offshore delivery as lower (see Figs. 11 and 12).

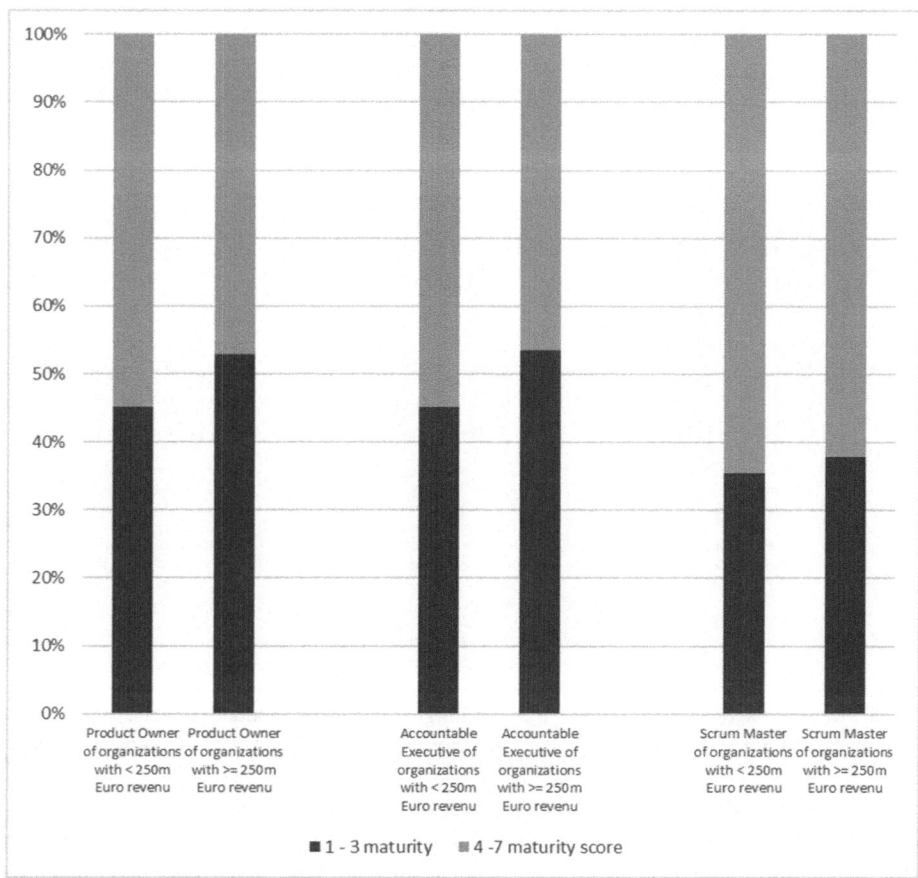

Fig. 7. Maturity score (2017 – low "1–3" and high "4–7") for Product Owners, Accountable Executives and Scrum Masters by revenue (<250m and >=250m Euro) (N = 89).

c. Changes in input/output contracting obligations profile

The percentage delivered by the internal organization remains for agile stable and the percentage of contractors drops (2017 versus 2020). The output obligations (predominantly fixed price and story points) for agile will increase 2020. Organizations are becoming more mature in contacting based on output obligations. There is minimal impact for agile of the size of the organization and the volume of the revenue outside the Netherlands. Also for DevOps per percentage of contractors drops (2017 versus 2020). In DevOps there is increased outsourcing and reduced inhouse service provision. The infrastructure services are not providing competitive advantage and are technical complex (requiring specific capabilities). Outsourcing is perceived as lower risk option. (see Figs. 13, 14, 15 and 16).

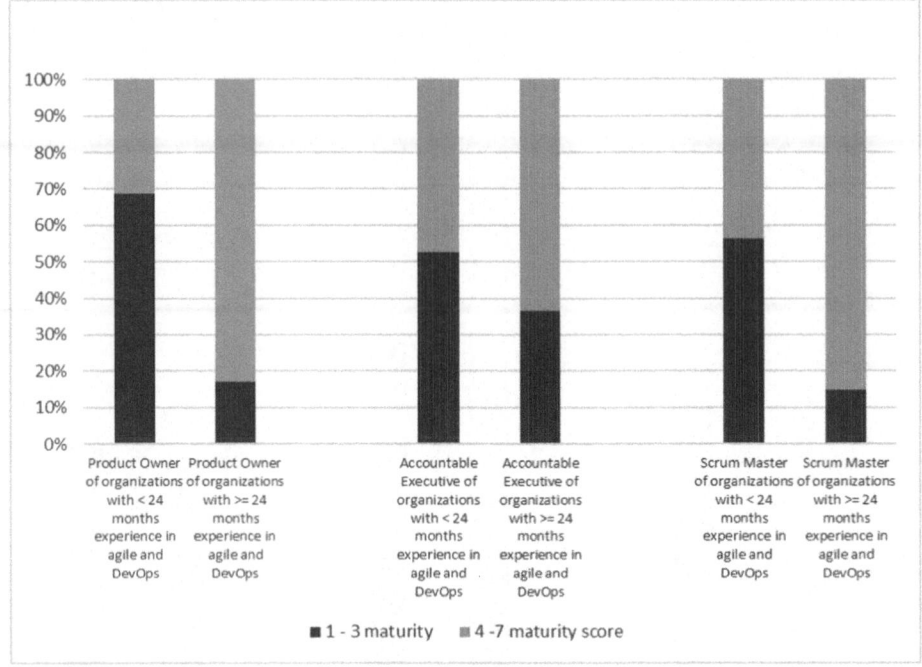

Fig. 8. Maturity score (2017 – low "1–3" and high "4–7") for Product Owners, Accountable Executives and Scrum Masters by agile experience (<24 months and >=24 months) (N = 89).

We conclude this discussion section with three observations related to contracting. Technical debt caused by inefficient application development of service providers should be at the risk of service providers. Nearly 80% of the outsourcing contracts have no clauses related to the costs of inefficient application development. Only 10% of the contracts include clauses protecting organizations fully for inefficient application development. In 11% of the contracts include clauses protecting organizations partly (see Fig. 17). For Chief Information Officers technical debt is an important service level to track and to incorporate in future contracts by transferring the risks to service providers.

Similar to technical debt, most contracts include no clauses for contracted but cancelled sprints and releases. This increases the risk profile for organizations. Only 6% of the contracts includes clauses detailing service providers are not entitle for compensation for contracted but cancelled sprints and releases. In 8% of the contracts service providers are partly compensated and in 4% of the contracts service providers are explicitly full compensated (see Fig. 18). For Chief Information Officers contract flexibility is important. In future Chief Information Officers should contract clauses allowing cancellation of contracted sprints and releases combined with sufficient notice. Notice periods can range from 1 to 3 months.

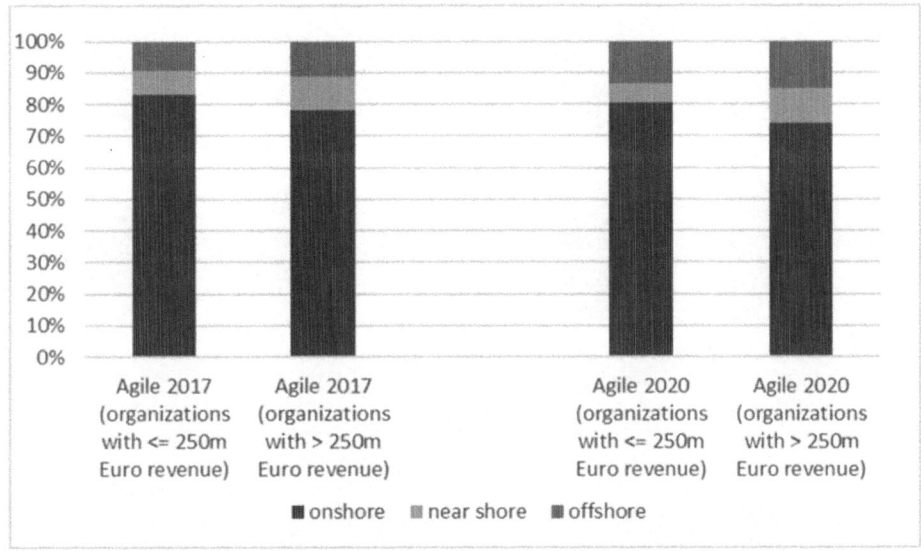

Fig. 9. Onshore/nearshore/offshore split for agile in 2017 and 2020 for small organizations (revenue <= 250 m Euro) and large organizations (revenue > 250 m Euro) (N = 89).

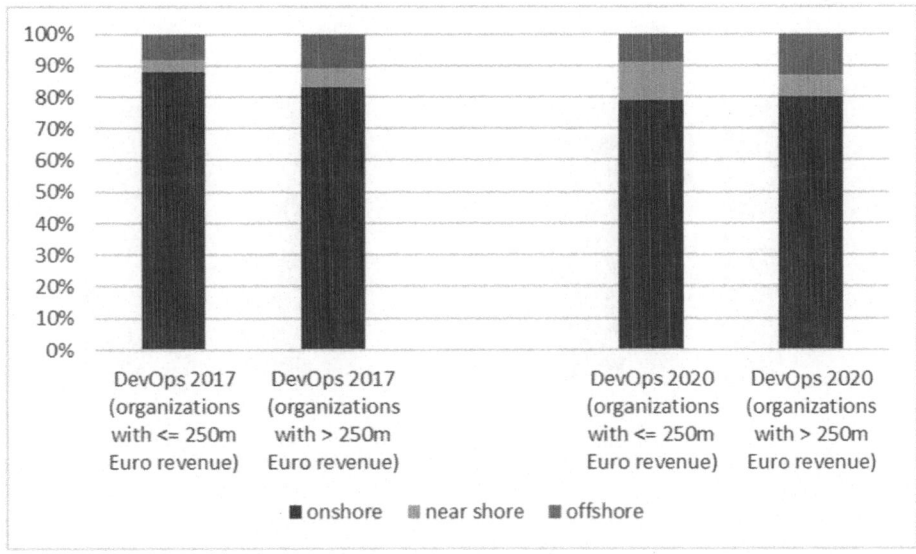

Fig. 10. Onshore/nearshore/offshore split for DevOps in 2017 and 2020 for small organizations (revenue <= 250 m Euro) and large organizations (revenue > 250 m Euro) (N = 89).

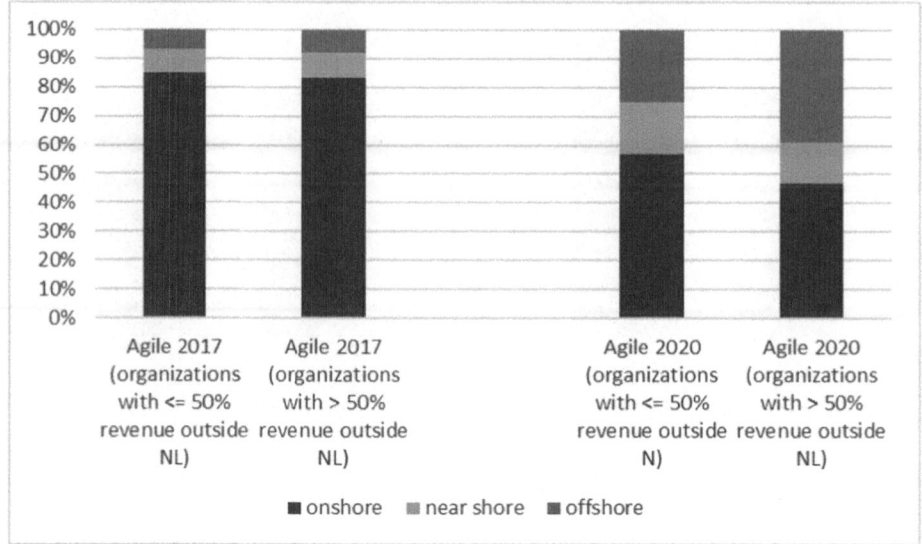

Fig. 11. Onshore/nearshore/offshore split for agile in 2017 and 2020 for organizations with revenues predominantly in the Netherlands (<=50% revenue outside the Netherlands) and organizations with revenues predominantly outside the Netherlands (>50% revenue outside the Netherlands) (N = 89).

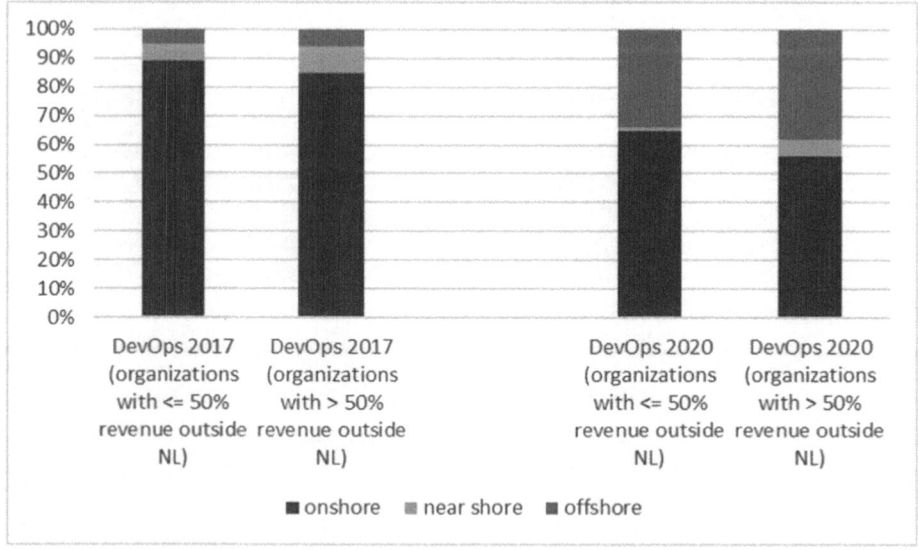

Fig. 12. Onshore/nearshore/offshore split for DevOps in 2017 and 2020 for organizations with revenues predominantly in the Netherlands (<=50% revenue outside the Netherlands) and organizations with revenues predominantly outside the Netherlands (>50% revenue outside the Netherlands) (N = 89).

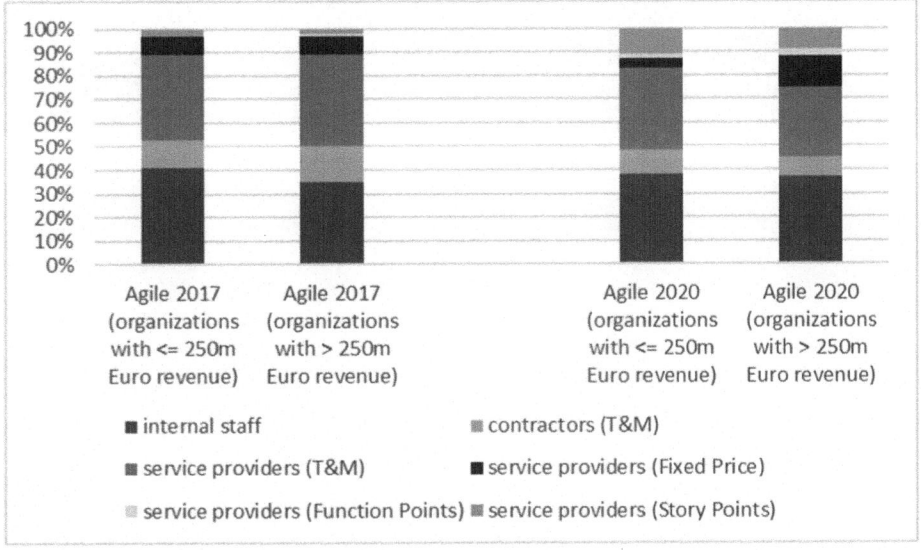

Fig. 13. Contracting for agile in 2017 and 2020 for small organizations (revenue <= 250 m Euro) and large organizations (revenue > 250 m Euro) (N = 89).

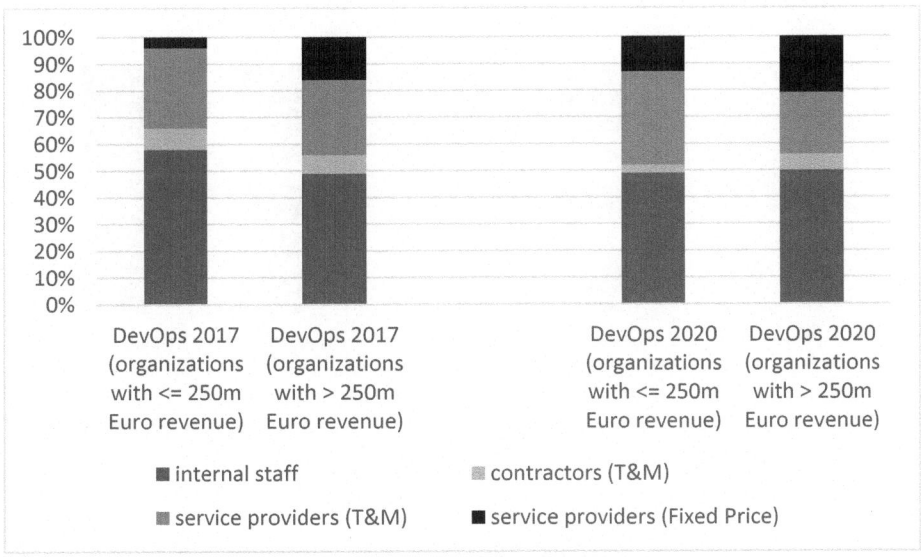

Fig. 14. Contracting for DevOps in 2017 and 2020 for small organizations (revenue <= 250 m Euro) and large organizations (revenue > 250 m Euro) (N = 89).

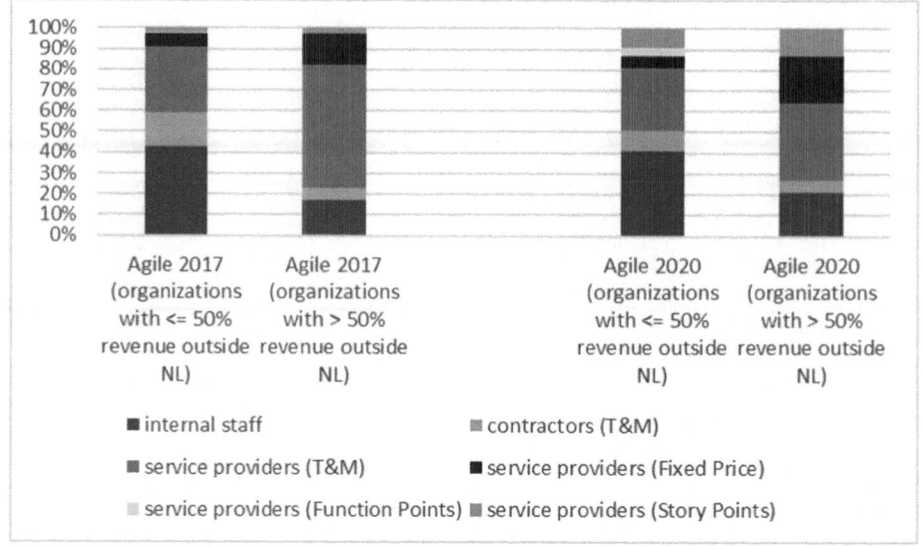

Fig. 15. Contracting for agile in 2017 and 2020 for organizations with revenues predominantly in the Netherlands (<=50% revenue outside the Netherlands) and organizations with revenues predominantly outside the Netherlands (>50% revenue outside the Netherlands) (N = 89).

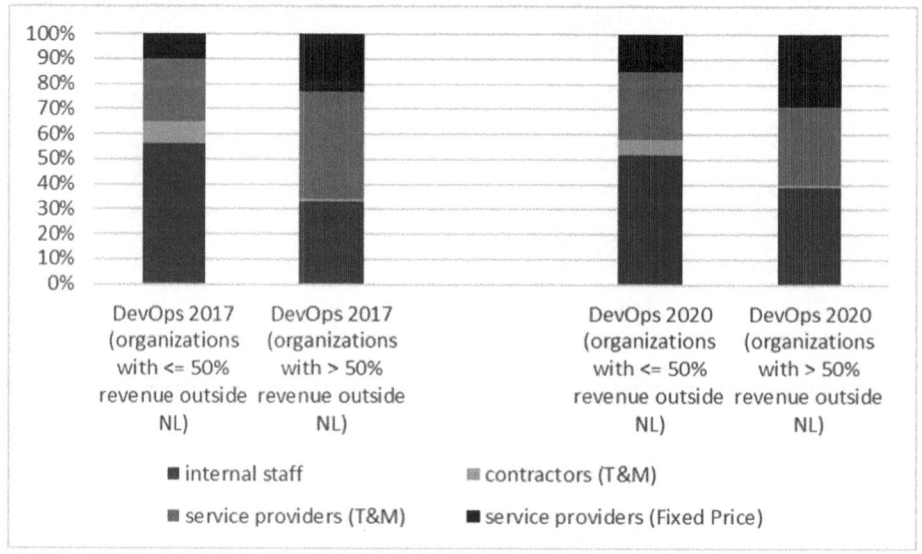

Fig. 16. Contracting for DevOps in 2017 and 2020 for organizations with revenues predominantly in the Netherlands (<=50% revenue outside the Netherlands) and organizations with revenues predominantly outside the Netherlands (>50% revenue outside the Netherlands) (N = 89).

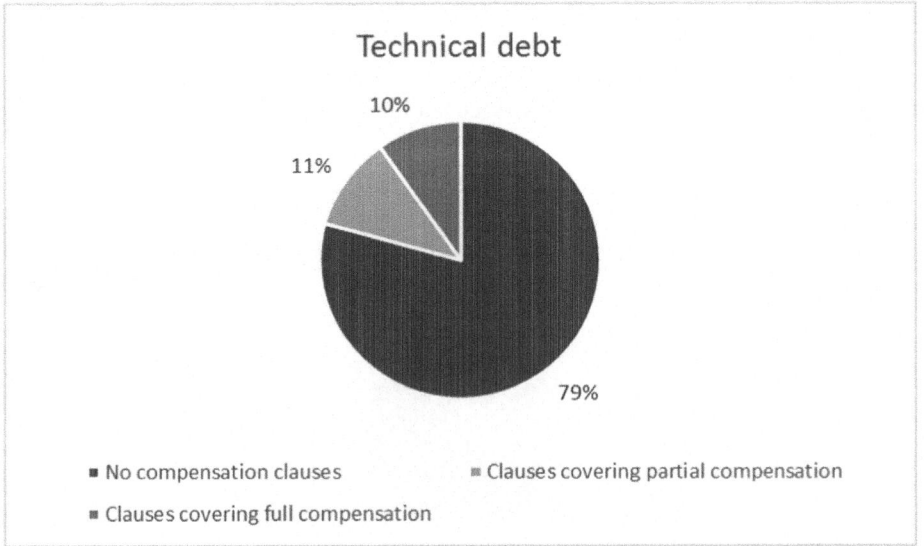

Fig. 17. Contract provisions for technical debt caused by inefficient application development of service providers (N = 89).

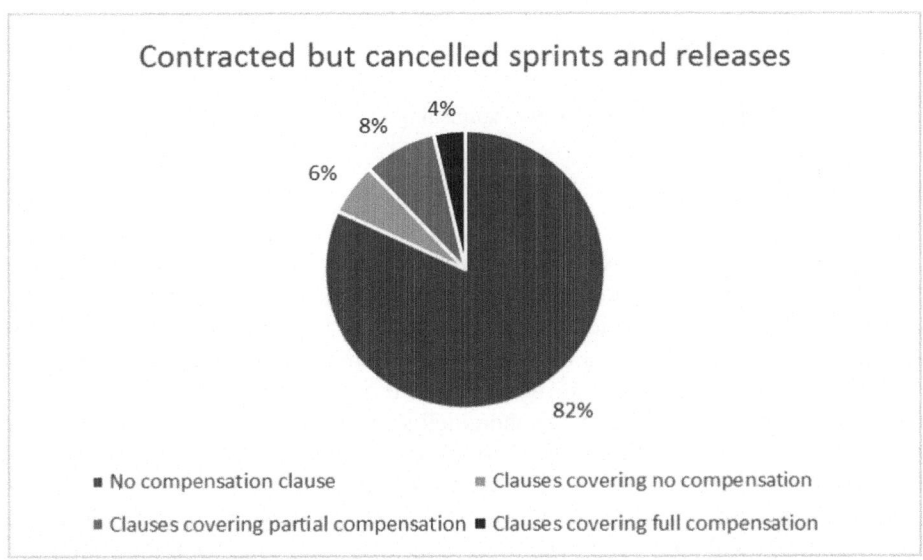

Fig. 18. Contract provisions for contracted but cancelled sprints and releases (N = 89).

The introduction of DevOps typically creates scope discussions for existing infrastructure outsourcing contracts, which typically include operations. Carving out of the operations requires contract re-negotiations of existing infrastructure contracts.

The majority of organizations has not re-negotiated their current infrastructure out-sourcing contracts. The experience with re-negotiating infrastructure contracts is mixed. About half of the organization experienced the re-negotiations as smooth where the other half of the organizations experienced the re-negotiations as difficult or even problematic (see Fig. 19).

Fig. 19. Re-negotiation contracting experience (N = 89).

8   Conclusions

Chief Information Officers need to ramp up capabilities to include agile and DevOps capabilities in their organization and capabilities to contract agile and DevOps services to facilitate digital transformations. The delivery model for agile and even more for the operations part of DevOps need to shift from onshore to offshore to ensure access to capabilities. Leveraging nearshore is questionable given increased risk profile com-pared to onshore and the limited nearshore delivery capabilities compared to offshore. Also, Chief Information Officers need to enforce output obligations including fixed price and price per story point, when both the organization and the service providers have built sufficient experience in delivering the service based on output obligations. Future contracts with service providers must include provisions for technical debt, if attributable to service providers, service providers must bear all the costs to resolve the technical debt. Also, provisions facilitating flexibility to cancel contracted sprints and release, with sufficient notice at no costs, are recommended.

9   Research Limitations and Future Research Direction

This research has been conducted in the Netherlands and included only a limited number of respondents - predominantly Chief Information Officers and their direct reports. Expanding the survey to other countries and business representatives will improve the representativeness of the data. Also collecting data in the years to come will help to understand the best practices for agile and DevOps better – annual survey. These surveys can be supplemented by case studies to understand better the underlying management decisions and issues organizations are facing.

Acknowledgements. The author would like to thank Rob Beijleveld, Sophie Haans and Arnoud van Gemeren from ICT Media (www.ictmedia.nl) for inviting the members of the ICT Media community to participate in the survey and for facilitating the execution of the survey.

References

1. Westerman, G., Bonnet, D.: Revamping your business through digital transformation. MIT Sloan Manag. Rev. **56**(3), 2–5 (2015)
2. Adner, R.: Navigating the leadership challenges of innovation ecosystems. MIT Sloan Manag. Rev. **58**(1) (2016)
3. Majchrzak, A., Markus, M.L., Wareham, J.: Designing for digital transformation: lessons for information systems research from the study of ICT and societal challenges. MIS Q. **40**(2), 267–277 (2016)
4. Schoemaker, P., Tetlock, P.: Superforecasting: How to upgrade your company's judgment. Harvard Bus. Rev. **94**, 72–78 (2016)
5. Berman, S.J.: Digital transformation: opportunities to create new business models. Strategy Leadersh. **40**(2), 16–24 (2012)
6. Utterback, J.: Mastering the Dynamics of Innovation: How Companies can Seize Opportunities in the Face of Technological Change (1994)
7. Hsiao, R.L., Ormerod, R.J.: A new perspective on the dynamics of information technology-enabled strategic change. Inf. Syst. J. **8**(1), 21–52 (1998)
8. Sambamurthy, V., Bharadwaj, A., Grover, V.: Shaping agility through digital options: reconceptualizing the role of information technology in contemporary firms. MIS Q. **27**, 237–263 (2003)
9. Liao, Y.W., Wang, Y.M., Wang, Y.S., Tu, Y.M.: Understanding the dynamics between organizational IT investment strategy and market performance: a system dynamics approach. Comput. Ind. **71**, 46–57 (2015)
10. Harvey Nash and KPMG Navigating uncertainty, research report (2017). www.hnkpmgciosurvey.com/
11. Bass, L., Weber, I., Zhu, L.: DevOps: A Software Architect's Perspective. Addison-Wesley Professional, Boston (2015)
12. Tamburri, D.A., Kazman, R., Fahimi, H.: The architect's role in community shepherding. IEEE Softw. **33**(6), 70–79 (2016)
13. Balalaie, A., Heydarnoori, A., Jamshidi, P.: Microservices architecture enables DevOps: migration to a cloud-native architecture. IEEE Softw. **33**(3), 42–52 (2016)
14. Vodanovich, S., Sundaram, D., Myers, M.: Research commentary—digital natives and ubiquitous information systems. Inf. Syst. Res. **21**(4), 711–723 (2010)

15. Fontana, R.M., Reinehr, S., Malucelli, A.: Agile compass: a tool for identifying maturity in agile software-development teams. IEEE Softw. **32**(6), 20–23 (2015)
16. Bass, J.M.: Artefacts and agile method tailoring in large-scale offshore software development programmes. Inf. Softw. Technol. **75**, 1–16 (2016)
17. Cunningham, W.: The WyCash portfolio management system. In: Addendum to the Proceedings on Object-oriented Programming Systems, Languages, and Applications (Addendum), pp. 29–30 (1992)
18. Kruchten, P., Nord, R.L., Ozkaya, I.: Technical debt: from metaphor to theory and practice. IEEE Softw. **29**(6), 18–21 (2012)
19. Behutiye, W.N., Rodríguez, P., Oivo, M., Tosun, A.: Analyzing the concept of technical debt in the context of agile software development: a systematic literature review. Inf. Softw. Technol. **82**, 139–158 (2017)
20. Johnston, W.J., Peters, L.D., Gassenheimer, J.: Questions about network dynamics: Characteristics, structures, and interactions. J. Bus. Res. **59**(8), 945–954 (2006)
21. Singh, K., Mitchell, W.: Growth dynamics: the bidirectional relationship between interfirm collaboration and business sales in entrant and incumbent alliances. Strateg. Manag. J. **26**(6), 497–521 (2005)
22. Cavalcante, S., Kesting, P., Ulhøi, J.: Business model dynamics and innovation:(re) establishing the missing linkages. Manag. Decis. **49**(8), 1327–1342 (2011)
23. Dosi, G., Nelson, R., Winter, S. (eds.): The Nature and Dynamics of Organizational Capabilities. OUP, Oxford (2001)
24. Gupta, A.K., Govindarajan, V.: Business unit strategy, managerial characteristics, and business unit effectiveness at strategy implementation. Acad. Manag. J. **27**(1), 25–41 (1984)
25. Bhatt, G.D., Grover, V.: Types of information technology capabilities and their role in competitive advantage: an empirical study. J. Manag. Inf. Syst. **22**(2), 253–277 (2005)
26. Santhanam, R., Hartono, E.: Issues in linking information technology capability to firm performance. MIS Q. **27**, 125–153 (2003)
27. Zhu, K.: The complementarity of information technology infrastructure and e-commerce capability: a resource-based assessment of their business value. J. Manag. Inf. Syst. **21**(1), 167–202 (2004)
28. Robey, D., Boudreau, M.C., Rose, G.M.: Information technology and organizational learning: a review and assessment of research. Account. Manag. Inf. Technol. **10**(2), 125–155 (2000)
29. Dewett, T., Jones, G.R.: The role of information technology in the organization: a review, model, and assessment. J. Manag. **27**(3), 313–346 (2001)
30. David, F.: Tables of the Ordinates and Probability Integral of the Distribution of the Correlation Coefficient in Small Samples. Cambridge University Press, Cambridge (1938)
31. Cohen, J., Cohen, P., West, S., Aiken, L.: Applied Multiple Regression/Correlation Analysis for the Behavioral Sciences. Routledge, London (2013)
32. Hayes, A.: Introduction to Mediation, Moderation, and Conditional Process Analysis: A Regression-Based Approach. Guilford Press, Guilford (2013)
33. Hedges, L., Olkin, I.: Statistical Methods for Meta-Analysis. Academic press, Amsterdam (2014)

Caring for Platform-Based Work: Changing Labour Relationships

Fay Davidson[✉] and Sharyn Curran

School of Management, Curtin University, U1987, Bentley, WA, Australia
fay.davidson@postgrad.curtin.edu.au,
Sharyn.Curran@cbs.curtin.edu.au

Abstract. The emergence of gig work and its acceleration by apps and every-thing 'i', has brought with it complex labour-market relationships, increased vulnerabilities of workers and industries, and created difficulties for legislative and governance systems. This research is an exploration of the current state of gig economy issues, and stakeholder relationships within and outside the industrial/employment framework. It is an overview of the interaction of gig work and the gig economy with government and labour relations. The findings contribute to the study of gig work and could be useful for organizations seeking to combine competing strategic goals to achieve efficiencies in the future of work.

Keywords: Gig economy · Platform-based work · Labour relations

1 Introduction

Leaving aside all workers who work for wages or salary, there remains a portion of the workforce who are paid for completion of an object, task, job, or service. We also understand this group as self-employed, contractors, freelancers or *gig-workers*. The *gig economy* is an expression that makes new our understanding of labour relationships that have always existed but have recently changed in frequency, style and process. In the gig economy, instead of a regular wage, workers get paid for the *gig*s they complete, such as a food delivery or building a website or even doing an audit. The work is distributed usually online after some tendering process, and success can rely on reviews of previous supply, the number of alternative suppliers available to supply a customer's request and in some cases less on the quoted price. The quoted pricing framework may have been agreed beforehand in the case of the *gig*.

Contracting for gigs is not so much a new thing, as a new tool and a new way to do more of something that has always been done (i.e. using contractors instead of paying ongoing employees). The gig economy as a term (that makes fashionable and inter-esting an old concept, see for example Finkin [1]) may be understood as beginning in the period following the 2007–2008 Global Financial Crisis (GFC) when there was a rush for quick-fix top-up work, urgent start-ups, and a passion for apps and everything d"i"gital. Agrawal et al. [2] argue that between 2009 and 2013 the quarterly wage bill on oDesk (the largest online labour marketplace) grew from $10,000,000 to almost $100,000,000.

© Springer Nature Switzerland AG 2019
J. Kotlarsky et al. (Eds.): Global Sourcing 2018, LNBIP 344, pp. 147–163, 2019.
https://doi.org/10.1007/978-3-030-15850-7_8

This was also a period just ripe for embracing new understandings of *disruptive technologies* which would challenge established cultures and make corporate organisational change inevitable. There was also an awakening of the scope and marketing psychology of apps, that included incentivising workers through rewards and the inclusion of game characteristics when marketing apps to customers.

Impending changes to the gig work model appear to be increased regulation (or deregulation in some cases) of service providers, self-organisation of workers into empowered groups, threats and risks to brand reputation, marketplace saturation, and collective or socially responsible expectations of consumers. This paper looks to the next disruption in this disruptive model.

2 Scope

The scope of the research is to summaries the issues and identify relevant research, within and outside the industrial/employment framework in the context of labour relations. This paper is an exploration of the current state of many gig economy issues, including potential issues within the gig economy operating through external platforms and the gig approach to the organization of work within organizations including public sector agencies. The paper summarizes (at a high level only) other work being undertaken internationally, some recent academic research, and research by some industry bodies.

3 Research Questions

Powered by the cloud, and with better access to digital technologies and platforms, work is increasingly enabled by many apps and platforms that are redirecting expectations and responsibilities of employment relationships. The gig economy is a labour market characterised by the prevalence of short-term contracts or freelance work as opposed to permanent jobs, where independent contractors work on a task-by-task basis for different employers concurrently [3].

The research questions arise from observations of the real world, and from the point of view of the public employer, as much as from identifying gaps in the literature. We aim to go beyond just an immediate solution for the state's engagement with the future of the platform economy in answering these research questions:

How is the gig economy changing labour relations?
Is there appropriate interaction with the gig economy for government?

4 Objectives

The state of Western Australia is part of a federal system of government. There are federal industrial relation laws that sit side-by-side with state labour relations laws and complex industrial relations systems. The state's engagement with the platform economy is threefold. The questions for the public service form the overarching objective of the inquiry at hand:

1. As a service provider and policymaker, what is the relationship of gig or platform-based work and government?
2. As a legislator, what does the expansion of this style of gig work mean to labour law and labour relations? and
3. As a business and service provider, how is the public sector able to interact with the gig economy.

This paper also questions the future of the business model inherent in platform-based work.

5 Method

The Commonwealth Scientific and Industrial Research Organisation (CSIRO) is an Australian Government corporate entity that carries out scientific research for Australian industry, community in respect of national objectives. CSIRO's world-renowned successes include Wi-Fi, the Hendra vaccine and polymer banknotes. The phases of this research are similar to CSIRO's stages of strategic foresight project [4], and form Sects. 6, 7, 8, 9, 10 and 11 below.

6. A background study (themes in the literature)
7. Environment scan (other organisations other research)
8. Identifying trends/themes
9. Narratives - discussions - analysed in the context of the WAPS
10. Inform strategy and decision making
11. Finally challenges, obstructions and gaps identified with a view to prioritising next steps and future work.

Outcomes
The findings of this research should point to key understandings for labour relations and market relations (if any) required for the operation of gig service delivery within Australian political economy, that may be transferable to other jurisdictions. The research at hand will also consider possibilities for the future of this kind of work and business model.

6 Themes in the Literature

Understanding the current focus of research and analysis in the area is crucial to better understanding how government can interact with the gig economy. Emergent themes in the literature can be broadly grouped:

Size and extent of gig economy and gig work.
Disruption to government and macroeconomics
Workers

Business engagement with the gig economy
The platform work marketplace.

These themes are discussed in the following sections.

6.1   The Size of the Gig Economy

Organisations like Uber are sometimes defined as belonging to the *sharing economy* or *platform economy* and sometimes the *gig economy*. The creative economy, the sharing economy and even the crowd or cloud economy have an underlying similarity in that all three rely on the internet connecting buyers (users) and sellers (providers) through a facilitator who usually operates an app or a website. Popular sharing economy examples include renting out cars, rooms, parking spots, tendering for odd jobs. Specific examples are Uber, Airbnb, Parkhound, Airtasker.

"There are five million people currently working in the gig economy in the UK – according to the McKinsey Global Institute (MGI). This figure represents around 15.6 per cent of the total full and part-time workforce (32 million people). As many as 30 per cent of workers across the United States and Europe are thought to make up the gig economy" [5]. These proportions are also apparent in Australia where it is estimated that the gig work contributes $51bn [6] to the economy and that in 2017 less than half of the labour force, and less than one-third (only 6 million Australians) of the working-age population held a paid, full-time job with basic entitlements [7]. This growth indicates new markets emerging where previously there was no market and the admission of new market participants.

6.2   Disruption to Government

"Employment in the gig economy involves a variety of digitally-mediated relationships ranging from semi-permanent employee relationships to anonymous crowdsourcing or on-demand labour relationships. Trust and reputation, as social resources, play a key role in facilitating reliable transactions…, and gig economy platforms are sensitive to the way in which social connections are maintained in the digital space" [8].

Platforms provide a mechanism for people to operate outside the system of taxes and counter to other regulation and laws. For example, international students who have visa restrictions on the number of hours they can work yet spend many hours waiting for work delivering takeaway meals. Similarly, Hunt et al. [9] when discussing gig opportunities for Syrian refugee women in Jordan say their research suggests:

"That despite existing labour regulation stipulating refugee labour market integration, notably work permits, refugees can in practice engage with gig economy platforms so long as they meet platform registration requirements. In the words of one company representative we interviewed, 'We don't really care that they have work permits or not" [9]. While enabling entrance to the market of those who would otherwise be excluded these practices can run counter to government policy and strategy to fully integrate migrant workers.

6.3   Worker or Contractor

According to the Australian Taxation Office, there are six factors (such as supplying your own tools and freedom to choose work hours) that taken together determine whether a worker is a contractor or employee of an organisation [10]. Gig-workers around the world are continually challenging organisations in courts and through civil actions to determine their rights as employees.

However, most gig-economy organisations call their workers independent contractors in order to maintain cheaper employment costs and less restrictive hiring and firing practices.

"Gig-workers have turned to the courts, hoping to secure employee protections, and judges have struggled to apply outdated multifactor tests to resolve these disputes" [11]. These factors are often contestable/contested especially when people have been contracting for the same partner for a long time and think that they are entitled to usual worker protections (e.g. severance pay, workers' injury compensation, parental leave etc.). Stewart and Stanford suggest there are five principle options for governments and labour relations scholars: "…enforcement of existing laws; clarifying or expanding definitions of 'employment'; creating a new category of 'independent worker'; creating rights for 'workers', not employees; and reconsidering the concept of an 'employer'" [12].

7   Environmental Scan

Gig work as contractor or freelancer means that the workers have no rights to redundancy payments, the national minimum wage, paid holiday or sickness pay or superannuation, and no protection against unfair dismissal. These factors have been contested in several jurisdictions by contractors seeking better conditions and entitlements. For example, Uber drivers in California [13], the UK [14], and Brazil [15].

The phrase *dependent contractors* [16] was suggested by the Taylor Review [17] to describe workers who are treated like contractors for the purposes of being paid, but act like employees in terms of being available to only one employer. The Taylor Review looked at fair work and decent work, in much the same way that the New Zealand Future or Work Commission Report [18] looked at *Decent Work*. Both reports point to the difficulty of an individual's reliance on gig work. There is a significant problem when people expect gig work to provide sufficient income to live off. "Rather, the apps and websites should be thought of as business connectors; these websites are connecting your business (of one!) with clients. Uber never meant for its independent contractors to have 'jobs' as Uber drivers—it's meant to put drivers of otherwise vacant cars in touch with car-less people who need a ride" [19].

These working participants can belong to one of four groupings [20]:

The Reluctants – those who participate, but would rather have a traditional working arrangement, haven't fully committed;

The Outsiders – those without usual working rights, vulnerable workers;
The Dependents – those who have embraced gig work as their only source of income;
The Top-Ups – those topping up other sources of income and can choose to gig or not.

8 Trends

The new gig economy is in part propelled by the ease of matching potential *independent workers* [21] with jobs quickly through the internet, and often without a third party involved. The literature indicates that gig work globally appears to be the domain of the young and displaced, and a panacea for bloated organizations looking for efficiencies and new lean business models. However, there are some challenges to these assumptions.

Not Just for Low Level Jobs; Gig Work and Automation is not Just Low Skilled Jobs Although the "swing chair" [22] tasks are ripe for automation and hiving off to even lower skilled workers, doctors and academics already move around for short-term gigs. There are a fresh batch of start-ups targeting doctors, legal workers and consultants for short-term contract-based work and interim executive solutions – "CFOs, CTOs can be really effective on a gig basis as it's an opportunity for organizations to bring in intellectual property (IP) if the business is lacking in a certain area" [23].

Age Intergenerational Expectations; Not Just for Millennials Generational issues surface in the different approach taken by Generation X and Y staff to work and careers. Gen Y (or Gen Me, the millennial generation born in the 1980s) take flexible work practices to the point of blending work-life, preferring to acquire "career security in lieu of job security" [24, 25].

There is an unrealistic expectation that millennials are particularly attached to gig work and the opportunities it provides to maximize leisure time and integrate work with all aspects of life. There is evidence that millennials are looking for different experiences at work, less hierarchical, more flexible, more values aligned, but there is also evidence that even young people want some security and a living wage. A recent report [7] about young people and the future of work reflects the need to prepare for less secure work. Interestingly there appears to be some alignment or fit of the expectations of millennials with the less rigid work practices and lack of equivalent progress in management skills often found in agile organizations.

"The key to success in the Gig Economy is to operate yourself as a business. Businesses are constantly looking for new work, they're identifying opportunities to increase profitability (becoming location independent), they aren't relying on one client (only cleaning houses for a single company for example) and they aren't getting bogged down by doing piece work for pennies" [19].

Like millennials, but without the age determinant, are professionals or iPros, who are working as consultants, or contractors linked to projects, through platforms of human networks. It is expected that this group would be seeking higher returns for their specialized labour than say *mechanical turks* [26]. iPros are highly skilled self-employed individuals who work for themselves but do not employ others. They range from journalists and designers to ICT specialists and consultants. iPros represent a significant segment of professional working generally, making up 25% of all those working in professional, scientific and technical work and 22% of all those in arts and entertainment. The growth in iPros in the EU since 2004 has been remarkable. Numbers have increased by 45% from just under 6.2 million to 8.9 million in 2013, making them the fastest growing group in the EU labour market [27].

Not for all Businesses
In the gig economy, business is trying to leverage the spaces between supply and demand of labour by minimising downtime and non-core expenses (e.g. OSH, Superannuation, training and development, performance management etc.) and not having commitment to maintaining a labour force and workers through market downturns. Other businesses that are actually providing a service or operating in R and D may need to own their own IP, develop talent or cutting-edge skills in order to operate or sell their product or service.

Regulation is Increasing
There is evidence (e.g. Uber) that start-ups can only leverage gaps in the market for so long before disputes, grievances, and other regulatory breaches become apparent and draw the attention of regulators and legislators. For example, Airbnb is coming under examination from Local Government Authorities concerned, for example, about the impact of unregulated business and the consequential burden on resources in residential communities, and strata groups dealing with short-term residential occupancies in domestic settings. Uber drivers may need to be registered in some cities, and *Working with Children* police clearances are required for some home care work.

Overcrowded Marketplace
The virtual world is subject to quick start-ups with little to no capital investment or resources, and as such is subject to flooding and overcrowding as innovative ideas are cloned, localised, targeted to market segments and drift away or are bought out by larger predator firms. This can mean a highly volatile marketplace and quick turn over of ideas and industries. "Uber originally arrived in London five years ago, but rivals like Lyft, Via, and Juno do not operate in the city yet" [28].

Global Market Shares
The market being serviced and the service providers are no longer just local. The company providing paper by courier to offices in Perth can be run out of Bangalore or Brisbane. The potential marketplace is expanding, but so too are the number of entrants into each market serviced. Each platform entry into a domestic market increases pressure on traditional suppliers.

"Germany's tough transport rules — involving health exams, security checks and state-issued licenses for all taxi operators — would never allow such a low-cost service to operate freely in the country, Europe's largest economy. In every country, you have to be prepared to change your setup," [29].

9 Narratives - Case Study

Using Western Australia's state government as a case study, the information and findings of this research target questions relating to the future of gig work against the backdrop of international trends in consumer, employment and contractor relationships. Australia has always had access to contract workers, and a long tradition of a mobile workforce linked closely to dependence on primary production. From shearers to insurance sales, back-packer fruit pickers to academics and engineers, contract work has been integral to the economy. The 2017 Western Australian state election returned a Labour government, which is a centre-left party, and the Ministry was sworn in on 17 March 2017. The change of government signalled a new *Plan for Jobs* [30] that has at its core aversion to privatization, outsourcing and sourcing labour offshore; and a message to cultivate inclusion and diversity. The agenda of the new state government included building *brand WA*, based on global business engagement particularly with Asia and the region, investment in tourism, and a focus on embedding community attitudes, sentiments and responses in policymaking.

In 2010 the state government was selling taxi-plates, the license to operate a taxi-vehicle, for AU$192,000 each. The taxi industry was heavily regulated and the number of plates available was limited and controlled. Plates could trade on the market for around AU$320,000. Ride-share came to Western Australia in about 2014. The increase in ride-share operators led to a significant drop in trade for drivers and owners of cabs, and the trade value of plates dropped to around AU$70,000. In 2018 the state government engaged in legislation reforms to buy taxi plates back from owners by applying a 10 per cent levy on all on-demand transport fares to fund its four-year $120 million taxi plate buyback scheme. [31] Taxi drivers responded quickly to the new ride-sharing model by changing their business model and adopting apps targeting their services, while the state is engaged in market outcomes and began taking steps to regulate and levy all on-demand transport services.

At this time of increased concern about Western Australia's financial future, focus on renewing an ageing workforce, and a general worldwide trend towards increased automation of service work, the new government's *Plan for Jobs* (along with other-election commitments) sits hand-in-hand with providing AUD$750 m in savings through Public Service efficiencies achieved mainly through staffing reductions. The drive for change fueled by the search for agile and lean workplaces has had the dual effect of moving workers out of ongoing employment in long-term roles, while at the same time increasing reliance on fixed-term workers and contractors that we now know as gig workers. Balancing worker expectations for more secure work with the drive to shed jobs requires a new way of looking at employment relationships, particularly implementing flexible work and generic skills and capabilities.

Australian Tax System Suffering and Growth in Black Economy
Where people are working for themselves, on piecework or over-investing in tooling-up or business investment there is the potential for gaps to open in recording and paying taxation, Goods and Services Tax, and payroll tax. Some Academics are raising questions about the future of Australia's superannuation schemes, tax base, and welfare

caused by vulnerable workers avoiding taxation, and predatory providers avoiding employer sponsored superannuation.

Benefits and Changes to Flexible Agile Organizations
Developed in 2002, an agile approach to restructuring organisations can be applied in public sector agencies and across the sector as a whole. Agile methodology brings with it a desire for lean easily deployable workforces and flatter management structures.

"Companies can enjoy numerous benefits from working with freelancers such as a fluid workforce adaptive to change, wider access to hyper-specialised talent, cost savings, and an increase in productivity. The relationship between managers and workers must evolve, ... even the complete abolition of formal hierarchies of rank. And as we increasingly self-organize alongside others, people start to experiment in various ways, from peer to peer and open source projects to social entrepreneurship initiatives, bartering circles and new forms of lending." [32].

Interaction with Public Sector Employees
Reform of the Australian public sectors is couched in a world of work that is more than ever engaged in the global distribution of work, automation of service work (Robotic Process Automation or RPA) and offshoring and outsourcing of bundled and unbundled business processes. Moving into the second decade in this century, academic theorists argue that the speed and disruption of change that is occurring now is the fourth industrial revolution [33]. The integration of the public sector with the gig economy involves achieving the goals of the government of the day, leveraging advantages of the gig economy, and evaluating the engagement of government with the gig economy. Pre-election material urged that: "... the consolidation of Government agencies will not specifically be driven by savings but by the ability to deliver a more efficient and robust public service better placed to address challenges presented by the cyclical and largely commodities-based Western Australian economy" [31].

This acknowledgment of service over savings echoes an A.T. Kearney study (2003) that reviewed 52 agencies from the governments of Australia, Canada, France, Germany, Italy, New Zealand, the United Kingdom and the United States. Kearney explored "what makes government organizations agile, what gives them speed, flexibility and responsiveness and how these characteristics can be developed...[and] to understand what stands in the way of change?" [34].

Sourcing workers as gig workers appeals to the agile notion of short-term, highly mobile, flexible workforce. The Kearney research found the most agile government agencies "attach high value to customer service, organizational change capabilities and leadership as drivers of speed, flexibility and responsiveness. " [34]. Kearney et al. also posit culture and values, e-government, and performance management as key aspects of agility for government agencies. The challenge for public sector agencies is in leveraging the advantages of gig work while maintaining traditional inclusive management relationships with workers.

"Labour law and institutions need to catch up to the new reality of this form of work and develop new tools to protect and enhance minimum standards for workers... Unions, business and government all have a role to play in the long term" [35]. These new tools have at their base the maintenance of trust in the working relationship with the public sector and service provision to customers. Other tools linked to trust include supporting workers through regulatory stewardship [35], and enabling workers to adapt to change through more generic capabilities and broader application of skills.

10   Discussion

Platform-based apps connect workers with people who are willing to pay to get some work done. There is a market created where none existed before because the work was too costly. This appears to benefit both the worker and the consumer, and the app provider. Increasingly gig workers are becoming disenchanted with a business model that sees them working for less and less reward.

10.1   Regulation

Regulators will continue to increase pressures for full engagement of app providers with local economies. For example, in North Carolina Uber lost its Federal Court challenge to avoid paying GST [36]. Similarly, regulators are beginning to look much more closely at the app providers to determine their obligations to workers and consumers and the state, and their overall effect on the economy.

London Transport Authority said it would not renew Uber's license to operate in London because Uber's "approach and conduct demonstrate a lack of corporate responsibility in relation to issues which have potential public safety and security implications" [37]. Those issues include "Uber's approach to serious criminal offences, medical certificates, disclosure and barring checks, and the company's use of its Greyball software that TfL [Transport for London] says blocks regulatory bodies from gaining full access to Uber's app for law enforcement duties" [37].

There are many other examples of regulation entering other platform markets, for example Airbnb is attracting the attention of local authorities, and Airtasker is drawing the attention of unions, other worker organizations and registration authorities for trades and licenses.

Such internal (users demanding more return on their investment) and external pressures (greater regulation) raise questions about the sustainability of business models based on the exploitation of unregulated gaps in the market. Regulation will continue to be a problem for platform services where there are concerns for civilian safety, avoidance of taxation, and the exploitation of vulnerable workers particularly where gig work enables breaches of immigration law.

10.2   Trust and Review

"Airbnb and Uber didn't spawn 'the sharing economy', the 'on-demand economy' or 'the one-tap economy' as much as usher in a new trust economy..." [38]. Because so much of the business model is based on published reviews of the transactions between user and provider, the integrity of the reviews is crucial to consumer safety and fairness in the marketplace. Trust in the service provider has been found to be a Critical Success Factor in Offshore Business Process Outsourcing. The element of *opaque indifference*

(OI) can improve trust and in the case of platform work, many of the elements of OI (e.g. location unknown) are found in the review of the service model [39].

"Consumer trust and review are central to the wellbeing and growth of gig users" [40]. Some activities are low-risk (such as sharing a parking space, or exchanging distant, cheap services online). Participants in these transactions may be willing to take a risk and rely solely on published reviews and collated feedback available on-line. Other more risky interactions, such as engaging carers, or workers on expensive highly skilled tasks, could call for higher level screening, reference checks, and personal and public liability-insurance.

There is a role here for the state to provide consumer protection and licensing of roles and minimum capabilities to ensure fair trading and fit-for-purpose exchange [41]. "When review platforms are independent (or transparent about their commercial relationships) they promote competition by helping consumers become better informed. Review platforms reward high quality and good value products and help expose bad dealings or poor value" [42].

10.3   Benefits and Changes to Flexible Agile Organizations

Just-in-time work, Human Intelligence Task (HIT) workers, and an easily enlisted not retained workforce has benefits for business, but for many older style organizations access to these flexibilities are at odds with workplace cultures and management techniques. Eventually, the impact on deliverables is at stake, and quality mechanisms must be in place to resolve inconsistencies.

"Companies can enjoy numerous benefits from working with freelancers such as a fluid workforce adaptive to change, wider access to hyper-specialised talent, cost savings, and an increase in productivity. The relationship between managers and workers must evolve, from traditional structures that are top-down, with employees doing what they're told, to newer ones that boast self-managing teams with managers counseling workers or even the complete abolition of formal hierarchies of rank. And as we increasingly self-organize alongside others, people start to experiment in various ways, from peer-to-peer and open source projects to social entrepreneurship initiatives, bartering circles and new forms of lending" [43].

11   Outcomes: Who Cares?

There is an argument that the gig economy has enabled marginalized groups access to work. For example, in the emerging and developing economies in the African states, gig work has opened market access to both providers and users, perhaps where no market existed before. In western economies, migrant populations who may otherwise be excluded from work because of language or skill deficits can also access work. However, these vulnerable workers are also at risk of exploitation and failure to meet immigration restrictions. Similarly, international students and those on visitor visas turn to gig work as a way around working restrictions. "This choice leaves them exposed to the whims of digital platform companies that regularly reduce the terms and conditions of food delivery work" [44].

On the other hand, private social-care company called HomeTouch currently uses a gig economy platform which, "despite charging less than traditional agencies, enables staff to make 67 per cent above the national living wage—this is in contrast with the average social-care worker, who in 2014 made an hourly wage around 8 per cent above the minimum wage. It also gives employees greater flexibility than those on zero-hour contracts experience. On zero-hour contracts, it can be difficult to juggle several sources of income, as hours can clash. In contrast, work acquired through online labour platforms is booked by workers themselves, encouraged to select unpopular hours by higher rates of pay" [45].

The state, workers, customers, business (the market) are stakeholders in the gig economy with competing positions and interests.

11.1   The State

To move governments to use work-based platforms they need to shift to become more flexible and able to compartmentalize tasks for sharing. Platforms can help develop lean agile organizational structures. There are also opportunities to develop e-government processes and develop a more client centered approach to service delivery. Ways the state can interact with platform work:

Regulate? License to operate?
Due diligence expectations on corporations and employees/contractors.
Min rates? Employees, contractors, dependent contractors
Protect most vulnerable of vulnerable workers

11.2   Workers

Early organized gig workers in Australia were shearers who went on to form one of the earliest and strongest unions in the nation. Grassroots organization of workers around rights, conditions and pay has a long tradition and strong emotional appeal to those workers involved in the field [46]. Uber tried to stop workers getting organized in the US but were unsuccessful. In Australia, the New South Wales unions worked with Airtasker to compose a list of minimum rates for certain trade tasks. Internal pressure on platform and gig models will increase as workers become more organized [47].

11.3   Customers and Consumer Penchant for Ethical App Providers?

There is a consumer trend toward preferring to buy services from an ethical or sustainable enterprise. This trend also extends to app providers, for example, those with good sustainability policies, ethical approaches to inclusive employment or profit sharing with charitable or community causes.

"Collaborative consumption, often associated with the sharing economy, takes place in organized systems or networks, in which participants conduct sharing activities in the form of renting, lending, trading, bartering, and swapping of goods, services, transportation solutions, space, or money. … In 2010, sharing systems had an estimated market volume of as much as USD100bn (Lamberton and Rose 2012). Bicycle sharing represents the fastest growing trend in transportation with about 400,000 public city bikes available worldwide in 2012 (Fishman et al. 2013)" [40].

11.4   The Market

The virtual world is subject to quick start-ups with little to no capital investment or resources, and as such is subject to flooding and overcrowding as new ideas are cloned, localized, targeted to market segments and drift away or are bought out by larger predator firms. This can mean a highly volatile marketplace and quick turn over of ideas and industries.

The platform market has grown enormously in just a few years. Uber is currently valued at $70billion [37]. MyTaxi currently has 45,000 drivers using its online platform, with half of them based in Germany. "That's why Uber failed here. They aren't willing to change when they enter a new country" [28].

Vanguard organizations have the capacity to develop market share by grabbing consumer attention and remaining a market presence for the long term. The market recognition of a brand name is an asset when organizations are made public. However, the longer these organizations are in the market the more options there are for newcomers to enter. Similarly, the existing traditional service providers can adapt to adopt platform tools and techniques. It is important for entrants to build their market share quickly and divest quickly. This mimicking behavior and 'phoenixing' requires attention from traders and regulators of public trading.

The Uber business model has faults and it is possible that these faults are transferable to similar platform business models.

"The core problems with the current business model of subsidizing drivers and riders… [will] catch up with them. The debate about their aggressive culture — where apparently there is strict emphasis on performance and deadlines, and very little on mutual respect, integrity and diversity — will further intensify. At the end of the day, the big question would become whether the board and the investors take any action" [37].

Many platform-based business models are easily cloned, and there is some analysis suggesting that the online platform economy has peaked, but there is no clear evidence as to why this may have occurred.

"between October 2012 and June 2016 … growth in online platform participation has slowed. First, growth in participation in the Online Platform Economy peaked in 2014 and has slowed since then. Second, while monthly earnings on capital platforms increased by 34 percent between June 2014 and June 2016, they decreased on labour platforms by 6 percent. Third, turnover in the Online Platform Economy is high: one in six participants in any given month is new, and more than half of participants exit within 12 months. Fourth, employed, higher-income, and younger participants are more likely to exit the Online Platform Economy within a year" [48].

While there appears to be access to an unlimited workforce some have argued that the digital workforce is nomadic and lacks commitment to an organization or culture. Described as "platform nomads" [49], workers are free to move from platform to platform. When employment rates are challenging more workers of higher quality are available, but when there are shortages of the right people the just-in-time certainty of platform work drops away.

Finally, non-employed individuals are more likely than the employed to participate in labour platforms, but represent a decreasing share of participants as the unemployment rate drops. In sum, growth in online platform participation is highly dependent on attracting new participants or increasing attachment of existing participants. As outside options improve, recruiting and retaining platform workers might become increasingly difficult [48].

12 Conclusions

This paper questioned the future of the business model inherent in platform-based work. The virtual world is subject to quick start-ups with little to no capital investment or resources, and as such is subject to flooding and overcrowding as new ideas are cloned, localised, targeted to market segments and drift away or are bought out by larger predator firms. These conditions can mean a highly volatile marketplace and quick turn-over of ideas and industries.

Many of the platform business models are based on providers accessing facilitated platforms to provide services to users. The model optimizes unregulated spaces in the market to create new cheaper markets where no markets existed before. However, maintenance of high levels of user trust and demonstration of corporate social responsibility appears to be increasing in importance as a factor of success. Consumers too are moving toward seeking out collective models and socially responsible platform providers. Such internal and external pressures raise questions about the sustainability of these business models.

Regulators are beginning to look much more closely at the app providers to determine their obligations to workers and consumers and the state, and their overall effect on the economy. Where the state as user engages with gig workers as providers the relationship must foster trust both in the state as employer, and the state as service provider. There is a role for the state as steward and regulator to provide independent review, and support honest and fair consumer review, of service providers, and licenses to operate particularly where protection and safety are at issue.

References

1. Finkin, M.: Beclouded work in historical perspective. Comp. LabL. Policy J. **37**(3) (2016). University of Illinois College of Law Legal Studies Research Paper No. 16-12
2. Agrawal, A., Horton, J., Lacetera, N., Lyons, E.: Digitization and the contract labour market: a research agenda. In: Economic Analysis of the Digital Economy, pp. 219–250. University of Chicago Press, USA (2015)
3. Chung, F.: Australia's freelance economy grows to 4.1 million workers, study finds (2015). http://www.news.com.au/finance/work/at-work/australias-freelance-economy-grows-to-41-million-workers-study-finds/newsstory/629dedfaea1334077c68822f4f2a469

4. Hajkowicz, S., et al.: Tomorrow's Digitally Enabled Workforce. Megatrends and Scenarios for Jobs and Employment in Australia over the Coming Twenty Years. CSIRO, Brisbane (2016)
5. Griffiths, J.: What is the gig economy and which UK companies are part of it? From Pimlico plumbers and Amazon to Uber (2018). https://www.thesun.co.uk/money/3985964/gig-economy-meaning-definition-temporary-labor-market-uber-deliveroo/
6. Edelman, D.J.: Quantify the number of people freelancing in Australia for the second year in a row (2015). https://www.slideshare.net/upwork/freelancing-in-australia-2015/
7. Stanford, J.: The future of work is what we make it: Submission to Senate Select Committee on the future of work and workers. Australia Institute, ACT (2018)
8. Sutherland, W., Jarrahi, M.H.: The gig economy and information infrastructure: the case of the digital nomad community. In: Proceedings of the ACM on Human-Computer Interaction, vol. 1(CSCW), p. 97 (2017)
9. Hunt, A., Samman, E., Mansour-Ille, D.: Syrian Women Refugees in Jordan: Opportunity in the Gig Economy?. Overseas development institute, London (2017)
10. Australian Tax Office.: Employee or Contractor (2017). https://www.ato.gov.au/business/employee-or-contractor/
11. Pinsof, J.: A New take on an old problem: employee misclassification in the modern gig-economy. MTTLR **22**, 341 (2016)
12. Stewart, A., Stanford, J.: Regulating work in the gig economy: What are the options? Ec. Lab. Rel. Rev. **28**(3), 420–437 (2017)
13. Johnston, C.: Uber drivers are employees not contractors, California rules: Uber to appeal California Labour Commission ruling that it is 'involved in every aspect of the operation' (2015). https://www.theguardian.com/technology/2015/jun/17/uber-drivers-are-employees-not-contractors-in-california-ruling
14. Kirka, D.: Uber just lost a legal battle in the U.K. and it could have a major impact for gig economy workers (2017). https://www.inc.com/associated-press/uber-drivers-employees-not-independent-contractors-freelancers-uk-london-united-kingdom.html
15. Woody, C.: A judge in South America's biggest city says Uber drivers are employees (2017). http://www.businessinsider.com/r-sao-paulo-judge-rules-uber-drivers-are-employees-deserve-benefits-2017-4?IR=T
16. de Plevitz, L.: Dependent contractors: can the test from Stevens v Brodribb protect workers who are Quasi-Employees? QUTLJ **13**, 263–275 (1997)
17. Taylor, M., Marsh, G., Nicol, D., Broadbent, P.: Good Work: The Taylor Review of Modern Working Practices. Department for Business, Energy & Industrial Strategy, UK (2017)
18. Robertson, G.: The Future of Work and Labour's economic vision (2017). https://www.labour.org.nz/speech_by_grant_robertson_the_future_of_work_and_labour_s_economic_vision
19. Page, V.: The Rise of the gig economy (2015). https://www.investopedia.com/articles/investing/102115/rise-gig-economy.asp
20. Manyika, J., Lund, S., Bughin, J., Robinson, K., Mischke, J., Mahajon, D.: Independent Work: Choice Necessity and the Gig Economy. McKinsey Global Institute (2016)
21. Cherry, M.A., Aloisi, A.: "Dependent contractors" in the gig economy: a comparative approach. Am. UL. Rev. **66**, 635 (2016)
22. Willcocks, L.P., Lacity, M.: Service Automation Robots and the Future of Work. SB Publishing, UK (2016)
23. Hopkins, C.: Understanding the 'gig economy' and the changing world of work (2017). https://insightsresources.seek.com.au/gig-economy-changing-world-work
24. Dries, N., Pepermans, R., De Kerpel, E.: Exploring four generations' beliefs about career: is "satisfied" the new "successful"? J. Man. Psych. **23**(8), 907–928 (2008)

25. Hill, B., Secker, J., Davidson, F.: Achievement relative to opportunity: career hijacks in the academy. In: Demos, V., Berheide, C.W. Texler, M. (eds.) Gender Transformation in the Academy, pp. 85–107. Emerald Group Publishing Limited (2014)
26. Amazon (2018). https://www.mturk.com/mturk/welcome
27. Leighton, P.: Future Working: The Rise of Europe's Independent Professionals'. European Forum of Independent Professionals (2013)
28. Warren, T.: Uber loses its license to operate in Europe (2017). https://www.theverge.com/2017/9/22/16349070/uber-london-tfl-license
29. Scott, M.: As Uber stumbles, German rivals prosper (2016). https://bits.blogs.nytimes.com/2016/01/04/as-uber-stumbles-german-rivals-prosper/
30. https://www.markmcgowan.com.au/files/Jobs_policy/WA_Labors_Plan_for_Jobs.pdf (2016)
31. Hastie, H.: Taxi and Uber fares to jump after levy hits parliament, WA Today (2018). https://www.watoday.com.au/national/western-australia/taxi-and-uber-fares-to-jump-after-levy-passes-parliament-20181019-p50are.html
32. Australian Industries Group Workforce Development.: The Emergence of the Gig Economy: Thought Leader Paper, AIG Australia (2016)
33. Schwab, K.: The Fourth Industrial Revolution., World Economic Forum Geneva Switzerland, Penguin Random House LLC New York (2017)
34. PR Newswire.: Reducing costs alone won't make government agencies more effective, according to new A. T. Kearney study on agile government (2003). http://www.prnewswire.com/news-releases/reducing-costs-alone-wont-make-government-agencies-more-effective-according-to-new-at-kearney-study-on-agile-government-73191277.html
35. Minter, K.: Negotiating labour standards in the gig economy: Airtasker and Unions New South Wales. Ec. Lab. Relations Rev. **28**(3), 438–454 (2017)
36. Winson, S.: Regulatory stewardship voice of the regulator. Policy Q. **13**(4) (2017)
37. Brown M., Stuart, R.: Uber loses Federal Court Challenge in Bid to Avoid Paying GST. ABC News (2017)
38. Golson, J.: Uber used an elaborate secret program to hide from government regulators (2017). https://www.theverge.com/2017/3/3/14807472/uber-greyball-regulators-taxi-legal-vtos
39. Warren, T.: Uber loses its license to operate in London: No ban until appeal process is finished (2017). https://www.theverge.com/2017/9/22/16349070/uber-london-tfl-license
40. Hawkins, A.J.: Can Uber be saved from itself? "They have dug themselves a very deep hole" (2017). https://www.theverge.com/2017/3/6/14791080/uber-sexism-scandal-strike-waymo-lawsuit-travis-kalanick
41. Stone, B.: Summary and Analysis of the Upstarts: How Uber, AirBNB, and the Killer Companies of the New Silicon Valley are Changing the World. Worth Books, New York (2017)
42. Wreford, J., Penter, K., Pervan, G., Davidson, F.: Seeking opaque indifference in offshore BPO. In: Kotlarsky, J., Oshri, I., Willcocks, L.P. (eds.) Global Sourcing 2012. LNBIP, vol. 130, pp. 175–193. Springer, Heidelberg (2012). https://doi.org/10.1007/978-3-642-33920-2_11
43. Möhlmann, M.: Collaborative consumption: determinants of satisfaction and the likelihood of using a sharing economy option again. J. Con. Behav. **14**(3), 193–207 (2015)
44. Cannon, B., Chung, H.A.: Framework for designing co-regulation models well-adapted to technology-facilitated sharing economies. Comp. High Tech L. J. **31**(1), 23 (2015)
45. Productivity Commission.: Data Availability and Use: Inquiry Report No. 82. Canberra (2017)
46. Resch, B.: Labour 2.0: Why we shouldn't fear the 'sharing economy' and the reinvention of work (2015). https://www.alexandria.unisg.ch/248433/1/labor-2-0-why-we-shouldnt-fear-the-sharing-economy-and-the-reinvention-of-work-46959

47. Goods, C., Veen, A., Barratt, T.: Being exploited and breaching your visa: The limited choices of the food delivery worker (2017). http://theconversation.com/being-exploited-and-breaching-your-visa-the-limited-choices-of-the-food-delivery-worker-82589
48. Sundorph, E.: The gig economy could save the public sector: It has come in for a hard time of late, - but the benefits are impossible to ignore (2017). https://www.prospectmagazine.co.uk/economics-and-finance/the-gig-economy-could-save-the-public-sector
49. Spinuzzi, C.: Working alone together: coworking as emergent collaborative activity. J. Bus. Tech. Com. **26**(4), 399–441 (2012)

Organizational Controls, Social Ties and Performance in Plural Sourcing

Ilan Oshri[1]($\boxtimes$), Eleni Lioliou[2], Alexandra Gerbasi[3], and Angelika Zimmermann[4]

[1] University of Auckland Business School, Auckland, New Zealand
ilan.oshri@auckland.ac.nz
[2] School of Business and Management, Queen Mary, University of London, London, UK
e.lioliou@qmul.ac.uk
[3] University of Exeter Business School, Exeter University, Exeter, UK
A.Gerbasi@exeter.ac.uk
[4] Loughborough School of Business, Loughborough University, Loughborough, UK
A.Zimmermann@lboro.ac.uk

Abstract. This paper seeks to shed light on the effect of organizational controls and social ties on sourcing performance in a plural sourcing setting. In plural sourcing, the controller makes organizational control choices for both internal and external sourcing providers. The plural sourcing context offers the controller the benefit of insight into the effectiveness of organizational controls in each sourcing mode (i.e., external and internal), thus allowing the controller to both mitigate risk and also attempt to enhance performance where risk is not present. We therefore posited that a plural sourcing controller has three strategies to improve performance when considering the use of organizational controls. First, a controller may follow a risk-mitigation strategy against specific hazards to defuse supplier opportunistic behavior, coined here as risk-mitigating controls. Secondly, the controller may use organizational controls that enhance performance (i.e., performance-enhancing controls), while not necessarily mitigating risk. Last but not least, the controller may improve relationships with controllees in order to improve the effectiveness of organizational controls. Based on the results of a survey of senior managers involved in plural sourcing in 122 large firms in the UK and USA, we find support for the use of both risk-mitigating and performance-enhancing controls in the internal provider setting, but no support for similar strategies in the external provider setting. Instead, stronger social ties demonstrate a greater moderating effect in the external provider compared to the internal provider setting.

Keywords: Plural sourcing · Organizational controls · Survey

1 Introduction

The use of organizational control mechanisms is assumed to motivate people to achieve desired outcomes. The recent IS literature has shown growing interest in the choice of organizational controls and their effect on performance (Choudhury and Sabherwal

© Springer Nature Switzerland AG 2019
J. Kotlarsky et al. (Eds.): Global Sourcing 2018, LNBIP 344, pp. 164–185, 2019.
https://doi.org/10.1007/978-3-030-15850-7_9

2003; Gopal and Gosain 2010; Tiwana and Keil 2009; Wiener et al. 2015). In particular, previous studies have sought to understand controllers' choice of organizational controls in software development projects under various sourcing settings. One research stream has focused on the controller's choice of organizational controls when an internal team is developing software (Kirsch 1997; Kirsch et al. 2002). A related stream of studies has examined organizational controls and their effect on performance in outsourcing settings, where the software development is carried out by a third-party provider (Choudhury and Sabherwal 2003; Gopal and Gosain 2010). Tiwana and Keil (2009) compared the effect of organizational controls on software development performance between internal and external suppliers. Regardless of the sourcing setting, these studies demonstrate the importance of control mechanisms in motivating the controllee to achieve desired outcomes and the effect of control mechanisms on project performance.

Recent developments in the outsourcing industry call for a re-examination of organizational control choices (Wiener et al. 2015). First, the emergence of plural sourcing in service outsourcing (Rai et al. 2015; Sako et al. 2016; Tiwana and Kim 2016), defined as a governance form in which firms make and buy more or less similar goods and services, has presented new opportunities to examine the controller's choice of control mechanisms under a governance structure that "does not sit between the individual governance modes, but rather is a combination of multiple governance modes in their full manifestation" (Krzeminska et al. 2013, p. 1614). Indeed, plural sourcing offers the opportunity to examine organizational control choices made by a single controller for both internal and external providers. As such, a single controller is aware of both the hazards and benefits of each sourcing mode and may therefore change organizational control choices as a result. One can assume that a controller is likely to be primarily concerned with mitigating risks associated with the performance of both the internal and external provider (Tiwana and Keil 2009). For example, when viewed as an equity partnership (Das and Teng 1996), the controller of an internal provider will attempt to mitigate performance ambiguity risk by elevating the transparency of outcomes delivered by the captive center. However in the case of a non-equity partner, i.e., an external provider, the controller will seek to mitigate relational risk by tightening its relationships with the external party. However, as past studies have demonstrated, relationships with internal and external providers are characterized by certain properties that are of relevance to the choice of organizational control. Broadly speaking, relationships with an internal provider are anchored in relational governance, while those with an external provider present greater risk of opportunism, thus requiring greater use of outcome specifications (Tiwana and Keil 2009). As such, the controller of a plural sourcing arrangement may benefit from acquiring knowledge from one sourcing mode and applying it to another (e.g., acquiring outcome specifications from the external provider engagement and applying them to the internal provider setting). In the context of making choices for organizational controls in order to improve performance, the controller will seek to mitigate risks but also enhance performance based on past experiences with both internal and external providers. While the premise for such a sourcing mode is attractive, it is not yet clear whether a plural sourcing controller perceives such opportunities to improve the sourcing performance.

Second, as our study posits that the controller of a plural sourcing setting is likely to choose organizational mechanisms that mitigate risk and enhance performance, we sought to examine the moderating role of relational governance, which is widely discussed in the IS outsourcing literature as positively affecting outsourcing performance. Strong relationships, examined here as strong social ties, may indeed enhance the positive effect of certain organizational controls on performance by mitigating relational risk and promoting collaboration and cooperation between the controller and controllee.

Our findings suggest that the controller is likely to mitigate performance risk in captive center setting by applying an outcome control, but no support was found for performance enhancement in the form of self-control. Instead, a plural sourcing controller will expect clan control to improve performance in an internal sourcing setting. We found no support for the use of clan control and behavioral control as risk-mitigating and performance-enhancing strategies, respectively, in an external provider setting. Instead, a plural sourcing controller associates the use of self-control as a controllee mechanism to enhance performance (Tiwana and Keil 2009).

We also found a selective moderating effect of social ties. Social ties strengthen the positive effect of clan, behavior and self-control on performance in the case of 3rd party service providers, and outcome control in an internal service provider, but weaken the positive effect of clan on performance in the case of an internal service provider.

We contribute to the IS outsourcing literature in two ways. First, we confirm that the choice of an organizational control in internal provider setting is guided by risk mitigation logic, complemented by an informal control as performance-enhancing control. On the other hand, our study suggests that in external provider, the choice of an organizational control is guided by performance-enhancing strategy. Secondly, we demonstrate that the effect of organizational controls on performance is subject to the strength of social ties between the controller and controllee.

The remainder of the paper is organized as follows. We first review the plural sourcing and organizational control literatures. We then develop a set of hypotheses for the effect of organizational controls in internal and external provider settings on outsourcing performance. We also theorize the moderating effect of social ties. The results of our survey will then be presented followed by a discussion and suggestions for future research.

2   Theoretical Background

2.1   Plural Sourcing

Plural sourcing is a governance form in which firms make and buy more or less similar goods and services (Krzeminska et al. 2013). Research on plural sourcing has so far examined the definition of this sourcing model (Krzeminska et al. 2013), the motivation for pursuing this sourcing model (Dutta et al. 1995; Heide 2003), optimizing the utilization of internal and external providers (Puranam et al. 2013) and more recently explored the conditions under which performance in plural sourcing can be enhanced (Tiwana and Kim 2016). Indeed, plural sourcing has attracted great interest in recent years (e.g., Parmigiani 2007; Puranam et al. 2013; Rai et al. 2015; Sako et al. 2016; Tiwana and Kim 2016) as firms have moved to adopt a governance structure that does not sit between the individual governance modes, but rather is a combination of multiple governance modes in their full manifestation (Krzeminska et al. 2013, p. 1614). Plural sourcing allows firms to consider certain benefits not available under the separate governance mode for external and internal providers. For example, Dutta et al. (1995) described how when producing a similar component in-house, the firm develops a monitoring capacity relevant to contracting the production of a similar product to an external provider. Harrigan (1986) claimed that the costs of contracting out could be reduced under a plural sourcing governance structure, as the client firm is fully aware of the production costs and can therefore effectively deter the external provider from over-charging. Puranam et al. (2013) also highlighted complementarities in incentives or knowledge as one outcome of the plural sourcing governance structure, whereby there could be "improvements in the competence of internal suppliers because of procurement from external suppliers and vice versa" (Puranam et al. 2013, p. 1152).

From a transactional view, plural sourcing may prevent opportunistic behavior by either the internal or external provider. Viewing external providers as non-equity partners (i.e., 'markets') and internal providers as equity partners (i.e., 'hierarchies'), Das and Teng (1996) suggested there is less opportunistic behavior (Ouchi 1980) within equity partnerships as compared with non-equity partnerships. In particular, the relational risk in an equity partnership, i.e., the potential of having a partner who does not co-operate or behaves opportunistically (Das and Teng 1996), can be better controlled because of joint ownership, monolithic control and diminished performance ambiguity. In contrast, firms will struggle to control performance risk in an equity partnership, i.e., the risk of not achieving the alliance objectives, even when partners co-operate fully (Das and Teng 1996). This is mainly because of the high initial investments in setting up the internal venture and then the relatively high costs involved in governing the venture. On the other hand, non-equity partnership, such as contracting out work to external providers, presents a high potential for opportunistic behavior. As suggested by Das and Teng (1996, p. 838), "[B]eyond the specifics identified by the contract ex-ante, non-equity contractual agreements rely heavily on the goodwill and voluntary co-operation from independent firms". Therefore, as partners realize that they lack the means to deal with such opportunism, a non-equity partnership will present challenges in controlling relational risk. However, non-equity partners can easily control performance risk by either exiting the relationship without incurring heavy costs, or by controlling for the level of commitment to secure their returns (Gopal and Koka 2012).

Controlling opportunistic behavior has been examined in the organizational control literature. In this regard, organizational controls have been described as the means through which firms "motivate individuals to achieve desired objectives [..] exercised via formal and informal modes" (Kirsch et al. 2002). We now turn to the literature on organizational control and its implications for plural sourcing governance.

2.2   Organizational Control Mechanisms

Most relevant studies refer to four main control mechanisms (Ouchi 1979), namely outcome, behavior, self and clan. Behavior and outcome are classified as formal modes of control, while self and clan are categorized as informal. Moreover, the extant literature (e.g., Gopal and Gosain 2010; Kirsch et al. 2002) assumes that there is a controller and a controllee in both intra- or inter-organizational settings, and the controllee is expected to respond to certain mechanisms, rituals and procedures put forward by the controller (Kirsch 2004). As a formal control mode, outcome-based control will see the controller specifying parameters of desired outcomes for the controllee and evaluating the controllee's performance based on whether these targets have been met, while giving the controllee the freedom to pursue his approach to achieving these goals (Kirsch et al. 2002). In behavior control, the other formal mode, the controller instigates rules, steps and procedures for the controllee to follow. Assessment of the controllee's performance is based on the degree to which the controllee adheres to the specified procedures (Gopal and Gosain 2010; Kirsch et al. 2002). Kirsch et al. (2002) argue that formal control modes "share a common underlying assumption that the controllers and controllees have incongruent goals, and they both align by providing appropriate incentives to the employees" (p. 486).

In terms of informal control modes, clan control takes place when controllees adopt the same values and beliefs and feel they belong to the same group within the organization and hence are committed to achieving the group goals (Kirsch et al. 2002). Individual members will then be assessed on the basis of whether they have acted in accordance with the group's values and norms. The self-control modes assumes intrinsic motivation on behalf of the controllee, who sets their own goals, monitors their own achievements, and rewards or sanctions themselves accordingly (Kirsch et al. 2002, p. 486). In this regard, the controller does not directly exercise control over controllees but rather encourages them to exercise self-control via personal development training or task definition and structuring (Kirsch et al. 2002). Controllers often use the various types of control in combination to create a portfolio of controls (Choudhury and Sabherwal 2003; Kirsch 1997).

The information systems literature has seen significant development in understanding choice of controls, their evolution over a project life and their impact on performance (Wiener et al. 2015). For example, Choudhury and Sabherwal (2003, p. 313) identified the evolution of a portfolio of controls over five outsourcing projects. They confirmed that in the context of outsourcing as well as internal software development, firms use a range of control mechanisms. Further, they concluded that many findings relating to the use of control mechanisms in an internal provider setting also apply to outsourcing, but with a greater emphasis on outcome controls in the beginning of the outsourcing project and behavioral controls coming into play later in the project. Gopal and Gosain (2010) examined the effect of control mechanisms on project performance in an outsourcing setting from the controllee's viewpoint (i.e., supplier). They identified a moderating role for boundary spanning activities in eliminating knowledge gaps between the vendor and the client firm. Tiwana and Keil (2009, p. 32) compared the use of controls between internal and external providers, although as separate governance modes. They found that "[…] controllers attempt to use controller-driven control mechanisms (outcome, behavior, and clan control) to a greater degree in outsourced projects relative to internal projects. Controllers also attempt to use controllee-driven control mechanisms (i.e., self-control) to a greater degree in internal projects relative to outsourced projects".

It is within this stream of research that our paper seeks to shed further light on the relationships between the choice of organizational controls and performance, but in the context of plural sourcing. Tiwana and Keil (2009) have asserted that control mechanisms achieve varied effects on performance depending on the setting. In the case of internal projects, the control relationship spans an internal departmental boundary, while in outsourced projects it spans an inter-organizational boundary. In this regard, plural sourcing poses a risk of opportunism by both internal and external providers (or equity and non-equity partners). Equity partnerships will find it hard to control performance risk because of performance ambiguity within the venture, while non-equity partnerships will struggle to control relational risk (Das and Teng 1996). In order to meet desired performance, the controller of a plural sourcing is likely to first and foremost mitigate either formal or informal risk. At the same time, a controller may seek opportunities to apply certain controls that enhance performance when either performance or relational risk is not present. For example, as risk mitigation in equity partnerships, the controller is likely to apply formal mechanisms that allow performance ambiguity risks to be eliminated, while encouraging the use of informal controls that enhance the positive effects on performance of the parent firm's social ties and joint objectives with the captive (Oshri 2011).

We seek to advance our understanding of how the application of various controls in plural sourcing both mitigates opportunism and enhances performance. The risk of opportunism exists in outsourcing relationships regardless of control strategies applied by the controller, simply because contracts cannot accommodate solutions for all exchange hazards without incurring the cost of being too complex to effectively govern the relationships (Gopal and Koka 2012). A stream of studies has persistently argued that non-contractual elements in outsourcing relationships, also known as the relational dimension in outsourcing (Tate and Ellram 2009), may safeguard against opportunism in outsourcing. Strong relationships between the client firm and the provider are seen as enacting the flexibility required to overcome stiff contractual arrangements (Gulati 1995). Several studies have argued for complementarity (as opposed to substitution) between relational and contractual governance (Goo et al. 2009; Poppo and Zenger 2002; Vlaar et al. 2007). As such, we will examine the role that social ties play in motivating individuals to achieve certain desired targets via the application of organizational control. The organizational control literature has so far paid little attention to the moderating role of the relational dimension in outsourcing, although relational governance has persistently been mentioned as having a positive effect on outsourcing performance (Lacity et al. 2010). To our knowledge, Gopal and Gosain (2010) is the only study to have examined such effects. They proposed that boundary-spanning activities in the form of interactions between the client firm and provider moderate the effect of modes of control on project performance. This is a critical interface in any outsourcing arrangement, however one that does not address the risk of opportunism in the client and provider relationship.

Alternatively, the relational dimension in outsourcing is commonly understood as the unwritten, worker-based mechanisms designed to influence inter-organizational behavior (e.g., Macneil 1980; Poppo and Zenger 2002). These manifest via the strength of social ties (Child 2001; Granovetter 1973; Storck 2000) between the client firm and the provider and may complement the contractual arrangement, offering relational flexibility (Gopal and Koka 2012) beyond the guidance and incentives available via organizational controls. The strength of social ties can be defined as the closeness and the frequency of interactions (Hansen 1999) between the provider and client firm. Developing strong social ties comes at a cost and they are not always viewed as necessary to mitigate a collaborative risk. As such, a client firm may only consider investing in relational governance via strong social ties to mitigate contractual risks if such an investment is less costly than the damages incurred by opportunistic behavior of the partner.

Having identified that the junction between organizational controls, social ties and performance is in need of further development, we now offer a set of hypotheses.

3 Hypotheses Development

Central to the hypotheses development is the assumption that a controller seeks to mitigate performance ambiguity and relational risk, thus maximizing performance, by exercising certain control mechanisms. In considering which control mechanisms will lead to better performance, the controller examines the nature of the risk in the partnership with the internal and external provider. In the face of high-performance ambiguity or relational risk, we argue that the controller will seek to exercise a mitigating control mechanism. On the other hand, the presence of low risk for either performance ambiguity or relational risk may lead the controller to exercise a performance-enhancing control in order to maximize performance.

In the case of equity partnership, the controller is likely to assume high performance ambiguity risk and high exit barriers.

Consider the case of a captive center that provides knowledge or business process services to a parent firm. Here the high dependencies between the parent firm and the captive center require the parent firm to invest effort in task coordination and knowledge sharing between the parent firm and the captive (Srikanth and Puranam 2011). Further, governing performance in captive centers is often shared between the parent firm and the captive center (Oshri 2011), thus elevating the level of ambiguity with regard to the captive center's contribution to performance. In addition, high initial investment in the captive center may result in limited flexibility to exit the equity partnership, thus elevating performance ambiguity risk because the controller will be unlikely to pursue an immediate termination of the venture in the case of negative performance. As such, the controller is likely to mitigate the risk of high levels of performance ambiguity by seeking to increase the degree of performance transparency through the exercise of outcome controls. Therefore,

H1: In a plural sourcing equity partnership, such as in a captive center setting, higher levels of outcome-based controls as the risk-mitigating strategy will be associated with higher performance.

An equity partnership suggests a joint set of objectives between the parties involved. Consider again the example of a captive center that provides knowledge or business process services to the parent firm. Similarly to internal development projects, it is less likely that the captive center will act in an opportunistic way that damages the parent firm (Tiwana and Keil 2009). Rapport between onshore and offshore captive center counterparts has been found to improve performance (Kotlarsky and Oshri 2005), with captive center employees reported to develop organizational identification and a collaborative attitude (Levina and Vaast 2008) critical to the success of the partnership. Other sources of concern that are often associated with worsening performance, such as security and confidentiality, have been found to be mitigated in the case of captive centers (Carmel and Agarwal 2002). As such, captive center counterparts are likely to develop a sense of trust with and belonging to the parent firm and identify with the parent firm's objectives and values. The controller is therefore likely to perceive the relational risk as low, posing little threat to the equity partnership performance. However, as trust between the parties is high, the controller is likely to encourage the controllee to assume further responsibilities to enhance performance by developing the unit's capabilities through offering its staff training, personal development and a career path (Oshri 2011). The controller will therefore expect the captive to set its own goals and objectives and develop a strategic path for growth and efficiency (Oshri and Van Uhm 2012) that is likely to lead to better performance. Therefore,

H2: In a plural sourcing equity partnership, such as in a captive center setting, higher levels of self control as performance-enhancing strategy will be associated with higher levels of performance.

Non-equity partnerships entail a relational risk (Das and Teng 1996). Consider the case of outsourcing a function to a third-party service provider. The lack of shared ownership of the outsourcing venture between the client firm and the supplier is likely to make it difficult to align their objectives, thus retaining a high degree of opportunistic behavior within the partnership (Choudhury and Sabherwal 2003; Das and Teng 1996; Tiwana and Keil 2009). On the other hand, the ability of the controller to assess performance through the monitoring of service level agreements and clauses in the contract is rather high. As such, there is little performance ambiguity with regard to the outcomes delivered from the outsourced function, as the responsibility to deliver resides with the supplier. However, the controller has little control over the behavior of the controllee in terms of processes and methodologies followed in the delivery of the service. It has therefore been suggested that as performance ambiguity is low in the case of non-equity partnership, a possible performance-enhancing strategy is to apply behavior control to "regulate the conduct of partners to prevent major surprises" (Das and Teng 2001, p. 261). A plural sourcing controller may have exposure to processes and methodologies from dealing with their internal provider, and therefore can benefit by applying these experiences when dealing with an external provider. We therefore posit,

H3: In plural sourcing non-equity partnership, such as in a third party outsourcing setting, higher levels of behavioral control as performance-enhancing strategy will be associated with higher levels of performance.

Non-equity partnerships are prone to relational risk, and the lack of joint objectives between the client firm and its suppliers has been reported to result in heightened relational risk in outsourcing. For example, the supplier's efforts to secure profitability may result in worsening performance of the outsourcing venture and thus deteriorating relationships with the client. Under such exchange hazards, the controller is likely to consider using a risk-mitigating organizational control in an attempt to restore the performance of the outsourcing venture. Further, as the outcomes of an outsourcing venture can be manipulated by the supplier through an opportunistic staffing strategy that secures acceptable levels of profitability, the controller is likely to apply measures that promote relational flexibility as an alternative strategy. In this regard, the controller will seek to improve relationships with the supplier by promoting and rewarding supplier behavior to create a sense of belonging to the non-equity partnership, and shared values, beliefs and norms within the partnership (Choudhury and Sabherwal 2003; Kirsch 1997). We therefore posit,

H4: In plural sourcing non-equity partnership, such as in a third-party outsourcing setting, higher levels of clan control as risk-mitigating strategy will be associated with higher levels of performance.

The IS outsourcing literature includes in-depth discussion of the positive effect of strong relationships on outsourcing performance (Lacity et al. 2010). These findings have implications for the study of control mechanisms and their impact of performance. On the one hand, the effectiveness of control mechanisms designed to motivate individuals to achieve desired performance can be undermined by one of the partners. For example, a supplier seeking to safeguard against performance hazards within a non-equity partnership may pursue a staffing strategy that distorts the effect of the outcome control mechanism. On the other hand, the effectiveness of a control mechanism can be limited, in particular when the conditions for behavior change of the controllee are not conducive to the nature of the control mechanism. For example, the application of outcome control in equity partnerships may not reduce performance ambiguity as the contribution of the parent firm and the captive center cannot be de-coupled, and under certain conditions may possibly erode the relationships between the units. In both cases, strong relationships between the controller and the controllee in the form of strong social ties may improve the effectiveness of a control mechanism applied by the controller. Strong social ties are likely to be developed within a partnership where there is trust between the parties and high frequency communications between the controller and controllee. Such a partnership is conducive to avoiding opportunism and will promote relational flexibility in the course of conflict resolution or negotiations. We therefore suggest,

H5: In plural sourcing equity and non-equity partnerships, strong social ties between partners will strengthen the positive effect of formal and informal modes of control on outsourcing performance.

Our theoretical model is depicted in Fig. 1.

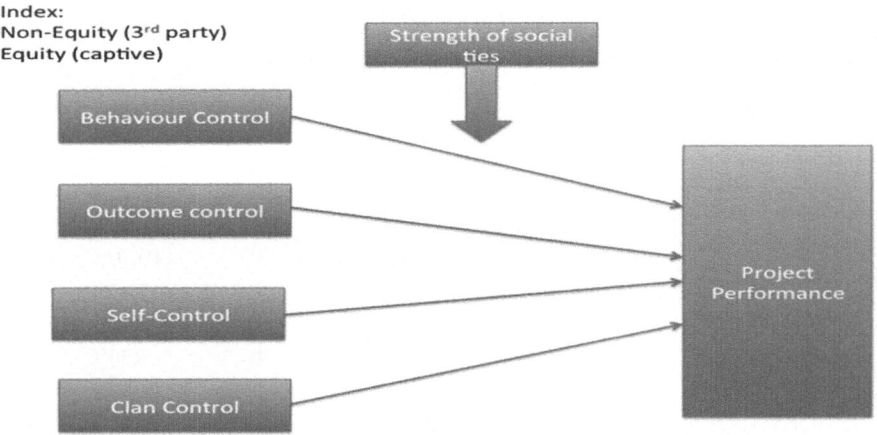

Fig. 1. Theoretical model.

4 Methods

4.1 Data Collection

We conducted an online survey of a sample of UK and US firms with more than 3000 employees in 2013. Senior managers involved in making decisions about both internal and external sourcing within the organization were asked to respond to a survey regarding: (a) the most valuable internal sourcing relationship; and (b) the most valuable external sourcing relationship. This study applied a "key informant" methodology for data collection (Goo et al. 2008; Kumar et al. 1993; Segars and Grover 1998).

Having completed the design of our questionnaire in June 2013, we performed content testing by collecting comments on the wording used in the questionnaire from several experts from academia and the outsourcing industry. This was followed by minor modifications of the questionnaire. We then conducted a pilot study using an online survey provider. Our pilot study took place at the end of June 2013. Over 100 firms were contacted initially and 20 fully completed questionnaires were obtained, resulting in a response rate of 19% for the pilot phase.

Following the pilot, over 980 firms were contacted, resulting in 150 fully completed surveys, a response rate of 15.3%. Of the 150 completed surveys, 28 were omitted because the firms did not use plural sourcing, hence our final sample of 122. Based on the data, there was not a significant difference between the demographic characteristics of the firms that responded and those that did not. Overall, the respondents represented a diversity of firms across multiple industries. For a full description of the firms, see Table 1.

The respondents worked in a range of areas within their firm: owner/board executive (6.67%), finance (9.33%), IT (69.33%), facilities (2.67%), marketing (1.33%), customer services (4%), human resources (2%), logistics (2.67%) and other (2%).

Services were sourced in the areas of: application management, software testing, data warehousing, ERP systems, finance and accounting, human resources, procurement, contact centers, legal services and research and development. Table 2 displays the proportion of each service provided by both equity and non-equity partnerships.

Table 1. Description of the sample

Description of the firms			
		Frequency	Percentage
Location	United Kingdom	60	49.18%
	United States	62	50.81%
Firm sector	Financial services	21	17.20%
	Manufacturing	23	18.90%
	Retail, distribution and transport	13	10.70%
	Pharmaceutical	9	7.40%
	Electronics	9	7.40%
	Energy	4	3.30%
	Insurance	14	11.50%
	Telecommunication	13	10.70%
	Public sector	4	3.30%
	Other commercial sector	1	0.81%
	Other non-commercial sector	11	9.00%
Firm size	3000 to 5000 employees	31	25.40%
	5000 to 10,000 employees	38	31.10%
	More than 10,000 employees	53	43.40%
Respondent characteristics			
Respondent position	Owner/Board executive	6	4.90%
	Finance	11	9.00%
	IT	86	70.50%
	Facilities	4	3.30%
	Marketing	2	1.50%
	Customer services	6	4.90%
	Human resources	2	1.60%
	Logistics	3	2.50%
	Other	2	1.60%

Table 2. Types of services provided by the sourcing arrangement

	Equity sourcing arrangement		Non-equity arrangement	
	Frequency	Percentage	Frequency	Percentage
Application management	71	58.20%	115	94.30%
Software testing	71	58.20%	111	91.00%
Data warehousing	71	58.20%	104	85.20%
ERP systems	54	44.30%	97	79.50%
Finance & accounting	45	36.90%	96	78.70%
Human resources	49	40.20%	93	76.20%
Procurement	40	32.80%	93	76.20%
Contact centers	45	36.90%	103	84.40%
Legal services	34	27.90%	93	76.20%
Research & development	35	28.70%	89	73.00%

Each of our respondents responded to a series of questions regarding both equity and non-equity partnerships. In order to more clearly present the results of the analysis, we have presented the analysis for equity and non-equity partnerships separately.

4.2   Measurement

Dependent Variable. Measures developed Grover et al. (1996) and Heckman and King (1994) were used to assess performance. Performance consisted of four items rated on a five-point Likert scale ranging from 1 (strongly disagree) to 5 (strongly agree): "the products/services delivered meet our expectations"; "we have met our goals"; "we have achieved our desired cost savings"; "we are satisfied with the overall benefits we have received".

Independent Variables. Modes of control were based on measures from Kirsch (2002). We measured four modes of control: clan control, behavioral control, outcome control and self-control.

The clan control segment consisted of three items rated on a five-point Likert scale ranging from 1 (strongly disagree) to 5 (strongly agree): "we actively participate in meetings with them to understand their values, norms and goals"; "we are a 'regular' member of the project team that includes them and our representatives"; "we place a significant weight on understanding their goals, values and norms".

Behavioral control consisted of three items rated on a five-point Likert scale ranging from 1 (strongly disagree) to 5 (strongly agree): "expect them to follow an understandable written sequence of steps in delivering their services"; "assess the extent to which they follow existing written procedures when delivering the outsourced service"; "anticipate that they apply acceptable practices and methodologies when delivering the outsourced service".

Outcome control consisted of three items rated on a five-point Likert scale ranging from 1 (strongly disagree) to 5 (strongly agree): "evaluate their performance by the extent to which services were delivered as defined in the contract, regardless of how this goal was accomplished"; "check regularly about progress achieved regardless of the actions taken by them"; "test intermediary and/or final outcomes/deliverables against criteria defined in the contract, regardless of how these outcomes were achieved".

Self-control consisted of three items rated on a five-point Likert scale ranging from 1 (strongly disagree) to 5 (strongly agree): "noticed that they defined specific proce-dures for delivering services, without our involvement"; "noticed that they decided on the methodologies to use for delivering services, without our involvement"; "noticed that they made changes where needed to ensure service delivery, without our involvement"[1].

Moderating Variables. *Strength of Social Ties.* We examined strength of social ties using a series of items rated on a five-point Likert scale ranging from 1 (strongly disagree) to 5 (strongly agree). Our measure for strength of social ties was based on

---

[1] This item was developed by the authors.

Chiu et al. (2006) scale, which combines closeness of ties and communication frequency (based on Hansen 1999). Respondents were asked to indicate the strength of the ties between their firm and their most valuable internal and external sourcing relationship based on the following items: "we maintain close social relationships with some members of the vendor/global in-house center"; "we know some members of the vendor/global in-house center on a personal level"; "we spend a lot of time interacting with some members of the vendor/global in-house center"; "we have frequent communications with some members of the vendor/global in-house center" (α = .880).

The means, standard deviations and correlations of all variables included in the analysis are presented in Table 3.[2]

Table 3. Means, standard deviations and intercorrelations of variables of interest

Equity partnerships	Mean	s.d.	1	2	3	4	5
1 Performance	4.06	0.76	–				
2 Clan control	4.04	0.86	0.48	–			
3 Behavioral control	3.98	0.86	0.58	0.65	–		
4 Outcome control	3.90	0.80	0.49	0.64	0.78	–	
5 Self control	3.47	1.08	0.21	0.27	0.31	0.34	–
6 Strength of social ties	4.01	0.86	0.51	0.53	0.59	0.61	0.22
Non-equity partnerships							
1 Performance	3.87	0.54	–				
2 Clan control	4.04	0.72	0.63	–			
3 Behavioral control	4.05	0.76	0.57	0.52	–		
4 Outcome control	4.01	0.71	0.05	–0.02	0.13	–	
5 Self control	3.83	0.67	0.67	0.53	0.62	0.24	–
6 Strength of social ties	3.82	0.81	0.71	0.44	0.42	–0.01	0.53

All correlations greater than ±0.16 are significant at the 0.01 level

4.3   Common Methods Variance

In order to test for common methods variance (CMV) we conducted Harman's single-factor test (Podsakoff et al. 2003). Common methods bias was not indicated as high, as more than one factor emerged to explain the variance in our analysis. In addition, no one factor accounted for the majority of covariance between the measures. Accordingly we met both criteria set forth by Podsakoff et al. (2003) for determining if a detrimental level of common method bias exists. We also conducted a second test to control for the effects of an unmeasured latent method factor. In this test, only four of the paths from CMV to single-indicator constructs were significant, indicating a small amount of CMV.

---

[2] Initially we controlled for firm size and sector, the services provided by the sourcing arrangement, the number and length of contracts between the firm and their sourcing vendor. We did not find that these variables had a significant effect on either the dependent or mediating variables. The inclusion or exclusion of these variables did not alter the magnitude, direction or significance of the variables of interest on the dependent variables, and hence we did not include these variables in the final models in order to preserve the parsimony of the models.

5   Analysis and Results

In order to test our hypotheses we estimated a series of linear regression models[3]. We included the modes of control in Model 1 in order to test Hypotheses 1–4. In Model 2 we added the effect of the strength of the social ties, and in Model 3 we included the

Table 4. Linear regression results predicting performance

Equity partnerships	Model 1		Model 2		Model 3	
	B	S.E.	B	S.E.	B	S.E.
Clan control	0.16	0.06*	0.35	0.10*	0.72	0.26*
Behavioral control	0.04	0.11	0.12	0.08	0.87	0.57
Outcome control	0.39	0.10**	−0.04	0.11	−1.74	0.52*
Self control	0.01	0.05	0.02	0.05	−0.45	0.32
Strength of social ties			0.22	0.08**	−0.64	0.22**
Clan control X strength of social ties					−0.16	0.07*
Behavioral control X strength of social ties					−0.12	0.14
Outcome control X strength of social ties					0.43	0.13**
Self control X strength of social ties					0.10	0.07
Constant	1.64	0.34	1.34	0.35	4.77	0.84
R^2		0.36		0.39		0.49
ΔR^2		0.35		0.03		0.10
Non-equity partnerships	Model 1		Model 2		Model 3	
	B	S.E.	B	S.E.	B	S.E.
Clan control	0.03	0.05	0.02	0.05	−0.37	0.22
Behavioral control	−0.01	0.07	0.02	0.06	0.89	0.29*
Outcome control	−0.05	0.05	−0.02	0.04	−0.07	0.18
Self control	0.42	0.08**	0.25	0.08**	−0.83	0.39*
Strength of social ties			0.28	0.04**	−0.38	0.29
Clan control X strength of social ties					0.15	0.05*
Behavioral control X strength of social ties					−0.23	0.07*
Outcome control X strength of social ties					0.00	0.05
Self control X strength of social ties					0.27	0.09*
Constant	1.27	0.27	0.95	0.23	3.93	1.19
R^2		0.61		0.72		0.74
ΔR^2		0.59		0.11		0.02

---

[3] Due to the nested nature of our data we initially estimated general linear mixed models (Hox 2002; West et al. 2007). We incorporated the firm level variables, as well as the sampling strategy at level 1 by including a random intercept. At level 2, we incorporated the types of control as well as the strength of the social networks. This tactic resulted in a series of complicated interaction effects, including three-way interactions, to test hypothesis 5. Subsequently, we split the samples, and tested the relationships separately for equity and non-equity partnerships. The results did not differ between the two methods of testing, so we have presented the linear regression models for ease of interpretation. The results from the general linear mixed models are available upon request.

interaction effects between modes of control and the strength of social ties in order to test Hypothesis 5 (all interaction terms were mean-centered prior to being entered into the equation).

In the upper half of Table 4 we present the results for equity based partnerships (Hypotheses 1 and 2), and in the lower half we present the results for non-equity based partnerships (Hypotheses 3 and 4). We found support for Hypothesis 1 in Model 1 for equity based partnerships. The higher the use of outcome-based controls, the higher the performance of the partnership ($b = 0.39$, $p < .01$). We did not find support for Hypothesis 2, as the relationship between the use of self-control and performance is not significant ($b = 0.01$, $p = $ n.s). In addition, we found a positive and significant effect of clan control on performance ($b = 0.16$, $p < .05$), but did not find a relationship between behavior control and performance.

As seen in the lower half of Table 4 focusing on non-equity partnerships, we did not find a significant relationship between behavioral-control and performance, thereby failing to support Hypotheses 3. Neither did we find a significant relationship between clan control and performance, thereby failing to support Hypothesis 4. In addition, we found a positive and significant effect of self-control on performance ($b = 0.42$, $p < .01$), but did not find a relationship between outcome control and performance.

For Hypothesis 5, Model 2 first tested the main effect strength of social ties on performance in plural sourcing equity and non-equity partnerships. We found that in both cases, the stronger the social ties the higher the performance (equity partnerships, $b = 0.22$, $p < .01$; non-equity partnerships, $b = 0.28$, $p < .05$). Finally, in Model 3, we focused on the interaction effects between modes of control and strength of the relationship proposed in Hypothesis 5.

For the equity partner condition, we found that the interaction between outcome control and strength of social ties is positive and significant ($b = 0.43$, $p < .05$), indicating that when there are high levels of outcome control and strong social ties, equity partnerships will likely show higher levels of performance (a visual depiction of this can be seen in Fig. 2). We found a negative interaction between clan control and the strength of social ties ($b = -0.16$, $p < .05$). This indicates that when there are high levels of clan control and strong social ties, performance is likely to be lower. We did not find a significant interaction between self-control and strength of social ties.

For non-equity conditions, we found that the interaction between behavioral control and strength of social ties is positive and significant ($b = -0.23$, $p < .05$), indicating that when there are high levels of behavioral control and strong social ties, non-equity partnerships show lower levels of performance (a visual depiction of this can be seen in Fig. 3). We also found a positive and significant effect for clan control and strength of social ties ($b = 0.15$, $p < .05$), indicating that when there are high levels of clan control and strong social ties, non-equity partnerships show higher levels of performance (a visual depiction is presented in Fig. 4).

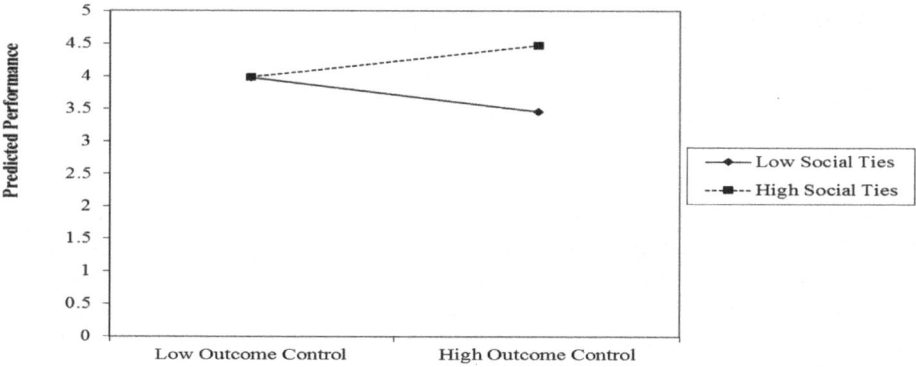

Fig. 2. Interaction of outcome control and strength of social ties in the equity condition

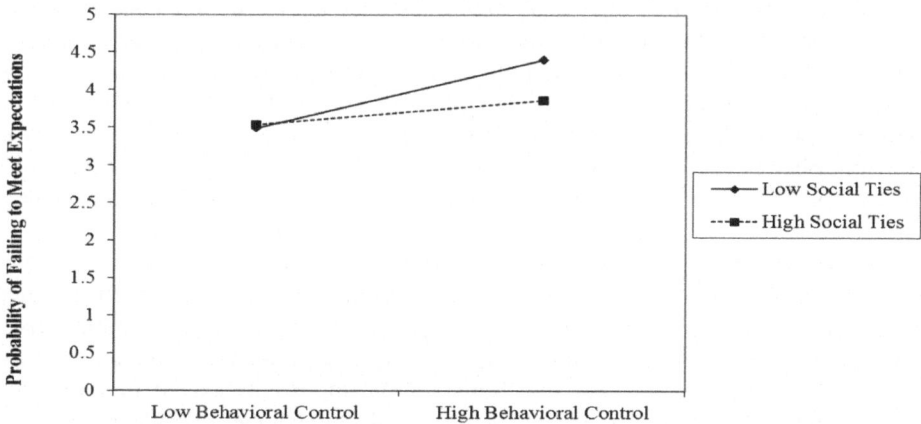

Fig. 3. Interaction between behavioral control and strength of social ties in non-equity partnerships

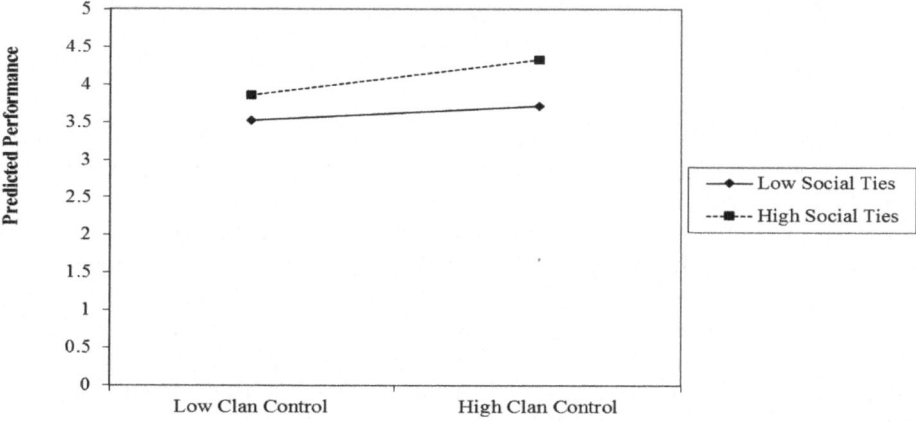

Fig. 4. Interaction between clan control and strength of social ties in non-equity partnerships

6 Discussion

We sought to examine the relationships between organizational controls, social ties and performance in a plural sourcing setting (Gulati and Puranam 2006; Krzeminska et al. 2013; Sako et al. 2016; Tiwana and Kim 2016). Our assumption was that the plural sourcing context places the controller in an advantageous position, where he or she will be able to consider both risk-mitigating and performance-enhancing controls in order to improve performance. Further, we assumed a plural sourcing controller will seek to enhance performance via strengthening social ties. Our results support the idea of using risk-mitigating controls in the form of outcome control in the internal provider setting, but offer no support for the use of risk-mitigating control (i.e., clan) in the external provider setting. Further, we did not find support for the use of performance-enhancing controls with either internal or external providers. Instead, with an internal provider, controllers seek to improve performance via the use of clan control, and for an external provider with the use of self-control. While risk mitigation strategy against performance ambiguity is evident in the internal provider setting, the use of performance-enhancing strategy in this setting is not the outcome of the controller learning from his or her external provider experience. Rather it is an attempt to maximize the effect of lower relational risk in the internal provider setting in order to maximize performance. The controller is also pursuing a performance-enhancing strategy when using self-control with his or her external supplier. However, this is possibly based on past experience in promoting initiatives and innovations from captive centers.

Indeed, our study found support for H1, whereby outcome control has a positive and significant effect on performance in equity partnership such as in a captive center setting. In such a setting, the controller will predominantly face less relational risk, however will be required to mitigate high levels of performance ambiguity risk by using an outcome control (Das and Teng 2001). Our results extend past findings (Tiwana and Keil 2009) to demonstrate that in plural sourcing the controller seeks ways to mitigate against performance ambiguity by using outcome controls. Such risk mitigation is an outcome of the plural sourcing controller's advantageous position from having observed outcome control applied in the external provider setting (Tiwana and Keil 2009). The controller is thus allowed to benefit from his unique position and re-apply knowledge acquired from one sourcing model to another (Puranam et al. 2013).

No support was found for H2, in which we hypothesized that the controller will seek to improve performance in equity partnership through the use of self-control as a performance-enhancing strategy. Equity partnerships have traditionally been characterized as offering high levels of trust and socialization between the parties (Das and Teng 2001; Kotlarsky and Oshri 2005). However, our study suggests that granting the controllee autonomy to pursue their own initiatives, further develop the captive center and seek growth opportunities will not result in better performance for the plural sourcing setting. One explanation for this rather surprising result is that self-control is unlikely to lead to higher performance because of the tight control the parent is likely to exercise over its subsidiaries in an attempt to limit investment in the subsidiary and restrain the subsidiary from pursuing initiatives and innovations that require injection of capital and resources (Oshri 2011).

In the case of non-equity partnerships, we did not find support for H3 in which higher levels of behavioral control, as a performance-enhancing act, would improve the performance of the plural sourcing setting. Our assumption was that the controller would aim to improve the controllee's performance by closely tracking certain behaviors and processes by the controllee (Das and Teng 2001). The lack of support for this assumption suggests that in non-equity partnerships, such as when outsourcing to a third-party provider, the controller lacks the ability to monitor how the third party provider performs the outsourced task, thus mainly relying on specifying desired outcomes as a risk-mitigation strategy. This result can be interpreted as demonstrating that the plural sourcing controller is unable to transfer the knowledge gained from managing a captive to the context of the external provider.

We did not find support for H4 either, thus concluding that the controller of a plural sourcing mode does not consider clan control as mitigating rational risk in non-equity partnership. As such, our results support past studies' claims that non-equity partnerships pose great difficulties in terms of spatial and cultural distance for the enactment of clan control (Carmel and Agarwal 2002; Chua et al. 2012; Wiener et al. 2015). Wiener et al. (2015) suggested that promoting clan control appears to be challenging in inter-organizational relationships, particularly in the offshore outsourcing context. They argued that while there can be frequent interactions and shared frames of reference between clients and providers, these may not be sufficient to promote the strong social cohesion and shared social norms essential for the enactment of clan control. As such, our results suggest that the unique case of plural sourcing does not offer the controller the opportunity to transfer experiences from the internal provider to the external provider setting.

Surprisingly, we found that in the external provider setting, performance is associated with self control, i.e., the external provider pursues initiatives to introduce changes and new methodologies while delivering the service. We see this result as relating to performance-enhancing strategies, in particular in areas where the controller may have had similar experience working with its internal provider (e.g., captive center) and such innovations emerged over time.

Finally, our study supports past observations that greater social ties between providers and clients are likely to enhance performance (Kotlarsky and Oshri 2005; Lacity et al. 2010). Further, we found selective support for the moderating effect of social ties on the relationships between control mechanisms and performance in plural sourcing (H5). In the case of equity partnership, i.e., internal provider, strong social ties between the controller and controllee magnify the positive effect of high levels of clan and outcome controls on performance, and of maintaining the risk-mitigation strategy while attempting to improve performance by using clan control.

In the case of non-equity partnership, greater social ties signify the positive effect of self and clan control on performance, but result in a negative effect on the relationship between behavior control and performance. Broadly speaking, we confirm past observations that relational governance positively affects outsourcing performance (Lacity et al. 2010). However, we have demonstrated that the positive effect of social ties on outsourcing performance can also be indirect, impacting the controller's choice of an organizational control vis-a-vis the sourcing model chosen, i.e., internal or external provider. Interestingly, the role of social ties in enhancing the effect of control mechanisms on performance in the external provider setting is greater than in the internal provider setting. Indeed, it appears that controls come into effect, either positively or negatively, in the external provider setting when social ties are strong. Last but not least, one surprising result is the negative moderation effect of social ties on the relationship between clan control and performance in equity partnership. Das and Teng (2001) argue that equity partnerships are ideal organizational settings for the enactment of social and clan control. This is simply because partner firms are open to the idea of employing similar socialization, communication and training mechanisms among their staff, often resulting in enhancement of partnership performance. However, our study suggests that strong social ties weaken the positive effect of clan control on performance in equity partnership, where an excessive investment in socialization may become counter-productive, resulting in a diminishing performance.

6.1 A Plural Sourcing View on Organizational Controls

The extant plural sourcing literature has so far focused on aspects concerning the optimization of the amount of work carried out by an internal and external provider, and the learning implications for the client firm that may diffuse opportunistic behavior toward the external provider. A common focus of the numerous studies on plural sourcing are the choices made by managers (e.g., the optimal ratio of outsourcing versus in-house development) as they weigh the risks and returns of such decisions (Krzeminska et al. 2013; Puranam et al. 2013; Sako et al. 2016; Tiwana and Kim 2016). Our study extends the plural sourcing literature by considering the effect of control choices on performance. More specifically, we show that a controller of plural sourcing may benefit from managing both internal and external providers. Indeed, in the case of an internal provider, a plural sourcing controller is mainly concerned with risk mitigation, thus applying outcome control, a property of the external provider setting (Tiwana and Keil 2009), in an attempt to improve performance. In the case of an external provider, a plural sourcing controller uses self-control to enhance performance, a property of the internal provider setting (Tiwana and Keil 2009). Indeed, our study shows that a plural sourcing controller is more selective in applying controls, choosing only those that mitigate risk or enhance performance, rather than widely applying various controls as reported for an individual governance mode (Tiwana and Keil 2009).

Our study emphasizes the combination of risk mitigation and performance enhancement in plural sourcing. In the equity context, the controller is therefore likely to prefer a balancing act between risk mitigation and performance enhancement, while in the case of an external provider a preference for enhancing performance is evident. These dynamics in control preferences come into effect in the unique case of plural sourcing as the controller assesses the range of hazards, both performance and relational, in his engagement with both internal and external providers.

6.2 Implications for Practice

The results of our study offer important implications for managers. First, contrary to common practice in internal IT, our study offers support for the professionalization of sourcing relationships between business units and the internal provider through the use of outcome specifications. Our study shows that when outcome control is used in internal provider settings, sourcing performance is enhanced. Secondly, while managers have been advised to invest in social ties as a mechanism to improve performance in sourcing relationships, this study shows that social ties can be selectively complementary to the application of an organizational control, thus enhancing performance subject to the nature of the sourcing mode and control applied.

6.3   Limitations and Future Research

There are several limitations of this study that could be addressed in future research. First, we followed Krzeminska et al.'s (2013) definition of plural sourcing in which two inputs are more or less similar. While such a definition can guide the selection of cases for hardware components (based on similar functionality, technology and interface), it is far more challenging to assess the similarity of service components as their functionality can change during delivery. One example is support service through a call center that becomes a sales service during the call. We therefore call for further refinement of the plural sourcing definition, in particular in the case of the service industry. Second, numerous studies on organizational controls have examined factors relating to controls by collecting observations from both the controller and the controllee. In this study we collected data only from the controller, thus drawing conclusions about controller and controllee behavior based on observations made by the controller. Future studies should consider collecting data from controller-controllee pairs in plural sourcing settings. Last but not least, our theorization has been guided by the argument that the controller is likely to seek ways to mitigate against relational and performance hazards. While this argument is highly supported in the IS outsourcing literature, our study did not include instruments that represent performance and relational risks. We therefore encourage future studies to examine for the presence of such risks as part of the data collection.

References

Carmel, E., Agarwal, R.: The maturation of offshore sourcing of IT work. MIS Q. Executive 1(2), 65–77 (2002)

Child, J.: Trust – the fundamental bond in global collaboration. Org. Dyn. 29(4), 274–288 (2001)

Chiu, C.M., Hsu, M.H., Wang, E.T.G.: Understanding knowledge sharing in virtual communities: an integration of social capital and social cognitive theories. Decis. Support Syst. 42(3), 1872–1888 (2006)

Choudhury, V., Sabherwal, R.: Portfolios of control in outsourced software development projects. Inf. Syst. Res. 14, 291–314 (2003)

Chua, C., Lim, W., Soh, C., Sia, S.K.: Enacting clan control in complex IT projects: a social capital perspective. MIS Q. 36, 577–600 (2012)

Das, T.K., Teng, B.: Risk types and inter-firm alliance structures. J. Manage. Stud. 33, 827–843 (1996)

Das, T.K., Teng, B.: Trust, control, and risk in strategic alliances: an integrated framework. Organ. Stud. 22, 251–283 (2001)

Dutta, S., Bergen, M., Heide, J.B., John, G.: Understanding dual distribution: the case of reps and house accounts. J. Law Econ. Organ. **11**, 189–204 (1995)

Goo, J., Huang, D., Hart, P.: A path to successful IT outsourcing: interaction between service-level agreements and commitment. Decis. Sci. **39**(3), 469–506 (2008)

Goo, J., Nam, K., Kishore, R.: The role of service level agreements in relational management of information technology outsourcing: an empirical study. MIS Q. **33**, 119–145 (2009)

Gopal, A., Gosain, S.: The role of organizational controls and boundary spanning in software development outsourcing: implications for project performance. Inf. Syst. Res. **21**(4), 960–982 (2010)

Gopal, A., Koka, B.: The asymmetric benefits of relational flexibility: evidence from software development outsourcing. MIS Q. **36**, 553–576 (2012)

Granovetter, M.: The strength of weak ties. Am. J. Sociol. **78**(6), 1360–1380 (1973)

Grover, V., Cheon, M.J., Teng, J.T.C.: The effect of service quality and partnership on the outsourcing of information systems functions. J. Manag. Inf. Syst. **12**(4), 89–116 (1996)

Gulati, R.: Does familiarity breed trust? The implications of repeated ties for contractual choices in alliances. Acad. Manag. J. **38**(1), 85–112 (1995)

Hansen, M.: The search-transfer problem: the role of weak ties in sharing knowledge across organization subunits. Adm. Sci. Q. **44**, 82–111 (1999)

Harrigan, K.R.: Matching vertical integration strategies to competitive conditions. Strateg. Manag. J. **7**(6), 535–555 (1986)

Heckman, R.L., King, W.R.: Behavioral indicators of customer satisfaction with vendor-provided information services. In: Proceedings of the International Conference on Information Systems, Vancouver, pp. 429–444 (1994)

Heide, J.B.: Plural governance in industrial purchasing. J. Mark. **67**(4), 18–29 (2003)

Hox, J.: Quantitative Methodology Series. Multilevel Analysis Techniques and Applications. Lawrence Erlbaum Associates Publishers, Mahwah, NJ, US (2002)

Kirsch, L.J.: Portfolios of control modes and IS project management. Inf. Syst. Res. **8**(3), 215–239 (1997)

Kirsch, L.J.: Deploying common systems globally: the dynamics of control. Inf. Syst. Res. **15**(4), 374–395 (2004)

Kirsch, L.J., Sambamurthy, V., Ko, D.G., Purvis, R.L.: Controlling information systems development projects: the view from the client. Manage. Sci. **48**(4), 484–498 (2002)

Kotlarsky, J., Oshri, I.: Social ties, knowledge sharing and successful collaboration in globally distributed system development projects. Eur. J. Inf. Syst. **14**(1), 37–48 (2005)

Krzeminska, A., Hoetker, G., Mellewigt, T.: Reconceptualizing plural sourcing. Strateg. Manag. J. **34**(13), 1614–1627 (2013)

Kumar, N., Stern, L.N., Anderson, J.C.: Conducting interorganizational research using key informants. Acad. Manag. J. **36**(6), 1633–1651 (1993)

Lacity, M., Khan, S., Yan, A., Willcocks, L.: A review of the IT outsourcing empirical literature and future research directions. J. Inf. Technol. **25**, 395–433 (2010)

Levina, N., Vaast, E.: Innovating or doing as told? Status differences and overlapping boundaries in offshore collaboration. MIS Q. **32**(2), 307–332 (2008)

MacNeil, I.: Power, contract, and the economic model. J. Econ. Issues **4**(4), 909–923 (1980)

Oshri, I.: Offshoring Strategies. MIT Press, Boston (2011)

Oshri, I., Van Uhm, B.: A historical review of the information technology and business process captive center sector. J. Inf. Technol. **27**, 270–284 (2012)

Ouchi, W.G.: A conceptual framework for the design of organizational control mechanisms. Manage. Sci. **25**, 833–848 (1979)

Ouchi, W.G.: Markets, bureaucracies, and clans. Adm. Sci. Q. **25**(1), 129–141 (1980)

Parmigiani, A.: Why do firms both make and buy? An investigation of concurrent sourcing. Strateg. Manag. J. **28**(3), 285–311 (2007)

Podsakoff, P.M., Mackenzie, S.B., Lee, J.Y., Podsakoff, N.P.: Common method biases in behavioural research: a critical review of the literature and recommended remedies. J. Appl. Psychol. **88**(5), 879–903 (2003)

Poppo, L., Zenger, T.R.: Do formal contracts and relational governance function as substitutes or complements? Strateg. Manag. J. **23**, 707–725 (2002)

Puranam, P., Gulati, R., Bhattacharya, S.: How much to make and how much to buy? An analysis of optimal plural sourcing strategies. Strateg. Manag. J. **34**(10), 1145–1161 (2013)

Rai, A., Arikan, I., Pye, J., Tiwana, A.: Fit and misfit of plural sourcing strategies and IT-enabled process integration capabilities: consequences of firm performance in the U.S. electric utility industry. MIS Q. **39**(4), 865–886 (2015)

Sako, M., Chondrakis, G., Vaaler, P.: How do plural-sourcing firms make-and-buy? The impact of supplier portfolio design. Organ. Sci. **27**(5), 1161–1182 (2016)

Segars, A.H., Grover, V.: Strategic information systems planning success: an investigation of the construct and its measurement. MIS Q. **22**(2), 139–163 (1998)

Srikanth, K., Puranam, P.: Integrating distributed work: comparing task design, communication and tacit coordination mechanisms. Strateg. Manag. J. **32**, 849–875 (2011)

Storck, J.: Knowledge diffusion through 'Strategic Communities'. Sloan Manag. Rev. **41**(2), 63–74 (2000)

Tate, W.L., Ellram, L.M.: Offshore outsourcing: a managerial framework. J. Bus. Ind. Mark. **24**, 256–268 (2009)

Tiwana, A., Keil, M.: Control in internal and outsourced software project. J. Manag. Inf. Syst. **26**(3), 9–44 (2009)

Tiwana, A., Kim, S.K.: Concurrent IT sourcing: mechanisms and contingent advantages. J. Manag. Inf. Syst. **33**(1), 101–138 (2016)

Vlaar, P., Van den Bosch, F., Volberda, H.: On the evolution of trust, distrust, and formal coordination and control in international relationships: toward an integrative framework. Group Org. Manage. **32**, 407–429 (2007)

West, B.T., Welch, K.B., Galecki, A.T.: Linear Mixed Model. Chapman Hall/CRC (2007)

Wiener, M., Remus, U., Heumann, J., Mahring, M.: The effective promotion of informal control in information systems offshoring projects. Eur. J. Inf. Syst. **24**(6), 569–587 (2015)

Author Index